THE AMERICAN PRESIDENCY 1945–2000

ILLUSIONS OF GRANDEUR

G.H. BENNETT

SUTTON PUBLISHING

Sutton Publishing Limited · Phoenix Mill
Thrupp · Stroud · Gloucestershire · GL5 2BU

First published 2000

British Library Cataloguing in Publication Data
A catalogue record for this book is available from the British Library.

ISBN 0-7509-2277-X

Typeset in 11/14.5 pt Sabon.
Typesetting and origination by
Sutton Publishing Limited.
Printed and bound in England by
J.H. Haynes & Co. Ltd, Sparkford.

Contents

Somewhere out there there is another fool – some idealistic sucker who still believes in us. After all the scandals, and party politics, and all of the bull there is someone out there who still believes that we care – that we will do what we promised to do. . . . If we lose that idealistic, gloriously deluded fool out there, hey, it's all over.

President Douglas to President Kramer in *My Fellow Americans*, © Warner Brothers, 1996.

For the sucker
For Ashbourne
For M.

Acknowledgments

In all academic studies the author invariably finds himself in debt to a large number of people and institutions. This author is no exception, and I would particularly like to thank George and Edward, the two most marvellous sons anyone could ever wish for. Thank you for reminding me repeatedly that "it's just a book" and there are far more important things in life such as football, watching the Simpsons, and hitting the beach. I must also thank Sarah, their mother, for keeping them from disassembling the computer, pouring coffee into the hard drive, and a host of other tricks.

My colleagues at the University of Plymouth, especially Jamie Munn, Jonathan Wood, Paul Lambe, Bill Leedham, Nick Smart, Kevin Jeffreys, Robert Hole, and Richard Williams, have been their usual helpful selves, and the staff in the library have been as efficient as ever. Thank you also to the staff at the Public Record Office, Kew, and Exeter University Library. Some of the students that I teach on the Master of Arts program at the University of Plymouth were very useful in their perceptive comments, especially Ann Arden, Lindsey Dalgety, and Dave Field. Heather Clarke was invariably helpful and superbly efficient in finding me everything from envelopes to the rough drafts that I would inevitably lose. Thank you also to my father, Roy, and his wife Sylvia. He read the book through in draft form, returning the chapters to me with the odd couple of hundred corrections and suggestions.

At Sutton Publishing I owe a great debt to Christopher Feeney, Anne Bennett and Ellen Simon who know how to push an author to deliver the best work that he or she can, and have an acute understanding of the bear-pit that is the publishing world.

In the United States I would like to thank the following for

Acknowledgments

making an Englishman feel welcome in a foreign country: Stephanie Endy, Margot Browning, and the staff at the Franke Institute for the Humanities, Frank Reynolds, Richard Strier, and Winnifred Sullivan, Fran Henschel, the Sheets family, Debbie and Officer McGreevy of the Chicago Police Department. A particularly warm and friendly welcome to Chicago was extended by the vice-president of the National Veterans Art Museum. I would also like to express my thanks to Forrest McDonald at the University of Alabama.

Introduction

Thomas Bennett of West Virginia was just 21 when he died in Vietnam on February 11, 1969. Despite his conscientious objections to war, Bennett had been drafted into the army to serve as a medic in the 2nd platoon of Company B, 1st Battalion, 14th Infantry. He arrived in Vietnam on January 8 – just over one month later he would be killed in action in Pleiku province. In a lengthy action from February 9–11 Bennett repeatedly risked his life to treat wounded comrades and remove them from the line of fire. It was while trying to help a wounded man who had fallen outside the company position that Bennett was mortally wounded on February 11. For his heroism and humanity he would receive the Congressional Medal of Honor, the highest award that his country could bestow on him. Bennett was a hero, but also a victim: a victim of a war that would cost over 58,000 Americans their lives; a victim, in some people's eyes, of a system that would allow the President of the United States to participate in the Vietnam conflict without Congress ever issuing a formal declaration of war. The award of the medal was fully justified by Bennett's outstanding heroism. But it still seemed somehow ironic to reward his bravery with the Congressional Medal of Honor in view of the role of Congress in giving the presidency *carte blanche* to wage the war in which he gave his life for his fellow countrymen.

In that same year of 1969, but a world away from Pleiku, Bobby Seale, and the other members of the Black Panthers preached "all power to all the people" and called for such things as full employment, decent housing, an end to discrimination, and an end to all wars of aggression. The political program of the Black Panthers placed them at the extreme end of the counterculture of the 1960s. The cry of "all power to all the people" was in direct conflict with the steady concentration of power at the apex of the American political system. J. Edgar Hoover, the director of the Federal Bureau of Investigation, considered the Panthers a threat to the national security of the United States and used the full weight of the FBI against them: some 2,000 Panthers were arrested between 1967 and 1972, and around 20 died in shoot-outs with the authorities or each other. In 1969 Seale and several other radicals found themselves on trial in Chicago on a charge of conspiracy after the 1968 Democratic Convention in the city had ended in mass violence.

Different as they may seem, Thomas Bennett and Bobby Seale were linked together by two common themes: power and national security. Bennett died in a war fought to contain the communist threat to American national security that had emerged in 1945, while the Panthers were considered an internal threat to that security. The lives of both Seale and Bennett were caught up in the issue of presidential power, about how powerful the president, as the embodiment of the American state, should be, and what he should do with that power – wage war or build a truly "Great Society."

This book looks at the rise and decline of presidential power in the mid- to late-twentieth century. It focuses particularly on presidential power in the field of foreign affairs, and how the imperative of national security came to be seen as a threat to the checks and balances of the US Constitution and to American democracy itself. It also examines the revolt against presidential power in the 1960s and 1970s, a revolt that Seale and so many others were a part of. The repercussions of this revolt in the Ford–Carter years are analyzed and set against the reemergence of strong presidency through foreign policy during the Reagan and Bush administrations. The book concludes with an examination of presidential power under the Clinton administration, and asks the question: What does the attempt to impeach Clinton in 1999 reveal about the state of the presidency at the end of the twentieth century? The book draws together the work of distinguished scholars of the presidency, the work of biographers, political scientists, historians, and other commentators. It presents an interpretation of presidential history from 1945 through to the end of the millennium.

Introduction

Presidential history has long fascinated scholars. Biographers such as Edmund Morris have analyzed presidential personalities, political scientists like Richard E. Neustadt have examined in great detail the workings of the American political system and the operations of particular administrations, while historians such as Arthur Schlesinger, Stephen Ambrose, and Robert Dallek have highlighted longer-term developments in the presidency. Former presidents including Truman, Eisenhower, and Johnson have written memoirs to explain their view of their life and period of office. Sometimes their wives, like Lady Bird Johnson, have made a significant contribution of their own to our understanding of the presidency.

In the decades since World War Two scholars of the presidency have chronicled fundamental and dramatic shifts in the power of the office. Arthur Schlesinger, writing in the early 1970s in the aftermath of Watergate, highlighted the rise of what he called *The Imperial Presidency*, which had steadily grown in power – culminating in the Vietnam War and the Watergate scandal. He described an increasing concentration of power in the hands of the president as a result of a hostile international environment since 1945, and the need to maintain America's position in the global economy. While few would have dissented from Schlesinger's view of an all-powerful presidency in the early 1970s, by the 1990s scholars were portraying an entirely different image of presidential power. In 1991 the distinguished political scientist Aaron Wildavsky wrote thoughtfully in the introduction to the second volume of his collected essays: "in rereading and reworking these essays . . . I was struck by their consistent theme: the presidency is in trouble, for criticism was rising and approval declining, while demands were impossible to meet" (Wildavsky, 1991, p. ix). Wildavsky entitled the volume *The Beleaguered Presidency.*

In the late twentieth century the transformation in the debate about presidential power has been striking. In twenty years we have gone from *Imperial Presidency* to *Beleaguered Presidency* and there is little doubt that the decline has continued into the late 1990s. Gary Rose's 1997 book *The American Presidency under Siege* perhaps captures the situation perfectly. He argues that the presidency is "under siege" from the combined forces of Congress, the bureaucracy, the media, lobbyists, and special interest groups. The presidency, in Rose's view, is increasingly unable to lead as it did, for example, during the Truman years. It is, then, small wonder that he and others have seen the need to reform the office. In the aftermath of the Lewinsky affair, the issue of presidential power is even more pressing. One cannot help but be struck by the contrast between perceptions of presidential power at the time of Watergate in the 1970s, and in the aftermath of the publication of the Starr Report in 1998. The apparent decline is cataclysmic, and the shifts in public and academic perception are remarkable. It is these shifts which form the context in which this book is set, and the work of previous scholars has defined the parameters of the debate to which this book makes a contribution. Yet the important thing for the reader to appreciate is the centrality of the subject of this book to the lives of ordinary Americans and others. Presidential power is not simply the preserve of political scientists and historians. For Thomas Bennett, Bobby Seale, and many millions of other people then and now, in America and beyond, presidential power and policy is a matter of life and death, of health and prosperity, or illness and poverty. This book is a history of one of the twentieth century's most influential institutions.

In many ways the Clinton administration brings to a close a great cycle of presidential history that some have characterized as the modern presidency. The concept is somewhat nebulous and there is no common agreement on precisely what is meant by the term. However, Joan Hoff's definition is perhaps the most useful:

> Modern Presidents have exhibited four new characteristics: (1) increased unilateral policy-making capacity at home and abroad; (2) centrality in national agenda setting; (3) increased media visibility, which often means increased influence over media content; and (4) increased reliance on a growing number of White House advisers (Hoff, 1994, pp. 9–10).

While there is some disagreement over what constitutes the modern presidency, there is a consensus that it was forged by Franklin D.

Roosevelt and Harry S. Truman. From 1933 to 1945 Roosevelt ruth-
lessly experimented with the country to find a way out of depression.
His presidency was typified by fundamental changes as he became
increasingly autonomous in the formulation of policy and increasingly
set the legislative agenda for Congress. Under Roosevelt and his
successors the president became the personification of the federal
government. At the close of the twentieth century the president
remains in this position, but the rigors of the press and public opinion
mean that almost no individual can shoulder the burden.

The dissection of the presidency in books such as this perhaps adds
to the problem faced by any presidential incumbent. Perhaps in taking
away some of the mystique from presidents, journalists and academics
have contributed to the decline of respect for and trust in the
presidency. At least the interpretation of presidential history presented
in this book is unusual in that it seeks to go beyond the traditional
confines of writing about this subject. Firstly, the book will involve the
views of not just the established scholars of the presidency. Too often
presidential history is the preserve of a small handful of brilliant and
well known scholars. Their expert opinions and learned works have
shaped America's understanding of itself. But there are wider truths
that the expert perhaps cannot capture with authority. Thus this book
will also include the views of those ordinary Americans who will
determine who will take office in January 2001: those that will vote
and, just as importantly, those who will not.

This book is also automatically positioned outside the American
establishment by the fact that it is written by an Englishman. It might
be asked what an English academic at the University of Plymouth in
Devonshire could have to contribute to the debate on the US
presidency. However, there are certainly some advantages in being an
outsider. American history is politicized to a far greater extent than
the history of any other nation. Elements of the past, such as the
treatment of native Americans, the slave trade, and the Civil War,
have the potential to be highly divisive, and in dealing with the
national story of the United States historians are handling potentially
explosive materials. The dangerous nature of US history was
highlighted early in the year 2000 as John McCain and George Bush

(Jr.) battled it out for the Republican nomination for the presidency. As the candidates arrived in South Carolina for the Republican primary in late February they were both asked to comment on the fact that the flag of the Confederate States flew over the state-house. The flag had been flying since 1962 when it was first flown as a reminder of the Civil War, but also as a powerful symbol of the South's resistance to desegregation. The flag signaled revolt against the union and against the presidency that was backing the cause of civil rights. McCain and Bush wisely avoided press invitations to fall into the trap of commenting on the flying of the flag, with McCain even-handedly declaring: "Some view it as a symbol of slavery; others view it as a symbol of heritage." To have said something more partisan would have been to risk a public furor and to invite defeat at the polls. As both candidates recognized, American history can be dangerous.

Robert Hughes, the Australian writer, has argued that the unique national origins of the United States are at the heart of this highly politicized history:

> The fact of immigration lies behind America's intense piety about the past (which coexists, on other levels, with a dreadful and puzzling indifference to its lessons); in America the past becomes totemic, and is always in a difficult relationship to America's central myth of progress . . . A culture raised on immigration cannot escape feelings of alienness, and must transcend them in two possible ways: by concentrating on "identity" . . . the past, or by faith in newness as a value in itself (Hughes, 1997, p. 4).

A society potentially divided by its origins needs an unchallengeable belief in progress and the future. When things go wrong, as with Watergate, the national reaction is more extreme than what would be felt in a European country in response to an event of similar complexity and importance. American historians are required to maintain the myth of the Republic of virtue and progress. Wrongdoing must be ascribed to an individual or a small group – the perfections of the American system and way of life are largely above question. Historians are thus in danger of becoming the peddlers of a comforting set of illusions about the past and, even though some of them are recognized for what they are, many ordinary Americans would sooner take refuge in them than contemplate less rosy realities.

The presidents since 1945 have faced similar problems. Just like some historians the most successful presidents in terms of popular esteem have been those who have dealt in illusions about themselves and about the progress of the nation. Straight-talking Jimmy Carter might be respected for his honesty, but the public preferred a Reagan who could present them with grand visions supported by illusions about the presidency and the extent of America's military rehabilitation after Vietnam. Likewise Kennedy was a master of illusion: the perfect family man hiding the serial adulterer; the man of charm, wit, and glamour who had Mafia help to get elected; the man of dynamism and vision whose legislative achievements were minimal.

And then there are those presidents who have tried to be more open, straightforward, and direct. Lyndon Johnson, for example, was in many respects the complete antithesis of Kennedy. His legislative achievements were remarkable and he styled his presidential image as almost the complete opposite to Kennedy – Texan simplicity and solidity replacing persuasive New England charm and suavity. Where Kennedy could, after a faltering start, deal in illusion to escape the policy dilemmas that must inevitably face a president, Johnson tackled them head on.

Some politicians have the happy knack of being able to define or present a problem in such a way that it ceases to be a major threat. This happened over Cuba after the missile crisis in 1962. Once the missiles had been withdrawn Castro's Cuba ceased to be the deadly bridgehead for a communist takeover of Latin America, which is how the Cuban problem had been portrayed before October 1962. Johnson meanwhile believed in a more straightforward approach. With him a problem, like communist subversion in Vietnam, needed to be dealt with like any Texas steer – by the horns. Issues such as communist expansion in Southeast Asia could not be neatly sidestepped. As a result of his determination to face realities, rather than deal in illusions to escape them, his presidency achieved much but ended in the pain and misery of public rejection. Being an outsider hopefully gives the author sufficient distance from which to view the illusions presidents make and fail to make.

In addition, Plymouth provides an excellent location from which to view US history. The city has long been a departure and arrival point for transatlantic crossings. The Pilgrim Fathers sailed from the city in 1620, and Charles Lindbergh flew over it during his epic first transatlantic flight in 1927. Thousands of Americans arrived in Plymouth during World War Two, and thousands left the city bound for Utah beach in Normandy in June 1944. Plymouth provides a remote, and yet deeply significant, location from which to make a contribution to American history. British history and constitutional practice informed the Founding Fathers as they struggled to draw up the American Constitution in the eighteenth century. Now, at the start of the twenty-first century, as Americans reassess their government in the aftermath of the Starr investigation, it is perhaps time to gather the broadest possible spectrum of views on the history of presidential power. With powerful voices in the United States, such as that of Pat Buchanan, calling for America to pursue a more restricted global policy, America's place in the world, and the institutions which have governed it, are being thoroughly reviewed. This book is an outsider's contribution to that debate.

G. H. Bennett
Plymouth, July 2000

ONE

The Development of Presidential Power

Many of the fundamental problems affecting the presidency in the twentieth century have always been inherent within the American system. The issue of presidential power has been especially thorny, and it has undergone great fluctuations since the eighteenth century. Particularly strong presidents have been compared favorably and unfavorably with less powerful incumbents of the office. Presidential power has been politically contentious even on the intra-party level. Moreover, the operation of a strong central government coexists uneasily with the libertarian element in the American psyche. Thus successive presidents have been beset by the fact that the level of power which they exercise is constantly contested, and that there is no such thing as a normative level of that power. Convincing the public that, in any given set of circumstances, they are exercising the right amount of presidential power, and that they are neither dictatorial nor weak, has been one of the tasks confronting the American president in the twentieth century. At the heart of this process lies the necessity of generating the right image of a presidency: one which suggests a strength of leadership and determination to use his powers which is appropriate to the tasks and difficulties facing the nation. Thus image has been an important aspect of the presidency since the days of George Washington. Where presidents have interpreted their constitutional powers liberally, creating an illusion to either mask the reality of the exercise of their power, or by portraying particular issues and circumstances in such a way as to merit strong presidential action, has been a necessary defensive response for successive presidents.

Of course, one of the central problems for a president, or for a book dealing with the history of presidential power, is the problem of how to define and then measure that power. The problem is

1

inescapable and its solution seldom satisfactory. Presidential power at its simplest involves the ability to decide, to determine the outcome of events, to shape national and international agendas, to be seen as being at the centre of events, and, with the modern presidency, to be seen as the personification of the federal government. But the word power is itself too limited, for one of the vital components of presidential rule is authority. The Constitution, within a system of checks and balances, authorizes the president to exercise certain powers. The election of the president by the electorate and party system creates a sense of democratic and political authority. Presidents have sometimes had the power of office but not the authority to govern effectively. Where the electorate chooses to appoint a president from one party, but a Congress dominated by the other, presidents have been handicapped by a lack of authority over Congress. The power relationship between the White House and Capitol Hill is defined by the Constitution, but without one party dominating both institutions the presidency lacks the political authority to force the legislative agenda. Likewise, during the Vietnam War Presidents Johnson and Nixon enjoyed considerable presidential power, but their moral authority to wage war on behalf of the American people was questioned.

It is a fact of the American political system that the power and authority of the president are constantly in a state of flux. The balance between Congress and the White House shifts from administration to administration, election to election. The nature of the presidential term of office means that presidents are more powerful at some times than at others. Human nature means that a newly elected president can count on a honeymoon period with the people and probably Congress, but inevitably this breaks down in time as issues arise that are politically divisive. The last 12 to 18 months of the term of office are often dominated by the incumbent's attempts to engineer his re-election. Thus controversial legislation tends to be introduced early in the term so that presidential popularity will hopefully peak in time for the election. With the emergence of the primary election system a proportionately greater amount of the president's effort had to be invested in electioneering.

In effect the structure of the presidential term places an important restriction on the president's authority and power for a substantial period of the his term of office. Stephen Hess in *Organizing the Presidency* has gone even further, to suggest a presidential life-cycle. He argues that presidential terms go through a series of distinct stages: honeymoon; controversy as issues arise to end the honeymoon; presidency dominated by foreign affairs as the domestic legislative agenda has largely been fulfilled or abandoned; electioneering; after re-election a renewed legislative drive; and finally in the last two years a loss of the political spotlight and a diminished authority as attention drifts to potential successors. Hess's ideas on the life-cycle of a presidency are important. They show how the four-year term contains an inbuilt series of peaks and troughs of presidential power and authority. They also point to the importance of foreign affairs in the presidential life-cycle. As Hess puts it, in the final two years of office the president will become steadily less visible and will perhaps lose something of his authority unless "there is a serious international crisis; otherwise he must try to manufacture interest through summit meetings, foreign travel (the more exotic the better), and by attaching himself to major events such as space exploits, disaster relief, or even athletic achievements that involve his countrymen" (Hess, 1976, p. 25).

If one accepts that the power and authority of the president are constantly fluctuating then there is the further problem of how to measure them. One way is to examine contemporary perceptions of presidential power from the speeches of opponents and supporters, press articles, and public opinion polls. They tend to be rather superficial and offer a snapshot of just a moment in time. In addition, the subject of presidential power is often referred to only indirectly. Another possible way to measure presidential authority and power would be to examine the comments of former presidents after they have left office. The late twentieth century has seen a number of ex-presidents, including Truman, Eisenhower, and Lyndon B. Johnson, write their memoirs. Some of these have been revealing and others not. Presidential memoirs are a particularly poor way of judging fluctuations in presidential authority and power because of the fact that they are the view of just one individual and they are not available for every administration. The retrospective assessments of historians and political scientists offer a third way of judging changes in the presidency over time, and indeed since 1945 there have been a number of attempts to canvass the opinion of the academic community to establish an intellectual consensus over who was the best president, the worst, the most charismatic, the most lucky, and the most powerful. However, such assessments have raised awkward questions about how, for example, a former president may manage to affect perceptions about his presidency by his activities after leaving office. After 1974 Richard Nixon managed to transform himself into something of an elder statesman with public and academic ratings improving as a result. His successor, Gerald Ford, meanwhile, was content to live out a peaceful and private retirement and perceptions of his presidency do not seem to have improved as a result. Thus the consensus of history about a particular president presents the student of presidential power with a problem. Using a mix of contemporary, personal and historic evidence seems to offer the only sensible, if not entirely satisfactory, means of gauging the shifting fortunes of the presidency.

This approach needs to be underpinned by close study of the Constitution and the way in which it has evolved over time. Changes in the Constitution offer a particularly clear insight into changes in presidential power, if not authority. That Constitution, inspired and informed by notions about the British system of government, sought to spread power between a presidential executive, a Congress to deal with necessary legislation, and an independent judiciary. This tripartite system created a series of checks and balances between the different elements that made up government in the United States. On those checks and balances rested American democracy. The Constitution also established further safeguards to ensure that the holder of the office of president would be suitable and would not grow too powerful. Limitation of the presidential term to four years, election by the people through the device of an electoral college, rather than by more direct means, and the imposition of residency and age qualifications on presidential candidates were designed by the founding fathers to ensure that the president would be a true American unswayed by what they saw as the dangers of popular politics. Under the Constitution the president was given wide-ranging powers, but they were wider in some fields than in others. In particular the president was to enjoy a freer hand in the conduct of foreign policy than he was in framing domestic policy. In domestic affairs the president had to work with Congress and "recommend to their Consideration such Measures as he shall judge necessary and expedient," whereas in foreign affairs the president could make the policy of the nation, and as commander-in-chief back that policy with force. However, presidential power in the field of foreign affairs was also subject to checks by Congress. Treaties and international agreements required the backing of two-thirds of the Senate before they could be ratified. Tension between president and Congress over the conduct and control of foreign policy was inherent in the Constitution. As the American historian Stephen Ambrose has explained:

> The president's most important asset in asserting control of foreign policy is Section 2, Article II, of the Constitution: "The president shall be commander in chief of the army and navy of the United States." The Constitution, however, also gives Congress power to shape foreign policy: Section 8, Article I, "The Congress shall have power to . . . declare war . . . raise and support armies . . . and maintain a navy;" and Section 2, Article II, which gives the president the power to "make treaties," but only "provided two-thirds of the senators present concur." These simple declarative sentences invite a constant struggle between the executive and the legislative branches for the control of foreign policy (Ambrose, 1991, p. 124).

The tensions inherent in the Constitution and the disparity between presidential powers in domestic and foreign affairs was quite intentional. The whole purpose of a federal government was to divide authority and responsibility between federal and state levels. Foreign policy, defense, and national treasury matters would be entrusted to a superior authority, whose power would be checked and balanced by Congress, while the states dealt with more local issues. Yet presidential power would for the most part be determined by success or failure in these federal responsibilities. This is a point which is both obvious and easily overlooked. As the federal government has become ever more important in the lives of ordinary Americans in the twentieth century, as it has assumed more roles and responsibilities, this basic fact has become obscured.

In foreign affairs there were no issues of states' rights that needed to be considered, no Congress in which the states were represented which the president would have to grapple with on a day-to-day basis. From its inception as part of a federal system, foreign and defense policy were the primary means through which the presidency could demonstrate its strength, especially since treasury issues have traditionally offered the chance to get it wrong rather than right. The necessary constitutional arrangements for a presidency dominated by foreign policy were always latent within the system devised by the founding fathers. David Nichols in his 1994 book *The Myth of the Modern Presidency* points out that the constitutional basis of presidential power and authority was sufficiently broad to allow the emergence of an imperial presidency. In some ways the constitutional basis of presidential authority is a poor way of measuring presidential power, especially as some elements of constitutional practice, such as that set down by George Washington that a president would only serve for two terms, were unwritten and could be dispensed with when expedient, as Roosevelt did in 1940 and again in 1944. However, the occasional changes to the Constitution do offer decisive evidence of shifting presidential power and authority. The framing of the Twenty-Second Amendment in 1947 formally limiting a president to two terms of office placed an important restriction on presidential power.

Using a slowly evolving Constitution, and a mix of contemporary, personal, and historic evidence as indices of presidential power it is possible to gain something of an understanding of how presidential power developed up to the end of World War Two. After the framing of the Constitution, presidential power was seldom an issue of political significance in the eighteenth and nineteenth centuries. Domestic affairs dominated the political agenda, as the economy and population of the United States grew, and the great plains were settled by white Americans. The United States was a long way from the diplomatic squabbles in Europe, and the world economy was nowhere near fully interconnected. America could get on with the business of business, and barring the war with the British in 1812 and the Alaska purchase, could leave the rest of the world to get on with its business too. In the late nineteenth and twentieth centuries this would change, as would the office of president.

Washington, the first incumbent of the office from 1789 to 1797, showed his determination to exercise strong leadership in both the domestic and foreign fields. Such leadership was necessary if the Republic was to prosper, and under Adams (1797–1801) and Jefferson (1801–9) the tradition of strong presidential leadership was continued. However, with the Republic firmly established, Jefferson's successors displayed less dynamism and determination, with the result that the balance of power between president and Congress shifted in favor of the latter. During the nineteenth century a succession of honest, hardworking, and yet deeply dull presidents came and went. In what might be described as the standard liberal narrative of presidential history, a good presidency is typified by activism – by great speeches, great legislation, and great actions. Most of the nineteenth-century presidents are thus considered to have been sub-standard. But there are often virtues in dullness. Safe unspectacular security is sometimes preferable to excitement. From the group of mid- to late-nineteenth-century presidents only two stand out: "old Andy Jackson" and Abraham Lincoln. Jackson, president from 1829 to 1837, believed in strong leadership both on the battlefield and in politics, and Lincoln, from 1861 until his murder at the hands of John Wilkes Booth, demonstrated his belief in a strong presidency in the events leading up to, and during, the crisis of the Civil War. Washington, Jackson, and Lincoln meant that before the United States had completed one hundred years as an independent state there was already a close association between the waging of war and what would be considered strong, arguably great, presidential leadership. After Lincoln the presidency returned to its deeply dull, but safe, ways, enlivened only by the scandals of the Grant administration from 1869 to 1877, and the shortness, at the hands of another assassin, of James A. Garfield's tenure of the White House. Rutherford B. Hayes (1877–81), Chester Arthur (1881–5), Grover Cleveland (1885–9 and 1893–7), and Benjamin Harrison (1889–93) for the most part carried out the role of president in quiet unspectacular ways.

Yet even in the late nineteenth century presidential power was becoming a contested issue. Lincoln's successor in 1865 was vice-president Andrew Johnson, who strove to carry out the dead president's plans for reconstruction of the South after the civil war. The Congress that convened in 1865 was dominated by radical Republicans opposed to Johnson's plans. They were concerned at such issues as the speedy return of former Confederates to political power in the South, and by wider fears that in his plans for reconstruction Johnson was encroaching on the authority of Congress. The struggle between Congress and president escalated with Johnson using his presidential veto to block radical legislation. The veto was, however, sometimes not enough and on March 2, 1867, Congress passed three acts dealing with reconstruction despite Johnson's use of the veto. The Military Reconstruction Act, the Command of the Army Act and the Tenure of Office Act amounted to a powerful congressional response against Johnson's plans for reconstruction. Johnson quickly fell foul of the Tenure of Office Act, by which the Senate had to give its approval to the removal from office of any office holder whose appointment it had already approved, when he dismissed the Secretary of War, Edwin Stanton, after he had refused to carry out a presidential order. The radical Republicans were outraged as Stanton was one of their sympathizers. Since the Senate had not given its approval for his removal from office moves were immediately made to impeach Johnson for, among other things, violation of the Tenure of Office Act. Johnson's lawyers countered by arguing that the Tenure of Office Act was unconstitutional. Finally the radicals failed by one vote (35 to 19) to get the necessary two-thirds majority to remove Johnson from office.

Johnson's survival helped to maintain the constitutional balance between Congress and presidency. However, his successors still preferred a conciliatory approach toward Congress. Clashes were to be avoided wherever possible and presidential power dwindled steadily. By the late nineteenth century the presidency was semi-impotent.

However, a complete transformation in the fortunes of the presidency was begun under William McKinley of Ohio, who became president in 1897. It was to gather pace under his successor in 1901, Theodore Roosevelt. When McKinley assumed office in 1897 there seemed no reason to suppose that he would not continue the pattern of ineffectual presidential leadership. But foreign affairs, and in particular the Spanish–American war of 1898, were to force McKinley to exercise his presidential power and to reassert strong presidential leadership of the country. During 1897 the situation on the island of Cuba, then part of the Spanish empire, had attracted growing concern in American circles. In 1895 a Cuban insurrection against foreign rule had broken out. As the Spanish sought to put down the revolt, stories of the maltreatment of Cubans at the hands of the Spanish military authorities were reported in the US press. After McKinley's election various factions from humanitarians to hawkish Republicans, who favoured American intervention, assailed the new administration. The press, especially W. Randolph Hearst's *New York Journal* and Joseph Pulitzer's *New York World*, also played a major role in putting pressure on McKinley to take action. McKinley eventually sent the USS *Maine* to Havana harbour as a symbol of US interest in Cuban affairs, and as a means to protect American lives and property on the island. Thus far McKinley had shown little desire to lead the nation into war. He was simply reacting to events and to the pressure on his administration. His reactions were limited and cautious. However, his hand was forced when on February 15, 1898, the USS *Maine* blew up while still in Havana harbour. To the factions in the United States that favoured intervention in Cuba the sinking of the *Maine*, with the loss of 260 of her crew, was clearly the work of the Spanish, even though the US Navy was subsequently unable to come to a conclusion about the cause of the sinking. Although McKinley wanted to avoid war he knew that failure to intervene in Cuba would split the Republican Party in Congress. Badgered by the popular press, a jingoistic public and pro-war factions in the House of Representatives and the Senate, on April 11 McKinley sent to Congress a message stating his opinion that the United States had to intervene in Cuba in order to establish peace. On April 19 Congress gave its support to the president's policy.

The resulting war between the United States and Spain lasted a matter of months: in August the United States and Spain signed a protocol arranging for a peace conference to be held in October. Five and a half thousand Americans had been killed, but from Cuba to the Philippines the Spanish had been comprehensively defeated. It was a war which had been forced on McKinley, and in the presidential election of 1900 he found himself being assailed by the Democrats for acquiring an American empire consisting of the Philippines, Guam, and Puerto Rico as a consequence of the war. McKinley had no other choice but to defend the war as a righteous crusade. Indeed, Theodore Roosevelt, who had distinguished himself in the war, and who had come back to win the governorship of New York, was nominated as the Republican candidate for the vice-presidency. McKinley had not wanted war with Spain, but now found himself being forced by the tactics of the Democrats to defend the exercise of strong presidential power in the field of foreign affairs. The people chose to endorse the idea of a strong American foreign policy, and what went with it: a strong presidency exercising national leadership. McKinley triumphed over his Democratic rival, William Jennings Bryan, by 292 electoral college votes to 155.

By force of circumstances McKinley had been compelled to exercise strong leadership. That leadership had been in the area of foreign affairs and had involved the president with congressional approval in using his powers as commander-in-chief to wage war against the Spanish. McKinley had not wanted war, but had ultimately reaped a rich electoral harvest. A strong presidency seemed to be what the people wanted. As the American economy had expanded and had become more enmeshed in global markets there was a growing need to defend US interests abroad. America was becoming less insular as the days of the frontier faded into popular memory, and the world was increasingly dominated by notions about the survival of nations in the competition between great powers. In Congress, business circles, and the country a subtle shift was occurring in the relative importance attached to domestic and foreign affairs. The popular agitation for war against Spain was one manifestation of it: the demand for an open door to American goods in China, which had been increasingly divided into spheres of influence by the European powers and Japan in the nineteenth century, was another.

After his election McKinley had little time to alter his policies, if indeed he wanted to. On September 6, 1901, he was mortally wounded by an assassin, an anarchist called Leon Czolgosz, while attending the Pan-American Exposition in Buffalo. He took six days to die. President Truman was later to comment: "They say he was a nice man, and I'm sorry he got shot. But [because he was not by his nature a believer in strong presidency] he was still a damn poor president" (Miller, 1974, p. 120).

McKinley's assassination brought Theodore Roosevelt to the presidency. Roosevelt was young, exuberant and dynamic. He also had an acute understanding of popular politics and had already developed a very close relationship with certain reporters. As governor of New York after 1898 Roosevelt had emerged as a leading progressive, and had understood the political lessons of the Spanish–American war. However, his nomination as vice-presidential candidate for the 1901 election had been unwelcome in some quarters:

Roosevelt had the kind of star quality that Republican organization men would have preferred to leave shining in splendid isolation. He had been promoted for the vice-presidential nomination in 1900 by machine politicians in New York who were anxious to get him out of the state house in Albany. On the receiving end of this deal, President McKinley and his political manager, Mark Hanna, were little more enthusiastic about having a "madman" so close to the throne, and, for a time they resisted the move. Still championing reform, Roosevelt was too independent to be embraced with open

11

arms; still basking in the glory of his Cuban adventures in the Spanish-American war, he proved too popular to be held at bay (Skowronek, 1993, pp. 233–4).

After McKinley's death Theodore Roosevelt tried to reassure the party that he was not going to be too radical. At the same time, he wanted to use the presidency to implement elements of the progressive program, and to exercise presidential power to its limits. He also realized that he could give a lead to the American public on many issues, and with the backing of the people Congress would be easier to manage. His State of the Union address delivered to Congress in December 1901 set the pattern for the rest of his presidency. It called for greater involvement of the federal government in the economic affairs of the nation and for a dynamic foreign policy. The extension of federal power to tackle the power and practices of big business was a progressive goal. There was a growing feeling that sections of the US economy were at the mercy of monopolies and combines whose only interest was in fleecing the consumer. Using the Sherman Antitrust Act of 1890 Roosevelt ordered the Justice Department to prosecute the so-called trusts to reinvigorate competition in such areas as the markets for oil, beef, and tobacco. Roosevelt's demand for a "Square Deal" did not transform the situation of the American consumer, but it was transforming the position of the presidency. Here was a president being proactive in the nation's affairs, interpreting his powers liberally, and involving the presidency in the ordinary everyday lives of Americans.

In addition, this extension of presidential responsibility was coupled with a foreign policy which, if not exactly dynamic by European standards, was at least remarkable by American standards thus far. Roosevelt gave *de facto* support to a Panamanian revolution against Colombia in November 1903 which paved the way for the building of a canal across the Isthmus of Panama. The canal would eventually be completed in 1914 just before the start of World War One. Roosevelt also continued to reassert the Monroe Doctrine in Latin America, springing into action when Britain, Germany and Italy sent warships to Venezuela in 1902 to pressure the South American government to settle the outstanding debts which it owed to the European powers. Roosevelt eventually got the European powers to settle for about 20 percent of what they thought they were owed. The Venezuelan issue followed hard on the heels of a similar crisis over the debts of the Dominican Republic in 1901 which had led Roosevelt to unveil a corollary to the Monroe Doctrine. In his first State of the Union address Roosevelt had declared that the United States was prepared to act as a police power within the region where order was threatened. This led the United States to assume a growing control over the affairs of the Dominican Republic. By 1905 the Roosevelt administration had negotiated an agreement with the Dominican Republic effectively placing key aspects of the management of the country's finances under American control. The Senate refused to ratify the treaty, but Roosevelt used his executive powers to put the terms of the agreement into force anyway. He was determined to be aggressive in his conduct of foreign policy and was not about to let Congress stand in his way. There were other aspects of this aggression. Roosevelt's rhetoric was more aggressive than his actual foreign policy and he did not really live up to his often quoted belief in the West African proverb "speak softly and carry a big stick." Roosevelt spoke anything but softly for the benefit of the American people and for European diplomats alike. Both constituencies were impressed, and as a further example of his showmanship in December 1907 significant elements of the American fleet were sent on a world cruise to fly the Stars and Stripes around the globe, and to demonstrate American military power to the Japanese who were more eager than ever to claim an expanded empire in China after their victory over the Russians in the Russo-Japanese war of 1904–5.

Roosevelt's political instincts that the American public wanted a new kind of presidency, aggressive abroad and proactive in domestic affairs, were borne out at the polls. The presidential election of 1904 had been fought on the basis of Roosevelt's style of presidency, and he had triumphed by 336 electoral college votes to his Democratic rival's 140. He would almost inevitably have won re-election in 1908 had he not decided to respect the convention set down by Washington that a president would serve for only two terms. Roosevelt's impact on the presidency was enormous. He had highlighted the twin bases on which presidential power would rest for most of the rest of the century: strong foreign policy and an expansion of presidential responsibility in the domestic field. The presidency was set on a course by Roosevelt that his successors could ignore at their peril.

Roosevelt's immediate successor was William H. Taft, whom Roosevelt nominated as his heir apparent. However, despite Roosevelt's endorsement and the hopes of the American people, Taft was not able to continue in the style of his predecessor. Many of the members of his Cabinet were lawyers, who not unnaturally professed concerns about the legal aspects of presidential action and power. They saw difficulties in carrying forward almost every aspect of the progressive agenda. The Republican Party, especially in the House of Representatives, increasingly found itself split between its conservative and progressive wings. It became harder to do anything. However, Taft continued to use foreign events as a means to bolster the presidential image. In 1912 Marines were landed in Nicaragua to bring peace out of the political chaos which reigned there, and the defense of American interests in China continued. In the same year that the Marines landed in Nicaragua, the American public delivered its verdict on Taft. In the run-up to the 1912 presidential elections the Republican Party split between those members who supported the incumbent President, and those who managed to persuade Theodore Roosevelt to run again. This culminated in the formation of a separate Progressive party, which held its first convention in Chicago in 1912. The presidential elections that followed were contested by Taft for the Republicans, Roosevelt for the Progressive Party, and Woodrow Wilson for the Democrats. Further spice was added to the election by Eugene Debs who ran as a socialist candidate. In the circumstances it was hardly surprising that Wilson, the Democratic academic from Princeton, should emerge as the winner. Wilson gained 435 electoral college votes to Taft's 8 and Roosevelt's 88. Debs gained no electoral college votes, although he did win 6 percent of the popular vote.

Wilson had a powerful mandate from the electorate and he was also a firm believer in strong presidency. He had made his name as an academic with the publication in 1885 of *Congressional Government*, in which he lamented the weak state of the presidency. Much more to his liking was the kind of leadership which had been shown by Roosevelt, and once in power Wilson was determined to seize the progressive mantle. He continued the policies of his predecessors in practicing an expansive foreign policy, especially in the Caribbean. In 1915 he sent troops to Haiti to take control of a republic on the edge of bankruptcy and collapse. An expedition against the Mexican bandit leader Pancho Villa was organized in 1916, and in 1917 the Danish West Indies were purchased at a cost of $25 million.

Wilson's policies were sufficiently popular to earn him reelection in 1916, but in 1917 the American people were to learn the ultimate cost of an expansive foreign policy when Wilson asked Congress for a declaration of war against Germany. Wilson's efforts to mediate in World War One, which had broken out in August 1914, had come to nothing, and tension between the United States and Germany had grown over the use of unrestricted submarine warfare by the Germans. Congress gave Wilson the declaration of war which he asked for and an American expeditionary force was sent to Europe. Some 117,000 Americans were to be killed in action or die from disease, while another 200,000 were wounded. Wilson's policies had placed the United States on the side of the victorious powers, had greatly benefited the United States economically and financially, and had given her a dominant position in world affairs. On January 8, 1918, Wilson unveiled before Congress a fourteen-point program for the peace that was to follow the war. In detail, the proposals called for the world to be remade according to American principles: the end of secret diplomacy and the creation of a League of Nations to regulate international relations and counter aggression struck at the heart of the old-style European politics that had led to the war. The importance of free trade was reaffirmed and Wilson's call for self-determination struck at the body of the European empires. Wilson's powerful assertion of the principle placed a time bomb under British rule over her empire from Dublin to Delhi. The president's fourteen points were to be guiding themes as the peacemakers tried to frame a postwar settlement. However, in the negotiations between the

15

victorious powers to frame a peace settlement for Germany in the shape of the Treaty of Versailles, Wilson's fourteen points were often compromised by political expediency and European *Realpolitik*. But as the Treaty of Versailles, and the other treaties covering the former central powers, ultimately were ratified, Wilson by mid-1919 felt that he was in a position to dominate international politics in the American interest as no US president ever had done.

If the American people understood that the balance of world power had shifted decisively in favor of the United States then they did not show it. By the standards of most of the European powers the total of 117,000 deaths suffered by the United States as a result of her involvement in the World War One was minute, but by American standards it was a national calamity. The country rejected Wilson's internationalism and the aggressive foreign policy which some blamed for the possibly needless deaths of so many American service personnel. Suddenly Wilson was the architect of American involvement in an unnecessary war: yet another, but rather bloodier, struggle between the ruling dynasties of Europe. Wilson wanted to dictate the future world order but eventually found that the American people had rejected his internationalism, and also the model of presidency that he had admired in Theodore Roosevelt, and which he had done so much to maintain. To the American public speaking softly and carrying a big stick was just fine so long as no one was called on to use the stick. Fighting the Spanish in 1898 or the Marines landing in Haiti in 1915 was one thing: fighting the highly trained and efficient German army quite another. A powerful presidency was all very well, but not if it meant another war on such a scale, and Americans saw that Wilson's internationalism might potentially call another generation of Americans to fight in the fields of Europe on behalf of the League of Nations.

By late 1919 Wilson was facing a massive struggle to get Congress to ratify the Treaty of Versailles, which he had negotiated at Paris, by the necessary two-thirds majority. He decided to bypass Congress and appeal directly to the American public. Thus in September 1919 he embarked on a public speaking tour of the Midwest. However, Wilson fell ill and had to return to Washington where he had a stroke which left him paralyzed. As Mrs. Wilson, the President's doctor, and the Cabinet tried to get on with the task of running the country, on November 19 1919 the Senate rejected the Treaty of Versailles. Further attempts to ratify the Treaty foundered on the need to secure a two-thirds majority, and the most powerful president up to that point in American history was forced to live out the dying days of his administration as a semi-invalid whose dreams had turned to dust. Wilson's departure seemed to draw an end to the era of activist presidency.

Wilson was followed by a succession of Republican presidents. Under Warren Harding, elected in 1921, and his successor in 1923 Calvin Coolidge, the presidency would be happy to drift slowly toward isolationism. The expansive and costly foreign policy of Wilson was to be eschewed. Harding and Coolidge did not even try to couple increasing isolationism with presidential vigor in domestic affairs: *laissez-faire* was to be the policy at home and abroad. In short, the president was seen but seldom heard or his presence felt. Whereas presidents after McKinley had been determined to intervene in the lives of ordinary people and show vigour in the field of foreign affairs, Harding and Coolidge thought it was best to leave the people to their own devices. There was a return to a nineteenth- century model of the presidency. The success of the economy from 1920 to 1929 kept the Republicans in the White House, and in 1929 Herbert Hoover succeeded Coolidge. However, in that same year came the Wall Street crash. After initially leaving the market to sort itself out Hoover took an increasingly interventionist line as he tried to guide America out of the growing world depression. He was not the man for the job, unfortunately. The economic successes of the 1920s had convinced many Republicans that the market could not be bucked, and that presidential interference would only make matters worse.

This gave the Democrats their opportunity. Franklin Delano Roosevelt's presidential nomination in 1932 was based on the promise of strong leadership and that the presidency would take continuous responsibility for the welfare of the people. Herein lie several interesting points: the disaster of World War One had convinced the Republicans that the nineteenth-century notion of a *laissez-faire* isolationist presidency should be followed; the disaster of the Wall Street Crash reconfirmed the conviction of many Democrats that it was the job of the president to lead. However, the isolationism of the American public meant that presidential vigor had to be focused on domestic affairs, and that an expansive foreign policy had to be eschewed. Roosevelt won the election of 1932 with a handsome show of support. Significantly, despite the isolationist tendencies of American public opinion, as he tackled the problem of the depression with the promise of a New Deal his political rhetoric was strikingly warlike. He called the emergency of the depression as serious as war itself and called for unprecedented power to be placed in his hands in order to meet the crisis. In his inaugural address on March 4, 1933, he referred to "this great army of our people dedicated to a disciplined attack upon our common problems," and as an early indication of his attitude toward the presidency he went on to say:

> It is to be hoped that the normal balance of executive and legislative authority may be wholly adequate to meet the unprecedented task before us. But it may be that an unprecedented demand and need for undelayed action may call for temporary departure from that normal balance of public procedure. I am prepared under my constitutional duty to recommend the measures that a stricken nation in the midst of a stricken world may require. These measures, or such other measures as the Congress may build out of its experience and wisdom, I shall seek, within my constitutional authority, to bring to speedy adoption. But in the event that the Congress shall fail to take one of these two courses, and in the event that the national emergency is still critical, I shall not evade the clear course of duty that will then confront me. I shall ask Congress for the one remaining instrument to meet the crisis – broad Executive power to wage a war against the emergency, as great as the power that would be given to me if we were in fact invaded by a foreign foe.

As Roosevelt struggled to come to terms with the depression he involved the presidency in the lives of ordinary people to an extent that had not been seen before. The President created millions of jobs, costing the taxpayer billions of dollars in the process. Congress was treated at times as little more than a rubber stamp for the president's wishes. Some Republicans claimed that under Roosevelt it seemed as though the Presidency was moving in the direction of a Soviet or Nazi model of leadership rather than conforming to the precedents of Cleveland and Coolidge. Thus Republicans attacked what they saw as too much presidential power. Regimentation, Communism, Fascism, were among the cries of the Republicans. The US Supreme Court joined in the attack on Roosevelt's New Deal, declaring some of the most important legislation to be in breach of the Constitution. After securing a second term of office in 1936 Roosevelt decided to tackle the Supreme Court by altering its membership to make it more amenable to New Deal legislation. Even the largely compliant Congress, including key sections of the Democratic Party, rebelled against this. A powerful president seemed hell-bent on tearing up the Constitution because of the checks on his actions imposed by the Supreme Court. To some Republicans it seemed that the President was about to become a dictator. The uproar was sufficient to convince Roosevelt to back off, although his threat to alter the Supreme Court was enough to ensure that it never seriously opposed New Deal legislation again.

Taking note of the state of public opinion, Roosevelt reluctantly had to maintain the isolationism of his Republican predecessors. The foreign policy rhetoric of Teddy Roosevelt, FDR's cousin, had been successfully transferred to domestic policy. It was also interesting to note that just as Teddy Roosevelt had cultivated a relationship with the popular press, FDR was to cultivate a relationship with the newsreel camera and the radio. The photogenic and natural actor in FDR made him a formidable holder of the office. He projected presidential power in a way that had not previously been witnessed. Before the camera he was the consummate actor: on the radio, in his occasional series of fireside chats to the American public, he was a reassuring father figure.

FDR perfected a style that was direct, lucid, friendly and inform-ative. Anxious not to blunt their effect by over-doing them, he gave only twenty-seven "fire-side chats" in his twelve White House years, six of them in the first eighteen months of the New Deal. So great was the impression they created that many people believed in retrospect that they had been almost weekly occurrences. His voice could be heard in every street in the land and his words lingered in the nation's imagination. His concern was that the federal government under a Democratic administration, should not only be active, but be known as active (Cunliffe, 1972, p. 265).

Both the newsreels and the radio gave Roosevelt a means to appeal directly to the American public, over the heads of Congress, in a way which poor Wilson could only have dreamed about in 1919. Under Roosevelt, new media emerged as powerful weapons in the presidential arsenal, but they were weapons that could cut both ways. Truman would later reflect during his presidency: "It seems that every man in the White House was tortured and bedevilled by the so-called free press . . . That old SOB who owned and edited the *St Louis Post Dispatch* and the *New York World* was in my opinion the meanest character assassin in the whole history of liars who have controlled newspapers . . . I had thought that pictures and the radio would cure the news liars – but they – the liars – have taken over both" (Ferrell, 1980, p. 136). Truman was never to enjoy the easy relationship with the media that Roosevelt did.

With Roosevelt the notion of a dynamic presidency reached its apogee – so much so that between 1939 and 1941, despite the state of US public opinion, Roosevelt made sure that America became steadily more involved in the war. Some commentators have argued that by 1941 he was actively trying to engineer incidents to bring America into it. By September 1941 Roosevelt was using his powers as commander-in-chief to send the United States Navy into the Atlantic to fight a private war against the German Navy. To some historians the Japanese attack on Pearl Harbor, on December 7, 1941, was the opportunity Roosevelt had been hoping for. From September 1939 onwards he had used the emergency of the war to supplement the emergency of the depression: both allowed him to become ever more powerful. In 1940 he had won an unprecedented third term as president, and in 1944 he would go on to win a fourth. Roosevelt's quest for power in both the United States and on the global stage seemingly knew no bounds as he attended international conference after international conference during the war years. Only his death in April 1945 could curtail his determination to stay in office and to ensure that the United States would continue to play a leading international role after the end of hostilities.

By 1945 the relationship between presidential power and foreign policy had undergone considerable twists and turns. Beginning with isolationism and the dwindling of presidential power in the nineteenth century, it moved toward McKinley's semi-accidental reinvigoration of the presidency in the Spanish–American war. Theodore Roosevelt learned the lessons of that war and governed accordingly, although the American people were to reject dynamic presidency through bold foreign policy after it led to US casualties in World War One. That war had demonstrated the potential pitfalls of the model of presidency followed by Theodore Roosevelt and Woodrow Wilson. The Republican presidencies of the 1920s, marked by *laissez-faire* at home and isolationism abroad, were in part a conscious reaction against dangerously dynamic presidential leadership. The nineteenth-century style of presidency which attracted Coolidge among others was dull, but it was largely safe, Lincoln being an exception to the rule. However, Franklin D. Roosevelt, who had served in the Wilson administration, was a man who wanted to be a dynamic president. The depression offered him the chance to exercise strong presidential leadership in the conduct of domestic affairs. Tojo, Hitler, and Mussolini later gave him the opportunity to be dynamic on the world stage, and to exercise his powers as commander-in-chief to the full. With Roosevelt's death in April 1945 presidential power reached another crossroads: would his successor, Harry S. Truman, try to continue his former chief's policies, and would the American people do as they had done at the end of World War One and react against the model of presidency followed by the architect of the New Deal and America's victory in World War Two?

21

TWO

Truman: Harry Gives 'em Hell

In the 1944 presidential election Harry S. Truman was nominated as the candidate for the vice-presidency by the Democratic Party. His senior running mate would be President Franklin Delano Roosevelt seeking election to the White House for the fourth time, having triumphed at the polls in 1932, 1936, and 1940. Truman was a respected figure but few saw him as presidential material: he was the able deputy rather than the main role. He seemed cut out for respectable mediocrity rather than greatness. His origins were humble and success had not come easily to him. He had been born on May 8, 1884, in Independence, Missouri, struggling to find a niche for himself as he grew up: the family livestock business did not appeal to him; his eyesight prevented him from going to West Point as he had at one time hoped; and the family was not wealthy enough to send him to college. After High School he spent five years in Kansas City from 1901 to 1906 doing various jobs before coming back to the family farm, which continued to sink deeper and deeper into financial trouble. After the death of his father on November 2, 1914, Truman tried and failed with various speculative investments that left him broke. By the age of thirty Harry S. Truman could easily be regarded as a failure. However, World War One helped to shape his personality. In 1917 he joined the army, and as commander of Battery D of the Second Missouri Field Artillery Regiment from July 1918 to the end of the war he made a reputation for himself as a tough, disciplined commander. War transformed him, but not his fortunes.

In 1919 he returned to America, married, and opened up a gentlemen's clothing store in Kansas City which by 1922 had failed. Truman then went into politics, managing to get elected as commissioner of Jackson County, Missouri. He followed this with a run for the US Senate in 1934, taking office in 1935. In the Senate he steadily rose in reputation and seniority, and made his name during World War Two as chairman of a committee investigating waste and corruption in the war effort. His efforts managed to save the taxpayer over $14 million. Hence he was thought suitable to be second on the 1944 Democratic ticket to Franklin D. Roosevelt. Truman was seen by some as a fine upstanding citizen who would make an effective foil for the more dynamic and charismatic Roosevelt. But others regarded him as a machine politician foisted on the party, and ultimately the country, by Roosevelt. In selecting Truman Roosevelt passed over a number of figures such as Henry Wallace, vice-president since 1940, and Harold Ickes, the Secretary of the Interior. Truman's nomination came as a considerable surprise in some quarters.

After the election, Truman was kept well out of the limelight by Roosevelt. His conception of presidential power was such that Truman was kept at the fringes of policy-making. The flow of information to him was restricted. Then on the afternoon of April 12, 1945, while the Vice-President was listening to a Senate debate, he received a telephone message saying that Roosevelt had died and that he was to go to the White House to take over. He duly took the oath of office shortly after 7 p.m., and found himself in a job for which he did not feel adequately prepared. On the day after Roosevelt's death he summed up the situation perfectly, and set the tone for the rest of his presidency, when he asked reporters: "Did you ever have a bull or a load of hay fall on you? If you have you know how I felt last night." In classic Jimmy Stewart fashion, Mr Truman would continue to play the ordinary guy from Independence, Missouri, through two presidential terms.

Truman excited considerable passions among contemporaries and among later scholars. Revisionist historians of the Cold War have blamed him for igniting the conflict and for fashioning a national security state which would help maintain the Cold War for more than forty years. Meanwhile, some contemporaries blamed him for being too weak on communism. This is bewildering – the slowness of his response to the communist threat to Europe, and the failure to prevent communist victory in the Chinese civil war in 1949, sit ill at ease with later allegations of Truman's Machiavellian responsibility for starting the Cold War. Against the image of Truman as a devious and clever president must be set the image of Truman as the little guy from Missouri which he cultivated for himself. Although it was accepted a little too uncritically in some quarters, in the aftermath of scandals involving Nixon, Reagan, and Clinton there has been a need among some sections of the American public to accept Truman at face value once again. He seems to hail from less troubled, simpler times when an honest and ordinary man could get elected. The myriad faces of Truman stem from the fact that he was a dealer in illusions – illusions about himself, about his presidency, and about the circumstances facing the United States at the end of World War Two. However Truman is viewed, there is a universal acceptance that the man from Missouri further transformed the presidency, playing a vital role in consolidating the re-emergence of strong presidency that had taken place under Franklin Roosevelt. What was particularly significant about Truman's exercise of executive power was that it was concentrated in the field of foreign affairs. He established an American commitment to fight communism that was to be followed by his successors until the 1990s. He also re-set the pattern of foreign policy serving as the definitive test of presidential strength, which had first appeared under Theodore Roosevelt.

Truman's impact on the development of the presidency was considerable, and it was testament to his considerable political skills. The mediocrity from Missouri was to prove anything but ordinary as a president. The first fact to be noted is that Franklin Roosevelt's death had not been so completely unexpected as is made out in the conventional narrative. During the 1944 campaign it had become obvious that Roosevelt's health was deteriorating. His eyes were a little more sunken than before and increasingly he seemed shriveled and fragile. If Truman knew that there was a fair chance that he might one day occupy the top slot, then he also understood the presidency and its history more fully than most of those who had occupied the post before, or would occupy it after, him. There is perhaps no such a thing as an ideal preparation for the presidency beyond the prerequisites of congressional experience or governorship of a state. Success in business, as in the case of Herbert Hoover and George Bush, are often touted as good omens. Truman, however, had been a singular failure in the commercial field. But, he had prepared himself thoroughly for the job by reading, reflecting, and observing. In his youth he had read voraciously. From the encyclopedias in the library at Independence he had moved on at age ten to a four-volume set his mother bought him entitled *Great Men and Famous Women.* To the knowledge gained from books he had added personal observation, and during his life he had witnessed fundamental shifts in presidential power and prestige. To him past presidents were not simply remote figures from history, but, like "old Andy Jackson," cherished friends about whom stories could be told, and from whom fundamental truths could be learned. He could remember Grover Cleveland's 1892 presidential campaign, even though he was just eight years old at the time. Truman was a student of the Constitution which determined the parameters of presidential power.

Despite his carefully cultivated appearance to the contrary, Truman was a savvy politician and a fighter. World War One had an important impact on his life, and World War Two was to have a still greater one on his career. When Truman came to the presidency World War Two was still raging and it was he who had to take the fateful decision to drop the atom bombs on Hiroshima and Nagasaki in August 1945. Truman understood the sorrow and the pity of war and had been tempered by it. He also perceived the way in which war had lifted the presidential authority of FDR to new heights. The war emergency had given Roosevelt the opportunity to strengthen his hold on power to an unprecedented degree. He could use it as an excuse to overturn the convention set by Washington that a president would only serve two terms, and he could use it to muzzle Republican opposition by the forging of a bipartisan coalition to see the war to an end. However, with the surrender of Japan on August 10, 1945, Truman would have to face the resumption of normal peacetime standards of government. It would be difficult to maintain presidential power and authority at the levels enjoyed by Roosevelt, and the Republicans would seek to attack elements of the New Deal.

The only way to maintain the inflated presidency, Truman's contemporary critics and subsequent historians have alleged, was to maintain the emergency – to generate either the reality or the illusion of danger to keep the United States on a war footing. The swift move from World War to Cold War, it has been alleged, was no accident, but a calculated move on Truman's part to maintain some of the features of Roosevelt's presidency, including its authority and power. The Cold War also served to prevent the American public from any retreat back into isolationism as had happened after World War One, and had important financial and economic impacts leading to the emergence of what Eisenhower would later describe as the military-industrial complex. The Republicans in 1952 openly maintained that America's prosperity was in part an illusion generated by the continuation of a war economy. The Republican Party platform for the presidential elections in that year argued: "They claim prosperity, but the appearance of economic health is created by war expenditures, waste and extravagance, planned emergencies and war crisis" (Caridi, 1968, p. 219). But though Truman was undoubtedly clever, his critics have perhaps been willing to ascribe to him rather too much unprincipled genius. There was no smooth transition from World War to Cold War, and in any case Truman did not create a conflict, or embrace it with alacrity.

The first problem of the peace that Truman faced was the call for immediate demobilization. Bringing the boys home was a politically popular move, but it did reduce America's ability to dominate the postwar world. By 1950 the size of the American military had shrunk to just 600,000 men from a wartime high of 12 million. But, at the same time as the American military was contracting, the commitments of US foreign policy were expanding as tension with the Russians increased in the late 1940s. Further problems were created by the growing sense of security felt by most Americans. The end of the war did not produce a return to the depression, thanks to a variety of factors including the Servicemen's Readjustment Act of 1944 which provided $13 billion to smooth the process of demobilization. Although as Garson and Bailey have pointed out "in the first ten days of peace nearly two million people lost their jobs and 640,000 claimed unemployment compensation" (Garson and Bailey, 1990, p. 39), thereafter the economy expanded rapidly. The gross domestic product of the United States more than tripled between 1940 and 1950. Security verging on complacency replaced fear of unemployment as a generation of Americans expressed their new-found confidence by having larger families to create the baby-boom generation. This confidence was not dented by a wave of post-war strikes, as for example when the United Automobile Workers went out on strike for a 30 percent increase in wages in view of the profits being made by General Motors. In fact, industrial militancy was a sign of confidence in the American economy. This confidence extended to every facet of US life including beliefs about the strength of the American military and the conduct of the nation's foreign policy. Truman repeatedly intervened in labor disputes to ensure that national prosperity was not harmed. His interventionism in the lives of ordinary Americans in 1945 and 1946 signaled that he intended to govern like Roosevelt. Indeed, in some respects Truman wanted to take the New Deal further.

However, Truman's comparatively serene progress from war to peace was interrupted by a growing dissatisfaction with the Democratic Party. The Republicans made the most of Truman's even-handed interventions in labor disputes which left both sides dissatisfied. Also, by 1946 the Republicans were able to gain much political capital by simply asking the question of the electorate, after thirteen years of rule by the Democrats, whether it was not simply time for a change. Claims that the government was full of communist infiltrators added a little spice to the Republican crusade against the Democrats, and in the 1946 congressional elections the Republicans gained control of both houses of Congress. Thus the political authority of the president over Congress threatened to diminish sharply.

The Republicans were determined to reverse some aspects of the New Deal and to cut the presidency down to size. Union power was the first item on the agenda, and it was closely followed by attempts to cut taxation. Despite the use of the presidential veto the Republicans were able to carry forward their legislative plans. More seriously, the determination of the Republicans to prevent the emergence of another Roosevelt led to the drafting of the Twenty-Second Amendment to the Constitution, eventually ratified in 1951, which placed a bar on a president running for office again after serving two terms. Truman was not altogether unhappy with the passing of the amendment. He later wrote in his diary: "Eight years as President is enough and sometimes too much for any man" (Ferrell, 1980, p. 177). Nevertheless, the passing of the Twenty-Second Amendment represented a significant and successful attack on presidential power. It highlighted the fact that in the wake of Roosevelt presidential power was once again becoming a contested issue. However, it was contested within the circles of American politics rather than by the wider public. To the majority, seeing their standard of living rise almost annually, strong presidency was entirely praiseworthy.

Truman's views on the nature of presidential power are fundamental to an understanding of his administration, the development of the modern presidency, and the Cold War. His eventual acceptance of the Twenty-Second Amendment would appear to support the view of scholars such as Colin Seymour-Ure who have commented that: "Truman never wanted the presidency nor apparently expected it even when Vice-President. Certainly he did not wish to aggrandize the office. With ten years' experience in the Senate he felt that the balance of power needed tipping back from the President to Congress; and he hoped to develop the potential of the Cabinet" (Seymour-Ure, 1982, p. 135). Without doubt, the image of having power thrust upon him was one that Truman wished to project, but, if it is accepted entirely, then we are left with the bizarre image of a man seemingly devoid of ambition somehow getting to the top of American politics. It was no accident that Truman reached the presidency. Likewise, whereas in public Truman did not make statements indicating that he wanted to maintain presidential power at the levels enjoyed by Roosevelt, or indeed to enhance that power, in private his thoughts sometimes amounted to exactly that intention. In particular, while he was willing to accept that the Twenty-Second Amendment was possibly a good idea, in other areas of presidential power he was much more aggressive in his defense of the *status quo*. In foreign affairs, especially, Truman thought that the president should have a still freer hand. He wrote in a memorandum on May 12, 1945: "I should like to see the Constitution amended to do away with all two-thirds rules" (Ferrell, 1980, pp. 22–3). Getting rid of the two-thirds rule, which had so bedeviled Wilson after World War One, would make the ratification of treaties and the execution of foreign policy significantly easier. But Truman was willing to offset an increase of presidential power in one area with new checks in others. The two-thirds rule could cut both ways, and by opting for simple majority voting it would make it easier for Congress to overturn presidential vetoes. Truman also favored simplifying the procedure through which a president could be removed from office through the impeachment process. His thoughts on the matter of presidential power are as sophisticated as the question demanded, but one thing is certain: he did not wish to see any overall diminution of that power. After he had left office he wrote to one senator about the proposed Bricker amendment to the Constitution limiting the treaty-making powers of the presidency: "If all the powers of the President are further limited by amendment as suggested the country may as well readopt the Articles of Confederation and go back to a Greek city state" (Ferrell, 1980, p. 314).

Truman understood the details of the Constitution which he revered, and appreciated that it gave the president considerably more freedom in the field of foreign affairs than in domestic affairs where the executive had to work more closely with Congress. He understood the contradictions at the heart of the Constitution, but also saw the need to see beyond. The Constitution might describe what a president could and could not do, but presidential power lay beyond such definitions. In his later years he commented:

About the biggest power the President has . . . is the power to persuade people to do what they ought to do without having to be persuaded. There are a lot of other powers written in the Constitution and given to the President, but it's that power to persuade people to do what they ought to do . . . that's the biggest. And if the man who is President doesn't understand that, if he thinks he's too big to do the necessary persuading, then he's in for big trouble, and so is the country (Miller, 1974, p. 10).

Truman knew that the presidency in large part depended on who occupied the office and how they chose to interpret their role. In particular, he had an active dislike of some of the nineteenth-century presidents who had followed Washington, but who had not chosen to exercise their powers as he had. Truman regarded the early- to mid-nineteenth century as a particularly unfortunate period in American history because of what he saw as the inactivity of successive presidents. He commented "If we hadn't had those weak Presidents, we might not have had a civil war" (Miller, 1974, p. 375). Truman was contemptuous of what might be described as the caretaker model of presidency. He was a firm believer in the president exercising strong leadership: setting the national agenda and leading rather than simply reacting to public opinion, and was determined to interpret his constitutional authority in the broadest possible way.

Beyond the Twenty-Second Amendment there were no successful moves to limit formally presidential power, but Republican domination of Congress after the 1946 elections still left Truman in a difficult position. How was he to maintain a strong presidential lead with a hostile Congress determined to cut him down to size? The answer was evident from Truman's studies of past presidents. Foreign policy offered the opportunity to assert his authority, and a strong lead in this field might enhance his position with the public to the extent that it would make Congress a little easier to deal with on domestic issues. During 1947 Truman pursued a bipartisan, increasingly anti-Soviet, line in world affairs. Republican anti-communism ensured that they would support almost any measure against the Soviet Union. During this period Truman set a course for the presidency that it was to maintain for over half a century. At the end of 1946 he had declared an end to the hostilities of World War Two. By March 1947 he had joined a new conflict with the Soviet Union. During 1945 and 1946 Truman had tried to work with Stalin. By the end of that year, Truman was convinced that confrontation, not partnership, was the only way to deal with the Soviets. Britain's admission in early 1947 that she could no longer go on supporting the Greek government in its struggle to contain communist subversion was in many ways a catalyst for the hardening of Truman's policy toward the Soviet Union. Faced with the prospect that a pro-western government might be overthrown, and that its fall would merely encourage communist ambitions elsewhere, Truman did not agonize over the decision of how to respond to the crisis. On March 12 he made a public pledge that the United States would "support free peoples who are resisting attempted subjugation by armed minorities or by outside pressures." The announcing of the Truman Doctrine signaled that the United States would rise to the challenge of meeting covert Soviet subversion and, if need be, overt aggression. Different presidents would maintain the commitment inherent in the doctrine at varying intensities but, periods of détente notwithstanding, the doctrine remained the cornerstone of American foreign policy from Truman through to George Bush. It was also significant that the doctrine gave a shape to the Truman presidency as the fog of World War Two began to clear. Franklin D. Roosevelt came to power in 1932 on the promise of a New Deal for the American public – an ill-defined promise to pursue domestic policies to drag America out of depression. What gave Truman's presidency a sense of direction was his doctrine and the commitment to fight communism which followed from it. The doctrine helped to underpin maintenance of presidential power at the levels it had reached during World War Two by fixing foreign affairs at the top of the political agenda, and by issuing a call to the American public to rally to the cause of defending democracy – a cause in which the president of the United States would play the key role. The call to the American public would be incorporated in an appeal to the western world to rally behind the American-led United Nations, created in 1945 at the San Francisco Conference, to defend the cause of liberty around the globe. The president was claiming for himself the role of guardian of the free world.

The Truman Doctrine was followed by the creation of the Marshall Plan. Although the war had been over for two years the economies of Europe remained unstable. The danger of complete economic collapse which could pave the way for red revolution could not be ruled out. Economic hardship provided the ideal conditions in which to recruit people to the communist cause. In addition, the fragility of the economies of Europe meant that western Europe was ill-prepared to meet a conventional Soviet threat to its security. Under the Marshall Plan, announced by the Secretary of State George C. Marshall, the United States provided economic aid to Europe to underpin an economic revival. Marshall aid, eventually worth more than $12 billion, was also offered to the Soviet Union and the emerging Eastern bloc, where it was refused. Stalin took the same attitude toward Marshall aid as could be summed up in the old proverb "beware of Greeks bearing gifts."

Acceptance of Marshall aid would be incompatible with Soviet economic policy and with the regime's political goals. Meanwhile western Europe, as well as Turkey and Iceland, accepted Marshall aid with alacrity. In Washington, Congress formed the Economic Cooperation Administration to oversee the aid program, and Europe in 1948 created the Organization for European Economic Cooperation to coordinate the revival of the European economy. Europe had taken the first substantial steps toward the formation of a European Community, whose primary goals would be economic prosperity and military cooperation, both of which were necessary to preserve its freedom. Truman's power was such that he was shaping the destiny of the continent which had dominated world affairs for over five hundred years. Marshall aid, which would continue until 1952, gave the United States a controlling interest in the affairs of western Europe, and Europe's agenda would from this time forth be dictated, in part, by the President of the United States.

To fight the Cold War effectively it was also necessary to reform the American government, and 1947 also saw the passing of the National Security Act. It militarized the American government, creating a Secretary of Defense and a National Security Council, composed of civilian and military personnel, to advise the president on security. The council's staff was headed by a national security adviser, and the council had special advisers including the head of the Joint Chiefs of Staff. The director of the Central Intelligence Agency, which itself came into being with the National Security Act, was also to be a special adviser to the NSC. The CIA was created to centralize the collation and interpretation of foreign intelligence. It was later complemented by the formation of the National Security Agency, set up by presidential directive in 1952. The agency was a separate entity within the Department of Defense under the control of the Secretary of Defense, and its role was to protect government communications and to produce overseas intelligence. Working alongside the FBI, the NSA and the CIA gave the United States the means to protect itself from internal subversion and to undertake covert intelligence-gathering and, if need be, military action against the overseas enemies of the American government. The phrase "national security" acquired new connotations – an imperative for national survival and the implication of a threat against those who would seek to threaten it. The president was at the apex of the new national security system. Senator Daniel Patrick Moynihan has written that the passing of the National Security Act in some ways marked the emergence of a new era of presidential and American history:

> And so the modern age began. Three new institutions had entered American life: Conspiracy, Loyalty, Secrecy. Each had antecedents, but now there was a difference. Each had become institutional; bureaucracies were established to attend to each. In time there would be a Federal Bureau of Investigation to keep track of conspiracy at home, a Central Intelligence Agency to keep tabs abroad, an espionage statute and loyalty boards to root out disloyalty or subversion (Moynihan, 1998, pp. 98–9).

The toll of the fight against communism on the American way of life would be heavy.

The Truman presidency was to be judged first and foremost by success or failure in the fight against communism. It was significant that it was not until 1949 that Truman attached the label "Fair Deal" to his campaign to increase employment, and to improve living standards, especially by better health care and by building new houses. The need to package his domestic policies, and the delay in doing so until after Truman's victory in a close race for the White House in 1948, shows that domestic issues were low on Truman's agenda. Indeed, the Fair Deal was partly reactive to the Republican program in Congress. In 1947 the 80th Congress, despite the use of the presidential veto, had passed the Taft-Hartley Labor Relations Act. The Fair Deal promised to repeal the act and was thus not an initiative but a response. The primacy of foreign over domestic issues that reemerged in the Truman Presidency was to continue for as long as the Cold War continued to be fought. This was of vital importance in the history of the presidency. By pledging the United States to maintain an international role after the end of World War Two, and by his subsequent policies, Truman ensured that there would be no retreat into isolation as had happened at the end of the World War One. It also meant that foreign policy issues would predominate in future presidential elections and in lesser electoral clashes between the parties. The primacy of foreign issues, and American economic and military strength which gave America leadership of the free world, in turn meant that successive presidents would have to take a proactive role in the office. With presidential power greatest in the foreign and military fields, an agenda dominated by such issues meant the maintenance of presidential power and authority at an enhanced level. A *laissez-faire*, or caretaker model of presidency, was impossible to pursue after the Truman doctrine.

However, as Truman well knew, it was all right for presidents to pursue expansive policies – but would the electorate back him? It was election year in 1948 and with Truman standing for re-election the signs were not auspicious. On June 23 Soviet forces stopped all land traffic heading from western Germany along the access corridor to Berlin. The pre-war capital of Germany, lying deep in the heart of communist-controlled East Germany, was split into American, British, French, and Russian occupied zones. The arrangements for the city mirrored those drawn up for Germany as a whole, divided between the four occupying powers. But in early 1948 the Americans, British, and French joined their zones to form a single entity and allowed elections to state assemblies and to a federal constitutional convention. The decision to blockade the access corridor to Berlin, the vital lifeline on which the re-supply of the city depended, was the Soviet response. Now that there were two Germanys, Stalin did not want a capitalist haven in the middle of the emerging Soviet bloc. Truman's response was to organize the re-supply of the city by air, rather than risk a confrontation by pushing a land convoy through to Berlin. From June 1948 to the Soviet decision to drop the blockade in May 1949 everything that the city required, more than 4,500 tons a day of assorted goods from potatoes, to coal, to clothes, was ferried in by air. By the end of the airlift a German Democratic Republic had been created in the East and the Cold War division of Germany was complete.

The Berlin airlift formed the backdrop to the Democratic Convention held in Philadelphia in July 1948. The party was deeply divided, not over Truman's exercise of presidential power to wage the Cold War, but rather over his use of presidential power to further the cause of civil rights. As president, Truman became only too well aware of the discrimination against black Americans being practiced in the Southern states. He was determined to use his constitutional powers to address the problem, and in his speeches he put the issue of civil rights firmly on the agenda. Many Southern Democrats resented Truman's interference in an issue of crucial importance to the South. Meanwhile Liberal Democrats were eager to encourage Truman down the path of extending civil rights. At Philadelphia the battle lines were drawn with Truman in the midst of a growing struggle. The struggle culminated with the delegations from Mississippi and Alabama publicly walking out of the convention. Afterward, on July 17, a party of Southern Democrats, labeled Dixiecrats, gathered in Birmingham, Alabama, and nominated one of their number, Strom Thurmond, governor of South Carolina, as a presidential contender. He was to campaign on the issue of states' rights, which Truman's civil rights policies seemed to infringe. Presidential power to intervene in the affairs of the South was being contested in a particularly public and potentially damaging way. Moreover, on July 23, a group of left-wing Democrats met in Philadelphia to put forward Henry Wallace as a progressive candidate. The Democratic Party had now been completely split over the issue of presidential power and policies. Some argued that Truman had gone too far: the progressives felt that he should use his authority to take the civil rights issue much further. Indeed, that is exactly what Truman did. In late July 1948 he issued an executive order ending segregation in the United States military. Racial discrimination in job interviews for federal employees was also forbidden under the terms of another presidential order. This was Truman's response to the splits within his own party, but it seemed likely to have little effect on the election which appeared a lost cause.

Truman seemed destined to lose the election right up to polling day. Despite his tour of the country by train, and despite his ferocious attacks on the Republican-dominated Congress, he seemed certain to lose to his Republican rival Thomas E. Dewey by a considerable margin. Yet in the event Truman defied the splits in the Democratic Party and the forecasts of the newspapers to gather 303 electoral college votes to Dewey's 189. The Dixiecrat and progressive candidates fared quite well, each gathering more than a million votes, and Strom Thurmond took the states of Mississippi, Alabama, Louisiana, and South Carolina. Truman's shock victory arguably masked some important features of the election. The South was no longer solid Democratic territory, but more importantly Thurmond had successfully demonstrated that Truman's interpretation of his constitutional powers was resented in some quarters and that it would be contested. Impinging on the rights and interests of some Southern states in the campaign for civil rights was one thing, but the issue would become more pressing when it involved a much greater cross-section of American society. Foreign policy, and the developing Cold War, offered exactly this chance.

In his 1949 inaugural address delivered on January 20 Truman broadened the campaign against communism when he described a four-point program to further counter the continuing threat:

First, we will continue to give unfaltering support to the United Nations and related agencies, and we will continue to search for ways to strengthen their authority and increase their effectiveness . . .

Second, we will continue our programs for world economic recovery . . .

Third, we will strengthen freedom-loving nations against the dangers of aggression . . .

Fourth, we must embark on a bold new program for making the benefits of our scientific advances and industrial progress available for the improvement of underdeveloped areas.

The four-point program promised to carry the Cold War into Africa and Asia where there would be a struggle between the United States and the Soviet Union for the friendship of those parts of the colonial empires of Europe moving swiftly toward independence. The points raised by Truman would eventually be one of the cornerstones of the foreign aid program of the United States.

Truman also felt it necessary to continue to galvanize the nations of western Europe to take more effective steps to defend themselves. Part of his inaugural address was aimed at rallying the forces of democracy against totalitarianism, and on April 4 the North Atlantic Treaty Organization came into being as the North Atlantic Treaty was signed in Washington. Twelve democracies signed the document by which they united to defend western Europe from attack. Congressional approval for the treaty was granted by 82 votes to 13, a remarkable gesture of approval for Truman's conduct of the Cold War.

Although 1949 saw a hardening of Truman's policy toward communism it also saw one of communism's greatest triumphs. By early 1949 it was increasingly obvious that the communist forces were gaining the upper hand in the Chinese civil war which had raged since the defeat of Japan in 1945. The Chinese nationalists, on whom American hopes for China rested, had been lavishly supplied with over $2 billion worth of aid since 1945, and the United States had also assisted them in other ways. Before the close of 1949 the nationalists had been soundly beaten, retreating to the island of Formosa, and only the United States Navy prevented complete victory for the forces of Mao Tse-tung. To many Republicans Truman's intervention was too little too late. The most populous country in the world had been lost to communism, and in global terms that represented a major defeat for the capitalist bloc. The strength of world communism had been massively augmented and a new front for the war of ideologies established in Asia. Under considerable criticism, the American government stepped up its efforts to contain communism, and indeed began to view the world in a starkly bipolar way. In the circumstances of the Cold War it was hard to accept that nations or movements might be non-aligned. Thus by 1950 the United States was backing the French in their struggle to eradicate the anti-imperialist forces of Vietnamese nationalism. Ho Chi Minh, the leader of Vietnamese Nationalism, was just as much inspired by the American revolution as by the Communist Manifesto, but in the circumstances of the Cold War he was labeled a communist first and a nationalist a distant second.

On top of the fall of China and the discovery that the forces of communism were becoming stronger and more threatening in Vietnam and elsewhere, in 1949 the presidency, Congress, and the American scientific establishment were shocked as they learned that the Soviet Union had managed to construct and detonate a nuclear bomb. This event had a number of profound repercussions, as it led to a deepening of the anti-communist hysteria that had been developing in the United States. Since 1938 the House Un-American Activities Committee had been probing the extent of foreign subversion in the United States. By 1945 its focus of attention had switched from Nazi sympathizers toward the puppets of the Soviet Union. Truman added to the sense of panic about internal subversion in March 1947 as he set up a program designed to ensure the loyalty of federal employees. Over three million of them had been investigated by 1951 and more than 2,200 had left their posts voluntarily or been fired. There were a number of spectacular criminal trials that followed the anti-communist witch hunt. In 1949 eleven members of the American Communist Party were found guilty of conspiring to encourage the revolutionary overthrow of the American government. The following year there was general satisfaction as an Anglo-American spy ring that had gathered atomic secrets for the Soviets was uncovered. Two alleged American members of the spy ring, Julius and Ethel Rosenberg, were executed in 1953. More damaging for the Truman administration was the Alger Hiss case. Hiss, president of the Carnegie Endowment for International Peace, who had served in the State Department, was identified as a communist spy in testimony to the House Un-American Activities Committee in 1948. Hiss denied the charges but was tried for espionage. The result was a mistrial. Nevertheless, he was subsequently tried for perjury and was convicted of lying about his un-American activities. In the course of these events Truman, and Secretary of State Dean Acheson, made statements that were taken as a sign of support for Hiss. The conviction of Hiss convinced many Republicans that Truman was indeed soft on communism and that the State Department and other branches of the government had been infiltrated by communist agents.

Some Republicans used the red scare as a means to further their careers. Richard M. Nixon made his name pursuing the Hiss case and won election to the Senate in 1950 on the strength of it. More dangerously, on February 9, 1950, Senator Joseph McCarthy of Wisconsin made a speech in West Virginia in which he asserted that the State Department was a nest of communists and communist sympathizers. When challenged about a list naming the subversives at work within the State Department he shifted his ground, extending his charges. It would take another three years for the bogus nature of McCarthy's continuing claims to be appreciated and the Senator discredited. In that time he would destroy and blemish the careers of a number of well-known Americans, including George C. Marshall. In the climate of hysteria few dared challenge the hammer of the reds from Wisconsin. That the presidency should remain silent in the midst of such a divisive personal campaign was particularly striking. At times McCarthy appeared more powerful than Truman, and while no-one could question the loyalty of the Senator from Wisconsin there were those who had their doubts about the anti-communism of the former Senator from Missouri. However, paradoxically, the red scare did further reinforce presidential authority and power. In the climate of fear, to voice open dissent from the policies of the US government became dangerous. The red scare helped to produce a certain conformity of views on the dangers of communism, American foreign policy, and the exercise of presidential power necessary to guard against the Soviet Union.

In addition to the intensification of the "reds under the bed" panic of the late 1940s and early 1950s, the explosion of a Soviet atomic weapon in 1949 also led to a reappraisal of American defense and foreign policies. The United States had lost its nuclear monopoly and the Soviet Union was now in a position to retaliate against American use of nuclear weapons. Soviet superiority in conventional forces could no longer be offset by the threat of nuclear weapons. The National Security Council reviewed the situation thoroughly in a secret document labeled NSC 68. This document took the Cold War to a new level of intensity as it called for a massive military build-up to ensure the security of the free world and hopefully to persuade the communist bloc to abandon the path of expansionism. NSC 68 made the Cold War truly global and noted that it was just as important to stop communist expansion in Asia and Africa as it was in Europe. The American historians Stephen Ambrose and Douglas Brinkley later commented:

> NSC 68 represented the practical extension of the Truman Doctrine, which had been worldwide in its implications but limited to Europe in its application. The document provided the justification for America's assuming the role of world policeman . . . NSC 68 was realistic in assessing what it would cost America to become the world policeman. State Department officials estimated that defense expenditures of $35 billion a year would be required to implement the program of rearming America and NATO (Ambrose and Brinkley, 1997, pp. 111–12).

NSC 68 was a fascinating and important document. It owed its origins to one of the new organs of the national security state, and the intelligence failure which led to it only reinforced the case for a greater emphasis on national security. By its implications it called for enhanced American vigilance and the maintenance of a war economy. The implications for the presidency were also profound. The public needed to be convinced that their tax dollars had to be spent on the military, and that strong presidential leadership was essential to the success of rearmament and the containment of the Soviet Union.

In June 1950 the Cold War heated up still further when communist North Korea attacked the capitalist South. The country had been divided as a temporary measure in 1945 between an American-occupied zone in the south and a Russian-occupied zone in the north. As the Cold War developed the occupied zones took on increasingly separate existences. By 1948 American and Soviet forces had withdrawn and mutually opposed regimes eyed each other across the line of division at the 38th parallel. With Stalin's approval, on June 25 North Korea launched an invasion of the South, rapidly sweeping before them the opposing military forces. Truman correctly interpreted the invasion as a vital test of his doctrine and all that it stood for: the resolve of a united western world to resist communist expansionism. If the western allies failed to respond effectively to this challenge there was the possibility of a follow-up against Berlin or elsewhere in Europe.

The United Nations rapidly condemned the North for its unwarranted aggression. It helped that the Soviet Union was at the time boycotting the United Nations over the failure of the latter to allow communist China to assume the position in the organization held by the Nationalist government, which in 1949 had retreated to the island of Formosa (Taiwan). On June 27 the Security Council of the United Nations called on all members of the organization to help South Korea repulse the armed aggression of the North. That gave Truman the opportunity to intervene, but the question was how far could he, or should he, go. Truman was assisted by the fact that it was the United Nations which was taking the lead over how to respond to the crisis in Korea. The United States could be seen to be upholding her international obligations rather than going to war against communism. Indeed, Truman would later represent the intervention in Korea as a police action, quite unlike war. The fact that US forces would subsequently be joined by those of fourteen other nations would further mask the realities of the fight in Korea. This camouflage in part would hide the constitutional realities of

41

intervention in Korea – this was war pure and simple, and for that congressional approval was required – and given the red scare there were plenty of people in Congress and beyond who would be happy to take refuge in that camouflage rather than risk accusations of being soft on communism.

On June 29 Truman took the decision to commit not just air and sea forces to Korea, but ground troops. He enlarged the commitment the following day. However, the constitutional issues now became grave. Did the president have the authority under the Constitution to commit the United States to a police action/war in Korea without obtaining the assent of Congress first? There were those in Congress such as Senator Kenneth Wherry of Nebraska who thought that he did not. By the end of June Truman faced the difficult choice of what to do next. As Arthur Schlesinger records:

Truman had evidently not made up his mind about the scope of presidential authority. Nor did he pretend to legal skills. But he had a most eminent lawyer at his right hand. His Secretary of State had been law clerk for Justice Brandeis, whom Truman had known and revered as a majestic explorer of the Constitution. Acheson, moreover, had been a senior member of Washington's leading law firm and was still a daily walking companion of Justice Frankfurter. On July 3 Acheson recommended that Truman *not* ask for a resolution [from Congress approving his action] but instead rely on his constitutional powers as President and Commander in Chief. On the same day the State Department churned out a memorandum listing 87 instances . . . in which Presidents had sent American forces into combat on their own initiative. Truman, impressed by the appearance of precedent and concerned not to squander the power of his office, accepted his Secretary of State's recommendation (Schlesinger, 1974, pp. 132–3).

Most commentators at the time believed that Truman would have gained congressional sanction for his actions, but by not requesting their support the president actively provoked some congressmen. Some believed that Truman had exceeded his authority as president and that the precedents that the State Department was happy to list, including the use of presidential authority to suppress piracy, bore no relation to the fighting of a major land war in Asia. Further harm was done as the administration used the urgency of the crisis to head off any potential debate about presidential authority and the commitment to South Korea.

The rather dubious status of Truman's intervention in Korea had some important repercussions. Firstly, it led to a significant and unnecessary division between the executive and legislative branches of government over Korea and presidential authority. Secondly, Truman's exercise of presidential power to wage war without congressional backing itself created a precedent that future presidents might invoke to sanction their own actions. Thirdly, Korea contributed to the growing breakdown of the bipartisan foreign policy that Truman had successfully followed since 1946. The Republicans, especially senior figures such as the veteran Senator Arthur Vandenberg, had been willing accomplices to the development of Truman's policies designed to counter the Soviet Union. But by the late 1940s the spirit of bipartisanship was being eroded:

> . . . the fall of China, and the explosion of the Russian atomic bomb were used by the Republican Party in the late 1940s and early 1950s to prove to the American people that the Democratic party was utterly unable to cope with the dangers confronting the nation. All of this helps explain the radical decline of bipartisanship, symbolized by Vandenberg's leadership in the passage of the Marshall Plan and the Truman Doctrine (Caridi, 1968, p. 14).

The intervention in Korea, and the fighting between a Democratic president and Republican Congress that resulted, strained this relationship still further.

Truman tried hard to rally public support behind the war effort in Korea but it was largely in vain. Korea was a long way from the United States and most Americans had not heard of it before June 1950. By the end of July some 4,000 Americans had died for the sake of South Korea, and American intervention had not prevented the

North from almost completely over-running the South. The price of defending South Korea seemed too high, even after the landing of American forces at Inchon on September 15 had led to a series of reverses for the North Korean army that saw them retreat back over the 38th parallel. The longer the war dragged on the greater the impact on the American economy. After years of wartime austerity America was in no mood to sacrifice the economic security and rising standard of living of the postwar period. Congress was sufficiently alienated to refuse Truman's requests to raise taxes to fund the war in Korea. Meanwhile the war effort was damaged by strikes and labor unrest. In addition, the war threatened to expand beyond the borders of Korea. On November 25, 1950, as United Nations forces completed the rout of the North and approached North Korea's border with China, a quarter of a million "volunteers" from the Chinese Red Army were thrown into the battle. United Nations forces suffered a series of reverses as they were pushed southwards. The inadequacies of the US army after years of neglect since 1945 were brought home brutally. General Douglas MacArthur, the theater commander, requested nuclear weapons to halt the Chinese onslaught. He also requested a naval blockade of China and the bombing of Chinese airfields in Manchuria, where in fact MiG jets piloted by Russians were flying in support of communist ground forces in Korea. American support for an invasion of the Chinese mainland by Taiwanese nationalists was also part of MacArthur's thinking. The Chinese attack and MacArthur's response to it threatened to expand the Korean action into a major war. The fighting there eventually stabilized back along the 38th parallel in March 1951, but Truman found himself at loggerheads with MacArthur. As the president strove to get negotiations for a ceasefire going MacArthur threatened that China would be attacked unless they made peace. MacArthur compounded his insubordination with public criticism of the President. On April 5 the House of Representatives listened as a letter attacking the president written by MacArthur was read out. Truman had no choice but to fire the General, which he did on April 11.

The dismissal of so distinguished a military figure as MacArthur produced an immediate backlash. Nowhere was this more strongly felt than in Congress, which had been the venue for MacArthur's act of insubordination and on his return MacArthur made a speech to a special joint session. He played the role of the career soldier perfectly and a significant strand of congressional opinion sided with him. Throughout the country Truman's support dipped sharply. However, a subsequent Senate investigation supported the administration's view that MacArthur had threatened to involve the United States in a wider war in a particularly unfavorable part of the globe. On July 10, 1951, armistice talks began at Panmunjom. By the time they concluded on July 27, 1953, 33,000 Americans would have died in Korea, 103,000 more would be wounded or missing and Harry S. Truman would have been out of the White House for over six months.

The Korean war meant that Truman left the White House under something of a cloud. The war was unsatisfactory in that it was a distraction and a threat to domestic prosperity. But more importantly it was a war that did not follow the same pattern as America's other foreign wars. Max Hastings has noted: "Many United Nations veterans came home from Korea to discover that their experience was of no interest to their fellow countrymen. The war seemed an unsatisfactory, inglorious, and thus unwelcome memory" (Hastings, 1987, p. 409). It had been fought in a relatively insignificant part of the world, and it had been hard to convince the voters that vital US interests were at stake. Yet with Chinese intervention, and the backing of Russia, the war in Korea had had the potential to escalate into a third world war, which (with both sides armed with nuclear weapons) promised to exceed vastly the brutality and destruction of every previous conflict on the planet. Worse still, after the loss of so many lives, by the close of the war it had appeared as though America had gained precisely nothing. There had been no victory to cheer or even peace to celebrate. An armistice along the 38th parallel, the point from which the war had originally started, was all that had been achieved. And Korea had served only to deepen the Cold War. As Richard Whelan writes:

> The Korean War resolved nothing. It had arisen in the first place out of the extreme tension and frustrations of the Cold War, and it

served mainly to intensify them. Before Korea, the United States and Communist China were adversaries; afterwards they were mortal enemies locked in a blood feud (Whelan, 1990, p. 373).

Yet here lay a fundamental difference in perception between the politicians and the public. While the public might see Korea as almost a defeat of sorts, in Washington there was a certain satisfaction. Communist aggression had been halted. The United Nations had withstood its first major challenge and the western world had rallied against communist expansionism. The West had demonstrated its willingness to pay a high price to stop communist aggression. Congress was caught in two minds between public and government perceptions, but it was unhappy at the way in which Truman had committed America to fight in Korea. There were also those in Congress that remained unhappy at the way in which the fighting had been conducted. Dismissing one of the most distinguished American soldiers of the twentieth century did not seem exactly conducive to the chances of victory in Korea. In a way MacArthur had been proved right – expanding the war was the only way to prosecute it effectively. Too few people saw that, in the circumstances of the Cold War, it was necessary for the president to couple the use of presidential authority to facilitate an effective military response to communist aggression with the use of that same authority to ensure that any conflict was strictly limited. The emerging rules of the Cold War, in part conditioned by the developing technology and speed of military action in the jet age, meant that the president had to take a lead in responding to any emerging crisis. Congress and the Constitution would have to follow in his wake. However, if humanity was to survive, the conflict had to be kept within certain boundaries. This was a new kind of warfare with new rules and new weapons. It called for a new approach to presidential authority, involving the more liberal interpretation of the Constitution and past precedent that Acheson gave to Truman before the latter intervened in Korea without congressional approval.

Moreover, American commitments to the United Nations and NATO also created a situation in which a president might have to choose between the international obligations of the United States and his obligation to the spirit and the letter of the Constitution. America's international obligations were binding, but to meet them with the necessary speed might raise grave constitutional issues. Those international obligations also clouded public perceptions: American citizens were not always certain whether their sons were being asked to lay down their lives for the sake of real American interests or for something more nebulous. In the far future, as the United Nations celebrated its fiftieth birthday, the issue of whether American troops were under the command of the president of the United States and the officers of the American military, or the United Nations and its appointees, would become a real issue in domestic politics.

During the Truman era a serious attempt was made to equip and mold the presidency for a new, more dangerous age. Truman continued to lead from the front as Franklin D. Roosevelt had done. He set the national agenda, and indeed played the leading role in setting the international agenda from the formation of the United Nations to the western responses to the dangers of communist expansionism. Truman interpreted his authority liberally, from using his veto to block Republican legislation to his authority as commander-in-chief to intervene in Korea. Many people did not like this, from the Dixiecrats with their concerns over states' rights, to those in Congress who thought that Truman went beyond the Constitution in intervening in Korea. In both cases Truman felt that there was a moral imperative which compelled the president to take action. There was a need to be decisive and speedy.

In later years Truman's interpretation of his office came under criticism. Korea appeared like a prequel to the still less popular war in Vietnam. But Truman's decision to intervene in Korea was based on a sound, practical assessment of the situation. He understood the emerging rules and tactics of the Cold War better than some of his critics. The challenge in Korea could not be refused. Yet even if Truman was wrong over the constitutional means of intervention in Korea, his interpretation of his office is still hard to criticize because the same view of the presidency that cost so many lives in Korea also led to improvements in civil rights. Truman, like Roosevelt, viewed the office as a dynamic catalyst for change, and as a source of national leadership.

Truman also made more concrete changes to the institution of the presidency with the National Security Act of 1947. The creation of a National Security Council was based on the perception that there was a clear and present danger to the United States and that the president required specialist advice. The formation of the CIA and NSA was designed to help the US government meet this threat. The red scare and the McCarthy witch-hunts were on the one hand disreputable, but also useful in that they created the kind of climate in which the American public would support the fighting of a Cold War against the Soviet Union. With the Truman Doctrine, the Marshall Plan, and NSC 68 the United States was put on a war footing that became ever more manifest after June 1950. Yet this was not a conventional war, as envisaged in the Constitution. The president was now the guardian of the free world, but Congress and the public did not see the world in quite the same way as the White House. So while presidential power was enhanced by the Cold War the very nature of that war meant that the enhancement was not accepted uncritically. The Cold War was at times something of an illusion rather than a reality. As a result, in the years after Truman the level of presidential power would become increasingly disputed and actively contested.

THREE

Ike: Covert Cleverness

Following the outbreak of the Korean war in 1950 the Truman administration became steadily more unpopular. The slogan "time for a change" had almost worked against the Democrats in 1948. By 1952 it was still more effective. In that year, as the war continued to drag on, a Republican victory in the forthcoming presidential election became a certainty rather than a probability. While Adlai Stevenson emerged as the front runner for the nomination of the Democratic Party, within the ranks of the Republican Party there was a much closer fight. One of the leading candidates was Robert A. Taft, son of the former Republican president William H. Taft. He was a party man through and through who had been elected to the Senate from Ohio in 1938. His opposition to the New Deal and his belief in right-wing Republican policies earned him the label Mr. Conservative. He was a real thorn in the side of the Truman administration and had been instrumental in the Taft-Hartley Labor Relations Act of 1947, restricting the bargaining rights of organized labor. As the standard-bearer of the Republican right it was natural that he should emerge as a candidate for the presidential nomination. However, the center and the left wing of the Republican Party were less than enthusiastic about Taft. The son of the former president threatened a return to an old-style presidency and an old-style foreign policy. Fewer foreign entanglements would be combined with less presidential meddling at home. The threat of a return to something approaching *laissez-faire* and isolationism, the hallmarks of the Republican presidency under Harding and Coolidge, led the left and center of the Republican Party to search for its own potential candidate for the party's nomination.

To their rescue rode Dwight D. Eisenhower – war hero, architect of D-Day and a key player in the organization of the defenses of NATO in 1949. Born in 1890, Eisenhower was a career soldier who had entered West Point in 1911. World War One finished before he reached France, but in the interwar period he rose steadily through the ranks of the officer corps of the United States Army. In 1941 he was promoted to the rank of Colonel and then to Brigadier-General. By July 1942 Eisenhower had been entrusted with the task of overseeing the invasion of North Africa, and by February 1943 he had reached the rank of four-star General. In recognition of his masterminding of the Allied invasion of Europe in June 1944, he had, on December 20 1944, been appointed to the rank of five-star General. After the war he had succeeded George C. Marshall as Army Chief of Staff late in 1945, subsequently playing a leading role in reorganizing the American military and ultimately the forces of the North Atlantic Treaty Organization. The General then faced a choice of whether to live out a quiet retirement, punctuated by a daily round of golf, or aspire to still higher office.

In early 1952 Eisenhower revealed that he was a lifelong Republican and that if he heard a clear summons from the electorate he would run for the presidency. Eisenhower's name was then put forward for the primary elections by enthusiastic Republicans. Those primaries, particularly in Minnesota, Nebraska, and New Hampshire, showed that the voters wanted Eisenhower. After resigning from command of NATO, and retiring from the Army, he launched his campaign for the Republican nomination in Kansas on June 4. Eisenhower's image as a clean-cut, uncompromising, war-winning hero was balanced by a genuine sincerity and father-like warmth. At the Republican Convention in Chicago the moderate Eisenhower was preferred to the more right-wing Taft. Eisenhower won narrowly on the first ballot. To balance the ticket Richard M. Nixon, who had made a name for himself as a virulent anti-communist, was appointed as vice-presidential candidate. Taft would die the following year.

The outcome of the contest between Taft and Eisenhower for the Republican presidential nomination was vital to the continuance of high levels of presidential power and authority. Republican opposition to the New Deal had involved opposition to Roosevelt's style of presidency and his willingness to interpret his constitutional authority in the most liberal way. Roosevelt's opponents did not like his willingness to ignore the spirit and, indeed, the letter of the constitution. Republicans protested against the ever-expanding interventionism inherent in the model of presidency pursued by Roosevelt and Truman. In 1952 Robert A. Taft, among others, wanted a more restrained presidency. Significantly his nemesis at Chicago came from outside the mainstream Republican Party. Indeed, Eisenhower appeared to stand above politics and sectional interest. He represented the mainstream and the mainstream wanted to maintain most aspects of the New Deal. The American public did not want a return to isolationism, *laissez-faire*, and minimalist presidency.

This was borne out during the election. The Republican Party united around the General's middle-of-the-road policies and, in particular, his pledge to find a way out of the Korean war. In November 1952 Eisenhower was elected in a landslide, winning by 442 electoral college votes to Adlai Stevenson's 89. The authority given to Eisenhower by such an endorsement from the electorate was indisputable. In addition, his election marked a resurgence of support for the Republican Party that enhanced his political authority and power. He was the first Republican president for twenty years and his election was capped by a Republican victory in congressional elections which gave them a small majority in both houses. In state and local elections the Republicans also did well. The message was clear: the electorate liked what Eisenhower stood for. That meant maintenance of the modern-style presidency created by Roosevelt and Truman, but a rather more restrained, cost-conscious, approach in the formulation of government policy. Within a matter of weeks after his election Eisenhower had made good his campaign promise to "go to Korea," and his search for a peaceful solution to the war would lead to an armistice in 1953. That triumph, and reductions in the international tensions generated by the Cold War, would be coupled with economic prosperity that would lead the Republican Party to re-nominate Ike unanimously in 1956. In the subsequent presidential election Eisenhower would defeat Stevenson even more emphatically than he had done in 1952 by 457 electoral college votes to 73. Despite losing control of Congress, the Republican Party sensed that the electorate showed few signs of wishing to return to the old-style presidency, and most Republican politicians came to recognize that there would be no future in campaigning for such a policy. Only by embracing the changes to the presidency wrought by the Democrats from 1933 to 1952 could they expect the enthusiastic endorsement of the electorate. A consensus among the parties and the people had been reached about the overall nature and exercise of presidential power and authority.

However, in his style of presidential leadership Eisenhower did his best to reassure the Republican right, creating a set of illusions about his presidency that were cunningly contrived and brilliantly executed. The role of president is composed of two parts: that of head of state and that of executive leader. In the Roosevelt/Truman years the executive leadership aspect of the presidency had been promoted sometimes to the detriment of the work of the president as head of state. Eisenhower highly effectively sought to redress the balance. Much of the scholarship on Ike divides into two clear camps: one that he was content to play the part of head of state who did not care too much for the hurly-burly of politics – a man who was more interested in his golf handicap than forcing through a political agenda; the second camp argues that this was merely a clever façade for the covert exercise of presidential power – a calculated public relations exercise behind which Eisenhower pursued his political aims including a lessening of Cold War tensions. Fred Greenstein has argued:

> On the assumption that a president who is predominantly viewed in terms of his political powers will lose public support by not appearing to be a proper chief of state, Eisenhower went to great lengths to conceal the political side of his leadership. He did this so well and played the part of nonpolitical chief of state so convincingly that until recently most writers on the presidency viewed him through the lens of his 1950s liberal critics as an aging hero who reigned more than he ruled and lacked the energy, motivation, and political know-how to have a significant impact on events (Greenstein, 1983, p. 5).

Eisenhower played this game of the covert exercise of presidential power with considerable talent. He had remarkable management skills, being able to charm, coerce, or persuade those with whom he came into contact to his chosen course of action. He was also able to craft a public image for himself that suggested only a limited engagement with the finer points of policy. The newsreels were happy to portray the head of state conducting official business on the golf course or receiving visitors at the White House, while Eisenhower's press conference performances were renowned for syntactical and grammatical errors and the briefest references to the policies of the administration. Some observers have taken these performances at face value. As Piers Brendon has written:

> Eisenhower was the first television president, and his wartime glamour melted away under the glare of the klieg lights. The crisp uniformed figure disappeared and in his place was an ailing, incoherent senior citizen, forever, as journalists liked to say, uttering "five-star generalities" and "crossing the thirty-eighth platitude" (Brendon, 1987, p. 4).

Yet such fumbling and inaccuracy was often deliberately employed by Eisenhower to mask his deeper intentions. In the circumstances of the Cold War, an off-hand remark in a press conference could cause a major diplomatic incident and Eisenhower knew it. General clarity in a response to a question combined with ambiguity about a particular point would invite different readings, some of which could be detrimental to the interests of the administration. However, if a response was generally ambiguous people would be less likely to try and second-guess his line on particular points. In his public performances Eisenhower was often sphinx-like: deliberately posing riddles and talking in generalities to conceal the details of policy. Throughout, Eisenhower built on his image as the distinguished general, albeit now a senior citizen, answering his country's call to further duty. Health problems, including a serious heart attack and an operation on his small intestine, also helped to add to the effect. His periods of illness and convalescence were carefully stage-managed. The public were reassured that the business of government was carrying on as normal, and after his heart attack the image on the newsreels of Ike in a wheelchair suggested a man putting country before self.

Eisenhower was also ready to resort to rather less subtle techniques of image-building and concealment. During the McCarthy versus the Army hearings in 1954 the President, after trying to appease the senator from Wisconsin, invoked the principle of executive privilege to deny information to McCarthy's committee. It was claimed that it was essential to withhold information on the grounds that to venture it would threaten "efficient and effective administration." Invoking executive privilege on these grounds meant a vast enlargement of presidential power, allowing the president to hide behind the principle whenever it was tactically useful. However, in 1954 liberals from both parties applauded Eisenhower's "stand" against McCarthyism. The hidden hand was determined to stay hidden wherever possible. So successful was this policy of concealed leadership, the exercise of power behind the image of the non-partisan elder statesman, that Eisenhower would serve two terms, and would enjoy an approval rating consistently above 50 percent.

Despite the change in style, in substance there was a smooth continuation of the policies initiated by Truman. As Supreme Commander of NATO Eisenhower had put into practice the necessary measures to give effect to the Truman doctrine. As president he saw no need to depart from the Truman line. Containment would continue, although with a heavier reliance on nuclear weapons than previously, in order to save costs on conventional arms. Many Republicans believed that the military build-up under Truman would eventually bankrupt the United States. Eisenhower appreciated the threat and evolved the New Look defense strategy placing greater emphasis on nuclear weapons as a result. The military posture of the United States and her allies would remain defensive. Deterrence was the watchword. There would be no rollback of communism, as some on the Republican right clamoured for. However, there was a substantial element of bluff in the New Look policy. One commentator has argued:

The policy, on its face, was incredible. Perhaps the United States conceived Berlin to be so crucial to American security that it would risk nuclear war to keep that city out of Russian hands. (Truman had responded to the blockade of 1948 – when the United States still possessed a nuclear monopoly – with nothing more belligerent than transport planes.) But it boggled the mind to think that the American leadership would put New York in jeopardy to preserve Seoul or Saigon (Brands in Bischof and Ambrose, 1995, p. 131).

While in public the United States would remain on the defensive, under Eisenhower aggressive covert action was increasingly used to secure policy objectives. In effect, the Central Intelligence Agency created by Truman in 1947 became the means by which the Eisenhower administration would go on the offensive. Covert action meant covert presidential sanction and use of his powers as president. It meant keeping the truth about foreign policy, and the threats faced by the United States, from the American people. It meant keeping Congress in the dark. It was true that most other presidents had authorized covert action and intelligence-gathering at one time or another, but under Eisenhower, and in the circumstances of the Cold War, the practice became well established. Allen Dulles, brother of the Secretary of State, John Foster Dulles, rose to become chief of the CIA under Eisenhower. The connection this created between foreign policy objectives and covert means of action was rather unhealthy, although both men were able and fully merited their appointment.

Within months of Eisenhower coming to office, the CIA had helped to overthrow the government of Iran headed by Mohammed Mossadegh who had made the mistake of challenging western oil interests:

Planning for a coup had been going on since November 1952, when the British secret service had approached CIA agent Kermit Roosevelt, the grandson of the first President Roosevelt and the cousin of the second. Partly because of his experience with wartime intelligence, partly because of his desire for efficient and inexpensive means to achieve American Cold War goals, Eisenhower decided to place far more emphasis than had Truman on covert operations. Operation AJAX in Iran was the CIA's first major test during the Eisenhower presidency. Under Roosevelt's direction, CIA operatives distributed Iranian currency to the equivalent of $100,000 to recruit street demonstrators who demanded Mossadegh's removal. The coup succeeded in mid-August, and the shah, who had fled the country only a few days earlier, returned from his brief exile (Pach and Richardson, 1991, p. 88).

In the following year the CIA, with Eisenhower's approval, helped to organize a military coup in Guatemala against President Jacobo Guzman who had come to power with communist backing, and whose rhetoric was too left wing for some in Ike's administration. A similar problem faced the administration over Cuba in January 1959 after the forces of Fidel Castro had come to power following a lengthy civil war against the dictator Fulgencio Batista. Castro's pledge that he would initiate a social and economic revolution alarmed many Americans. Land redistribution and nationalization of foreign companies smacked of communism. Even though Castro coupled this with seeking help from the United States, Eisenhower was put off by claims that Castro was a communist. The signature of a trade agreement between Cuba and the Soviet Union in 1960 seemed conclusive evidence of Castro's leanings. During his last year of office Eisenhower scaled down imports of Cuban sugar and then they were stopped altogether, as were exports. On January 3, 1961, Eisenhower severed diplomatic relations with Cuba. However, even before this he had authorized the training of a force of anti-Castro Cuban exiles that might be brought into play at some point in the future. Meanwhile the CIA were busy undermining the Cuban economy by covert action and were investigating ways to kill Castro. Presidential power had now reached the point where the murder or removal of foreign heads of state could be contemplated and indeed carried out. The possible complications that might arise from covert action were not fully thought through. Nor were the implications for the Constitution. Eisenhower instinctively chose the hidden-hand way. In public presidential power was held in check, but with the resort to covert action the president was free to do almost anything as long as it was not subjected to the glare of the media or public opinion. Under Eisenhower's successor in 1961, John F. Kennedy, the General's secretive policies toward Cuba would produce a disaster.

The same was also true in respect to Eisenhower's approach to East Asia. Eisenhower was as good as his campaign promises in 1952 in that he went to Korea and in July 1953 managed to conclude an armistice to bring the fighting in Korea to an end. Yet even in doing this the hidden hand was significant. In May 1953 he stepped up the bombing of North Korea, and used John Foster Dulles to convey a threat in secret that the use of tactical nuclear weapons against China was back on the agenda. Secrecy, the avoidance of public scrutiny of presidential policy and power, was a significant feature of the Eisenhower years. One year after the threat to bomb China, the administration was again wrestling secretly with a problem – whether or not to intervene in Indo-China. Since 1946 French troops had been engaged in fighting a nationalist movement inside Vietnam that sought to end decades of French colonial rule. French control over Indo-China had been established in the mid- to late-nineteenth century only to be humiliatingly replaced by the Japanese during World War Two. On September 2, 1945, Ho Chi Minh proclaimed the birth and independence of the Democratic Republic of Vietnam. Attempts to reach a compromise with the French proved hopeless and in 1946 a war between the French colonial forces and Vietnamese nationalists broke out. The war went badly for the French, culminating on May 7 with the overwhelming of the French fortress at Dien Bien Phu. Prior to this, Eisenhower had flirted with the idea of using American airpower to relieve the garrison, and since 1953 America had been providing most of the funds needed to keep the French war effort going. Although Eisenhower refused to listen to suggestions that American nuclear weapons should be used to support the garrison at Dien Bien Phu, the CIA was actively involved in the fight against Vietnamese nationalism which was automatically condemned as being part of the communist monolithic conspiracy against western capitalism. In effect, by May 1954 the United States was fighting a war in Vietnam using the French military, with appropriate CIA backing, as little more than anti-communist mercenaries. The United States was at war, but not in the way that the makers of the Constitution had understood it back in the eighteenth century. The new method of conflict involved in the Cold

War meant that some of the checks in the Constitution were being bypassed. If the president camouflaged his actions carefully enough he would never be called to account for them.

French defeat in Vietnam led to an agreement, negotiated at Geneva, which partitioned Vietnam at the 17th parallel, creating a communist state in the north, and a pro-western state in the south. The division was only supposed to be temporary until elections scheduled for 1956 which would lead to the reunification of the country under a single popularly elected government. However, Korea had proved that temporary divisions had a habit of becoming more long-standing. Korea had also demonstrated to many that communism was inherently expansionist and that South Vietnam, if left to its own devices, might become subject to subversion or outright assault from the North. Thus increasing amounts of American aid were channeled to South Vietnam to help it withstand the communist onslaught which was considered inevitable in the long term. The formation of the Southeast Asian Treaty Organization (SEATO) on September 8, 1954, was intended to create an Asian version of NATO with the aim of containing communist aggression against South Vietnam, or any other Southeast Asian state. An internal State Department paper of April 29, 1960, defined America's ambitions in the region as being:

To prevent the countries of Southeast Asia from passing into or becoming economically dependent upon the Communist bloc; to persuade them that their best interests lie in greater cooperation and stronger affiliations with the rest of the Free World; and to assist them to develop toward stable, free representative governments with the will and ability to resist communism from within and without, and thereby to contribute to the strengthening of the Free World (Glennon, 1986, p. 412).

SEATO was complemented the following year by the signature of METO (the Middle East Treaty Organization). With NATO, METO, and SEATO John Foster Dulles had created a series of defensive pacts designed to contain the communist world. Congress endorsed the decision, but overall it meant a massive extension of America's responsibilities in the world. By the end of the Eisenhower administration the United States was specifically pledged to go to war to defend over forty other states, quite apart from her commitments under the charter of the United Nations.

Presidential power and the circumstances of the Cold War were creating a situation in which events around the globe were seen in strictly bipolar ways. An event had to be either good for the Soviet Union, or good for the United States and the western world. There could be no neutrality, nor could there be any quarter given or compromise sought with the opponent. The lessons of pre-war appeasement were not lost on the policy-makers. This produced a mind-set in which Eisenhower exercised ever greater powers, not just in the United States, but more importantly in global terms. Dulles's pactomania meant a significant extension of American power across the globe and, by implication, that of the president who would have to choose whether or not the United States should uphold its obligations. Whenever Eisenhower asked for congressional support against communism he got it, most especially in 1955 when the President was authorized to take necessary steps to prevent Taiwan and its related islands from falling to Communist China. Although McCarthyism had come to an end with Senate condemnation of the Senator's tactics and campaign on December 2, 1954, there were few who wanted to be perceived as being weak on communism. Thus Eisenhower enjoyed considerable authority over Congress in pursuit of his foreign policy objectives, even though the Democrats had gained a majority in 1954. In some ways, the Democrats gaining control over Congress actually helped Eisenhower. In 1953 Senator John Bricker of Ohio had put forward an amendment to the US Constitution by which any treaty that conflicted with the Constitution would be declared automatically invalid. The Bricker amendment also promised to give new powers to Congress to control the making of executive agreements. The amendment was a clear threat to presidential power, and was put forward by Republicans who feared that the Democrats would continue to maintain their stranglehold on the presidency. It was also a sign of a widespread and growing feeling that the presidency was too powerful. Eisenhower, who opposed the amendment, felt that:

> The Bricker amendment would have denigrated the status of a legitimate treaty. Every treaty of the future and possibly of the past would be subjected to ceaseless challenge by any of the states, under Article X. Lawsuits, controversy, and confusion would replace the simple and efficacious processes visualized by the Founding Fathers, and, I believed, chaos in international affairs would result. As the months wore on, I was visited by many individuals and groups whose purpose was to urge my support for, or my opposition to, the amendment – mostly the former. From these meetings I soon learned that there was a great gulf of misunderstanding between the experts who clearly realized what the effect of an amendment would be, and those who, in the stress of fear that the Constitution would be betrayed and destroyed without the amendment, made great personal sacrifice of time and travel money to acquaint me with their concern. For a time there was a tremendous emotional upsurge in the country and this was in itself a matter of grave concern to me. . . . [There was a] popular fear that our entire Constitution could be overridden by a treaty (Eisenhower, 1963, pp. 281–2).

In the event Bricker failed by one vote to reach the two-thirds majority to bring his amendment into law. Thereafter, with a Republican safely ensconced in the White House, Republican fervour for the Bricker amendment declined, and in any case after 1954 they no longer controlled Congress. However, the battle over the Bricker amendment had highlighted the continuing struggle between legislature and executive over the latter's power.

To try to appease congressional concerns Eisenhower tried to follow a bipartisan line in foreign policy which slowly but surely won him considerable influence over the Congressmen. Eisenhower was also helped by the changing nature of the Cold War. As Stephen Ambrose has described:

The threat posed by the Soviet Union, the development of nuclear weapons and long-range bombers to carry them . . . , combined with the Pearl Harbor fear of surprise attack, made Congress content – even eager – to leave foreign policy decisions to the president. Eisenhower informed, rather than consulted with congressional leaders about his major decisions. . . . A majority of Republicans and perhaps of Congress as a whole wanted Eisenhower to adopt different policies. But thanks to his immense prestige and congressional fears he got his way (Ambrose, 1991–2, p. 125).

As Ambrose points out, the real issue of the Eisenhower presidency, after the conclusion of the Korean war, was the relationship with the Soviet Union. China, Vietnam, and Cuba were simply side issues to the state of Russo-American relations. The death of Joseph Stalin on March 5, 1953, less than two months after Eisenhower had been inaugurated, was certainly a great help. It paved the way for the emergence of a more enlightened leadership in the Kremlin. By the mid-1950s Nikita S. Krushchev felt sufficiently secure to begin to explore the possibilities of a more lasting and harmonious peace. Likewise, Eisenhower, although he despised communism, believed that the most pressing problem facing the President of the United States was that of the Cold War. The explosion of a Russian atom bomb in 1949 had begun an arms race that neither side could afford to lose, and which humanity could not afford to see won. Eisenhower hoped that, if he could establish his good faith with the Russians, he might be able to negotiate an arms limitation agreement. With the formation of the Warsaw Pact in 1955 to rival the US negotiated security pacts designed to contain communist aggression, two armed camps nervously faced each other across the globe. Even a comparatively small incident at a host of possible flashpoints scattered around the world had the capacity to generate a third world war. Eisenhower felt that he had to do something.

In July 1955 he went to Geneva for a summit conference with the Russians. Although nothing concrete came out of the summit (the Soviets dashed Eisenhower's hope for an open skies agreement to facilitate aerial reconnaissance to determine each other's intentions) the meeting did produce a great deal of good will on both sides. The summit fostered an atmosphere in which East–West relations were seen to improve, but the improvement was of short duration. In 1956 the Anglo-French-Israeli expedition against Egypt to crush the pan-Arab pretensions of General Gamel Abdel Nasser led to a dramatic increase in Russo-American antagonism. On October 29 the invasion force entered Egyptian territory, leaving Eisenhower with the problem of how to respond. The president was furious with the British and the French who had given a supposed ally no warning of the attack. He was particularly angry because of the way in which he perceived the invasion to be playing into the hands of the Russians. The Anglo-French assault gave the Soviet Union the chance to pose as the protector of all newly independent former colonies that might have something to fear from their former masters. More immediately, the crisis was a highly convenient cover for a Soviet crackdown in Hungary, where the emergence of a pro-democracy movement provoked a military intervention in October by the Soviet Union which did not like the direction of events in one of her most important satellites. Hungarian freedom fighters bravely battled Soviet tanks with molotov cocktails but the rising was short-lived. With the headlines dominated by events in the Middle East, the Eisenhower administration was unable to exploit events in Hungary. This outraged many Republican hardliners who had repeatedly listened to Dulles's rhetoric about freeing Eastern Europe from the yoke of communism. The hidden hand had been virtually powerless in respect to Hungary.

After the events of late 1956 it took some time for East–West relations to improve and just as they were doing so the Soviet Union launched the first orbiting satellite on October 4, 1957. A few weeks later Sputnik II was launched carrying a dog into space. It was not until January 31, 1958, that the United States was able to respond with the launch of its own satellite. This provoked a fierce controversy in the United States where allegations were hurled by Democrat and Republican alike that the administration had allowed a missile gap with the Soviet Union to open up. This was largely an illusion, but it was damaging to Eisenhower's authority as president. Much of that authority rested on the benign paternal image that was projected to the American public, and on his wartime reputation. The missile gap suggested that the general was behind the times, and that there was a certain indolence in his approach to the Soviet Union. He had failed to anticipate that the Soviets would have the technology to launch a satellite into space, and the response of the administration seemed like too little too late. Congress felt that the president needed to be persuaded of the dangers of the missile gap. In 1958 Congress gave Eisenhower more money than he asked for in the defense and domestic budgets. This was after that same body in 1957 had slashed $4 billion off the overall federal budget. The missile gap led to a complete change of heart, as the National Aeronautics and Space Administration was created by Congress in 1958 to boost America's performance in the field. In the same year the National Defense Education Act was passed to give federal financial support to learning in mathematics and the scientific disciplines.

The Sputnik episode served to underline one area of real weakness in the Eisenhower presidency. The President was a firm believer in reducing federal spending. He believed that the federal budget had to be reined in from the days of Roosevelt and Truman, if America's prosperity was not to be compromised. In both the foreign and domestic fields he tried to reduce spending, but he was unable to make the kind of progress he had hoped at the outset. The Korean war had underlined the case set out in NSC 68 for a major increase in defense spending. At the end of the Korean war defense expenditure accounted for 12.9 percent of the gross national product of the United States. By the end of the Eisenhower years it had fallen to 9.1 percent. Despite this fall historically the amount was still very high, and was testament to the fact that the expansive foreign policy pursued between 1945 and the 1950s had resulted in so many commitments that it was hard to scale down the forces necessary to meet them. Those commitments continued to multiply under Eisenhower. For example, in 1958, as Middle Eastern tensions reached a new crisis point, Eisenhower formulated a new doctrine allowing him to give financial and other aid to Middle Eastern countries. The Eisenhower doctrine, which received congressional approval, also gave the president the power to intervene with armed forces to counter a Soviet invasion. Also in 1958 a renewed threat to the security of Middle Eastern countries from Nasser's Pan-Arab drive led to the commitment of American ground troops to the Lebanon, all making it hard to reduce the federal budget. High defense spending also produced further complications with Eisenhower giving grave warnings against the military-industrial complex. It also made it harder to make progress on lessening Russo-American tensions. However, by the late 1950s other circumstances were pressing Eisenhower to make a renewed effort with premier Krushchev.

With the Democrats controlling Congress, the president found it easier to take the initiative on foreign policy rather than in domestic affairs. The 1958 mid-term elections, influenced by Congressional investigations which uncovered evidence of financial corruption and the trading of favours for influence by some figures in the Eisenhower administration, were particularly damaging for the Republicans. The White House Chief of Staff, Sherman Adams, was forced to resign and the Democrats eventually came out in the mid-term elections with 282 seats to the Republicans' 153 in the House of Representatives. In the Senate the Republicans mustered only 34 seats to the Democrats' 64. Although it proved possible for the administration to work successfully with the Democratic majorities on such issues as the Landrum-Griffin Act which sought to counter corrupt union practices, Eisenhower was left in a difficult position. Given the scale of the Democrat majorities in Congress, and the general's style of presidential leadership, it would have been all too easy after 1958 to perceive Ike as a lame duck president. This added impetus to Eisenhower's search for de-escalation with the Soviet Union.

The need for progress was further underlined by an increase in Russo-American tensions in November 1958. Krushchev made threatening references to the question of the status of Berlin at a public rally in Moscow. The Eisenhower administration had to contend with the possibility that Berlin might be blockaded once again. In an honest attempt to seek a solution, while refusing to give in to Krushchev's threats, Eisenhower opened talks with the Soviet Union. The talks prevented the situation over Berlin from reaching another crisis, even if they did not resolve the anomalous status of the city. In September of 1959 Krushchev made a public tour of the United States, and during a stay at Camp David the Soviet leader indicated that he was ready to pursue the doctrine of "peaceful coexistence." A further summit was scheduled for May 1960. It seemed as though, at the close of his presidency, Eisenhower had the chance for an historic breakthrough on East–West relations. The end of the Cold War was even a possibility. It would be a fitting end to the career of a distinguished soldier, and a perfect note on which to retire with his prestige and authority dramatically enhanced.

Yet at this point the dangers in the hidden-hand presidency became manifest. American aircraft had been overflying the Soviet Union on intelligence gathering missions since 1945. On May 1, 1960, one of them, a U-2 photo reconnaissance spy plane piloted by Francis Gary Powers, a CIA pilot, was shot down over the Soviet Union. Against expectations, and the designs of the CIA, Powers survived being shot down, and was captured by the Russians along with the remains of his aircraft. Krushchev manipulated the release of information about the shooting down of the U-2 to cause maximum embarrassment to the American government. Details about the flight, the aircraft, and its pilot were revealed after the State Department had put out a fictitious cover story to explain the loss of the aircraft. Throughout the course of events Eisenhower was consistently one step behind the game. The president had been assured that the U-2 was virtually invulnerable to Soviet air defenses and that the pilot could not possibly have been taken alive by the Russians. Eisenhower eventually decided that honesty was the only option and on May 11 he took personal responsibility for the incident. Krushchev tried to offer Eisenhower a way out of the developing diplomatic impasse by calling on the President to censure those of his subordinates who had obviously executed a dangerous mission without the President's knowledge or approval. Yet at this point Eisenhower refused to go along with his public image as being rather above the control of such matters of detailed policy. There was to be no censure. Although the two did meet briefly before Krushchev walked out, the summit was finished, as was further progress on East–West relations. Eisenhower was dismayed, and cross with himself, for missing a major opportunity to secure an improvement in Russo-American relations. It was, however, significant that, given the chance to save the summit by blaming his subordinates, the general had refused. Despite his image as a laid-back leader, where his honour was at stake Eisenhower felt compelled to dispense with the illusions that he had so carefully crafted about his role as president and to be seen for what he really was: the man in charge.

The U-2 episode provided the American public with a glimpse behind Eisenhower's presidential façade. An important parallel could be found in domestic affairs. For most of his presidency Eisenhower had to be careful to work with the Democratic majorities in Congress. Inaction rather than action was the general tendency. However, on some domestic issues Eisenhower could be very decisive. In particular, the issue of civil rights provoked a bitter conflict between federal and state authority into which Eisenhower was inexorably drawn. Eisenhower believed in desegregation and during his first administration public services in Washington were desegregated. Then in May 1954 the Supreme Court made a landmark ruling against the principle of segregation in the provision of local schooling. The schooling of blacks and whites had been separate, although rarely equal, but it was the very practice of segregation which Chief Justice Warren singled out for attack. The Court subsequently ordered that there should be reasonably swift progress made toward integration in the schooling of black and white children.

This helped to provoke an upsurge in racial tension. Respectable southern whites organized themselves into citizens' councils which used economic means to coerce blacks from crossing the carefully defined racial boundaries. Unsurprisingly there was virtually no progress made toward desegregation of schools in the Deep South. At the same time southern blacks responded to white intimidation. In December 1955 a young pastor named Martin Luther King played a leading role in organizing a bus boycott in Montgomery, Alabama, because under local laws black Americans were forced to surrender their seat on a bus to their white compatriots when asked to do so. The boycott eventually proved successful, and federal courts repeatedly ruled against the practice of segregation.

Throughout these events Eisenhower was deeply skeptical of the tactics of the civil rights movement. He favored gradual evolution and a general policy of leaving southern opinion to change slowly. He did not believe in landmark rulings and thought that coercion would produce only more racial intolerance. However, he was aware of the political repercussions of the civil rights issue. The Democratic Party had been torn apart by civil rights in 1948. Thus in 1956 Eisenhower proposed a civil rights act. After a year of Congressional wrangling the 1957 Civil Rights Act was less than revolutionary or comprehensive, establishing a brief-lived civil rights commission and a civil rights division in the Department of Justice. Its purpose was really to exacerbate tensions in the Democratic Party, rather than to make real progress on the issue of civil rights, and in political terms it was a success. But like the Civil Rights Act of 1960 it was not a success in terms of improving the position of African Americans. The 1960 Act was a sop to the civil rights movement, allowing the appointment of federal court officials to register black voters where a court had found that discrimination was making registration difficult or impossible. The Act did little to improve the situation of the potential black voter.

While Eisenhower was not eager to promote the civil rights agenda, where the issue of civil rights and presidential power and authority became linked the President proved that he could take decisive action. In Little Rock, Arkansas, in 1957 the state governor called out the National Guard to prevent nine black students from entering the Central High School, which they were entitled to do by a federal court order. Eisenhower tried to persuade the governor, Orval Faubus, to see sense. Eventually it took a further court order to force Faubus to withdraw the guard. The nine students should now have been able to enter the school, but on Monday, September 23, a mob gathered outside the Central High School determined to prevent them from entering. After serious rioting, the police, on the orders of the mayor of Little Rock, pacified the crowd by taking the children out of the school. The authority of the federal government had again been flouted, leaving Eisenhower with the choice of whether he should he seek a compromise solution or use his presidential authority to ensure that the State of Arkansas complied with the demands of a federal court. Eisenhower had no doubts:

> The issue had now become clear both in fact and in law. Cruel mob force had frustrated the execution of an order of a United States court, and the Governor of the state was sitting by, refusing to lift a finger to support the local authorities. Under the law, the Attorney General advised me, the Governor had a mandatory duty to suppress violence and remove "any obstruction to the orderly enforcement of the law." "This Constitution," Article VI reads, "and the laws of the United States which shall be made in pursuance thereof . . . shall be the supreme law of the land . . . all executive . . . officers . . . of the . . . States, shall be bound by oath or affirmation to support this Constitution. . . ." This particular governor, however, saw in the mobs not his duty but rather his vindication for having called out the National Guard in the first place. But here again he was on the wrong side of the law: "A state government," a Minnesota district court decision of 1936 read, "cannot suppress disorder the object of which is to deprive citizens of their lawful rights, by using its forces to assist in carrying out the unlawful purposes of those who create the disorders . . . the use of troops or police for such purposes would . . . constitute an assurance to those who resort to violence . . . that, if they gathered in sufficient numbers to constitute a menace to life, the forces of law would . . . actually assist them in accomplishing their objective." The result would be anarchy (Eisenhower, 1965, pp. 168–9).

Having reached a decision Eisenhower sent in federal troops to keep order. They would stay for the whole school year. At the same time the National Guard was put on federal service. Although Faubus would close the schools in 1958 rather than desegregate, and it would not be until 1959 that they would reopen after lengthy legal proceedings, Eisenhower had demonstrated that the federal government would enforce compliance with the demands of a federal court. The image of the hero of Normandy sending in his paratroopers to enforce the wishes of the federal government against those of a state was one which Eisenhower had wanted to avoid. But in Little Rock the hidden hand became the mailed fist, very publicly brought down in anger at the defiance of federal authority.

Despite the hopes of some Republicans that the end of the Truman administration would provide an opportunity for a new president to reinterpret the role of that office along less vigorous lines, in Eisenhower they produced a Republican president whose interpretation of the presidency followed closely the precedents set by Roosevelt and Truman. The presidency remained vigorous and proactive, albeit with a certain sleight of hand to conceal just how far Eisenhower was continuing to lead and direct policy as his Democratic predecessors had done. The New Deal and Fair Deal were not subjected to a revisionist onslaught, and in foreign policy Dulles continued to add to the commitments of American foreign policy. To the Truman doctrine was added the Eisenhower doctrine – the fight against communism continued. Yet there were considerable dangers inherent in the situation. Covert operations from Iran to Cuba had the potential to generate unforeseen consequences. The Constitution was being undermined by stealth as the United States waged war on its enemies. This was concealed from the American people, and the extension of executive privilege in the McCarthy versus Army hearings created a precedent that seemingly almost any president could invoke when they objected to the release of information to Congress or a court. Even though McCarthy had shot his bolt by the end of 1954, the atmosphere of mistrust, secrecy, of the enemy within, created a climate in which practices alien to the principles of American government could develop. By 1960 the American intelligence community was increasingly autonomous in its activities, despite occasional efforts by Eisenhower to bring it more firmly under his control. For the sake of national security the American people were increasingly ignored by their government, kept in the dark about policy and subjected to propaganda to maintain their support for the crusade against communism and the kind of presidency necessary to carry it out. Congress was largely willing to trust the president, and by doing so the legislature was subordinating itself to the executive to the ultimate detriment of American democracy.

FOUR

JFK: The Case against Presidential Charisma

The power and authority of a President of the United States come from a variety of sources in addition to the formal, written provisions of the Constitution. Some have enjoyed the luxury of a solid majority in Congress. The personal attributes of an incumbent are sometimes important – sometimes not. Eisenhower possessed, because of his wartime exploits, an image of authority that Truman had lacked. Sometimes the personality of an individual alone can be sufficient to generate that same authority. John F. Kennedy, who was elected to succeed Eisenhower as president in 1961, fell into this latter category. As Seymour Hersh has argued, Kennedy, with his charm, wit, intelligence, and good looks, possessed "the power of beauty." He was the "most charismatic leader" in the history of the United States, leaving "otherwise strong and self-reliant men and women" seduced by his "magnetism" (Hersh, 1998, pp. ix–x). During his presidency he projected an image of dynamism and the vitality of youth, enjoying a consistently high approval rating. With his murder his place among the presidential greats was assured for ever. And yet there is also another side to the Kennedy presidency that challenges his mythic status. In the 1990s revelations about his womanizing, related wrongdoings, and reliance on injections to reinvigorate him when he was tired began to erode the popular illusions about the wholesome, clean-cut icon. It was also significant that in Kennedy's administration historians could point to the seeds of the Vietnam war and all the evils that followed from it. To some, Kennedy was the first true imperial president, creating a type of presidency that would be followed by his successors Lyndon Johnson and Richard Nixon. Yet for all that, popular and scholarly judgments on Kennedy are still

70

largely favorable. As one recent biographer of President Kennedy has explained:

> To many historians at least, the Kennedy glitter and promise and the tragedy of the assassination have given way to the realities of Vietnam, excessive presidential activism, and the perceived limitations of liberalism at home – all of which were rooted in the Kennedy presidency. [But] . . . for those of us who reached adulthood in the early 1960s, John Fitzgerald Kennedy will always be remembered as a remarkable person, if not as a great president (Giglio, 1991, p. 287).

The remarkable level of Kennedy's authority as president requires close examination. In part it stemmed from his membership of a Massachusetts family steeped in politics and money which had helped him gain a seat in the Senate in 1952. It stemmed from the right Harvard education and a distinguished war record as commander of the motor torpedo boat PT109. It stemmed from a keen intellect: His senior year thesis was turned into the bestselling *Why England Slept*, and in 1955 he had won a Pulitzer Prize for another book, *Profiles in Courage*. It also stemmed from his marriage in 1953 to the attractive Jacqueline Bouvier. With that John F. Kennedy became one half of the nation's favorite romance, and later, as children were added to the scene (Caroline in 1957 and a son, John Fitzgerald, seventeen days after Kennedy was elected president of the United States in November 1960), Kennedy became head of the nation's favorite family. In part, Kennedy's authority owed something to his humility: he suffered from the crippling Addison's disease which nearly killed him on several occasions before he became president. Kennedy knew how transitory life could be, something emphasized by his Roman Catholic faith. He was also extremely lucky. In 1956 he had narrowly failed to be nominated as the Democratic Party's vice-presidential candidate. The 1956 presidential elections saw a handsome victory for Eisenhower, and so Kennedy had been fortunate to avoid a damaging defeat. In 1960, when Kennedy made a fresh run for the Democratic nomination for the presidency, he was the right man in the right place at the right time. His youth, optimism, and charm offered a real contrast to an Eisenhower administration which was increasingly perceived as stale and behind the times. Kennedy seemed to offer a fresh approach, and one that was badly needed if the United States was to meet the challenges of a continued Cold War and rising expectations at home. Kennedy also had the singular gift of being a good communicator, able to charm audiences with the warmth of his personality. He could appear affable and relaxed, whether at a press conference, small gatherings, or mass meetings. Unlike Eisenhower, he was completely at home with television cameras. Whatever the setting, Kennedy could create a sense of warmth and intimacy with his audience. Kennedy considered that journalists were important as a two-way channel from and to the people. Mindful of the practices of Theodore and Franklin Roosevelt, he cultivated a close relationship with the press. "Kennedy took to heart the example of the Roosevelts both on the style and substance of presidency" (Brogan, 1996, p. 220).

Following his failure to gain the Democratic nomination in 1956, Kennedy had worked tirelessly for a run at the nomination in 1960. With the backing of his brothers, Robert and Edward, Kennedy's national stature and standing within the Democratic Party had increased to such an extent that in 1960 he won seven primary elections. The Democrats nominated him on the first ballot as their candidate for the presidential elections against Eisenhower's chosen successor, Vice-President Nixon. The election was dominated by the state of international relations, the economy, and the level of defense spending. In particular Kennedy alleged that Eisenhower had allowed a missile gap to open up with the Soviet Union that had left the United States in a dangerously inferior position. The allegation was largely groundless, as Eisenhower was fully aware of the state and extent of the Soviet missile arsenal, but the charge still had a powerful effect on an American public which had experienced fifteen years of warnings about Russian intentions. Kennedy promised to get the country moving again after what was portrayed as the indolence of the Eisenhower administration. On September 20, 1960, Kennedy and Nixon met in a televised debate. Seventy-five million viewers saw

Nixon defend the record of the Eisenhower administration and charge that Kennedy was too young and inexperienced to be entrusted with the running of the country. The difference between old and new was emphasized by the visual impact of the two men: Nixon looked rather worn, haggard, and under considerable stress whereas Kennedy was the complete opposite, looking healthy, groomed, and relaxed. The televised debate gave Kennedy a slight edge and on polling day Kennedy's popular vote of 34,226,731 was just large enough to eclipse Nixon's 34,108,157. Kennedy's victory in the electoral college was larger, by 303 votes to 219, but there could be no doubting that with such a slim popular majority Kennedy at least subconsciously wanted to build up his authority and relationship with the American people. Over the next thousand days until his murder in Dallas in November 1963 he was to do this with spectacular effect.

Kennedy's presidential authority mattered a great deal to him because he was a firm believer in an activist presidency. He wanted not just to lead, but to make a difference, as Franklin Roosevelt and Truman had done. In the opinion of Ted Sorensen, a Kennedy insider:

> One of John Kennedy's most important contributions to the human spirit was his concept of the office of the Presidency. His philosophy of government was keyed to power, not as a matter of personal ambition but of national obligation: the primacy of the White House within the Executive Branch and of the Executive Branch within the Federal Government, the leadership of the Federal Government within the United States and of the United States within the community of nations. And yet he almost never spoke of "power." Power was not a goal he sought for its own sake. It was there, in the White House, to be used, without any sense of guilt or greed, as a means of getting things done. He felt neither uplifted nor weighed down by power. He enjoyed the presidency, thinking not of its power but its opportunities, and he was sobered by the presidency, thinking not of its power but its obligations (Sorensen, 1965, p. 389).

Kennedy wanted to follow in the footsteps of Roosevelt and Truman, championing the cause of social justice and maintaining the commitment to contain communism. This was only possible through a strong presidency. Kennedy was no inauguration convert to this view. Throughout his life he had been consistent on the question of presidential power:

> As a Senator he had supported more power and discretion for the President in foreign aid, trade, item vetoes and national emergency disputes, and opposed curbs on the President's treaty-making power and electoral base. As an author and historian he had praised the independent Presidency and the men who stretched its limits and preserved its prerogatives. As a candidate he both launched and closed his campaign with addresses focused upon Presidential responsibility as the No. 1 issue. And as President he both expanded and exerted the full powers of that office, the informal as well as the formal (Sorensen, 1965, p. 389–90).

One example of this came with his first executive order, designed to improve the distribution of surplus food to the poor. Eisenhower had refused to make such an order because he feared that he did not have the proper statutory authority and that it might be subject to a challenge. Kennedy's just went ahead and did it, signalling that, like Teddy Roosevelt, he would act rather than let constitutional and legal niceties stand in his way.

Foreign policy and social justice were to be the twin themes of his presidency. From his inaugural speech on January 20, 1961, to the speech which he should have given at the Dallas Trade Mart on the day he was assassinated on November 22, 1963, these themes were at the forefront of the Kennedy agenda. In 1961 he told the world "Let every nation know whether it wishes us good or ill, that we shall pay any price, bear any burden, meet any hardship . . . to assure the survival of liberty." In November 1963, as he prepared for the presidential elections in the following year, he was to have assured his audience that America was better prepared to meet any military or economic challenge which might face her. At the same time he was to have warned "only an America which practices what it preaches about equal rights and social justice will be respected by those whose choice affects our future." Only an assertive presidency, defending America abroad while championing the cause of equality at home, could make good on Kennedy's hopes of a New Frontier: a new national mission for the United States. Moreover, in the 1960 presidential elections Kennedy had promised drive and dynamism to go with his youth and charm. In every way possible Kennedy was personally and politically committed to an activist presidency.

In forming his new administration Kennedy was determined to signal a break with the past, putting together a team of some of the best brains the United States had to offer. Dean Rusk would serve as Secretary of State under Kennedy and his successor in November 1963, Lyndon Johnson. Rusk had been a student of politics at Oxford University and a career diplomat. During World War Two he had been involved in intelligence operations in Burma. After it, he joined the State Department, becoming an expert on Far Eastern affairs, and he had played an important role in drawing up the armistice arrangements for Korea. In his belief that the United States should be resolute in standing up to the communist menace abroad, while promoting social equality at home, Rusk's views reinforced those of Kennedy. Another interesting appointment was that of Robert McNamara who was brought in to do to the Department of Defense what he had done to the Ford Motor Company. McNamara would need all his skills as an innovative manager to get to grips with the problems of defense facing the United States during the early 1960s. Other appointments included Robert Kennedy to the post of Attorney General, and McGeorge Bundy as Special Assistant for National Security Affairs. Bundy's appointment signalled that Kennedy would make particular use of the National Security Council to determine national policy.

In his appointments Kennedy combined liberal intellectuals such as Arthur Schlesinger and J.K. Galbraith with career managers and administrators such as Rusk and McNamara. So many Harvard academics were appointed to posts in the administration that it was a standing joke that the faculty was virtually empty by the time the President had finished with it. There was widespread approval for Kennedy's appointments, although there were also problems over particular selections. More generally there were problems generated by the increasingly complex structures and procedures of the national security state, instigated by Truman and expanded under Eisenhower under the influence of the red scare. As Harris Wofford observed:

> Once Kennedy had decided upon an appointment, it was not supposed to be announced until the FBI had reported on the man's loyalty, character and background. Even on a crash basis, a full field investigation would take weeks, during which the appointee could not take office. Before the era of Alger Hiss and Joe McCarthy such investigations of top level people were minimal; in the Truman–Eisenhower transition they had been a problem, but now they threatened to be a major log jam (Wofford, 1980, p. 74).

So intractable did the problem of appointments and transition from one presidency to another prove that in 1963 a Presidential Transition Act was passed to try to alleviate the problem. In fact it was only to make matters worse.

Who a president picks to serve in his administration, and who he does not, is an important but often overlooked aspect of presidential power. The president retains the right to determine policy according to his convictions, but a cabinet united behind a line of policy is psychologically and politically important. Back in 1867 Andrew Johnson's disagreements with his Secretary of War precipitated the impeachment of the president. With Kennedy determined to return to the model of open presidential activism, as opposed to Eisenhower's hidden hand, the 1961 presidential appointments were particularly significant. In Rusk he selected a man broadly in sympathy with his policies, but who would generally defer to the president in argument. In McNamara he had a manager par excellence whose understanding of how organizations worked Kennedy valued highly. McNamara was consistently more influential than that other center of political power in the defense field, the Joint Chiefs of Staff. With McGeorge Bundy, Kennedy appointed a man who he confessed was the second cleverest person he knew. Consequently he was, through the National Security Council, highly influential. In Robert Kennedy he had the ultimate loyal colleague. Vice-President Lyndon Johnson considered that John Kennedy valued his brother's advice far more than his or any one else's. Although there would be occasions when Bundy, Rusk and the other influential figures in the Kennedy administration would violently disagree with the President (indeed, at times Kennedy would be entirely alone in his choice of policy options), Kennedy's circle of advisers was perhaps too narrow, and the president valued their opinions just a little too highly for comfort. It was perhaps inevitable that Kennedy would select people whose abilities he valued and with whom he enjoyed a good working relationship, but this factor has constituted a perennial problem for presidents. For example, Warren Harding packed the White House with wealthy men from business backgrounds, in the belief that businessmen knew best how to run the economy, only for his administration to become embroiled in a series of financial scandals.

The transition from one administration to another caused Kennedy considerable difficulties in terms of making appointments, but there were also potentially more serious ramifications. American strategists had identified the transitional period as a highly dangerous moment of which the Soviet Union might seek to take advantage. Their thinking was that a new president settling into the White House might lack the self-assurance to respond effectively to any Soviet gambit. Such a gambit might involve a *coup de main* against Berlin, or it might even take the form of a Soviet first strike against the United States. Would the new president feel sufficiently in power and possess the necessary belief in his own authority to take appropriate action? Despite the fears of the strategists, something very near the opposite was to take place: precipitate American action against the communist bloc. The precise location of this event would be the Bay of Pigs on the coast of Cuba.

On assuming office Kennedy was informed of the extent of the Eisenhower administration's covert efforts to undermine Castro's Cuba. During the election campaign Kennedy had supported Castro's removal. After his inauguration he was presented with a CIA plan to use specially trained Cuban exiles as a force with which to invade the island in the hope of sparking a popular uprising against what was seen as a communist dictatorship. The plan was put to him by Richard Bissell, the agency's Director of Operations. Kennedy was assured that it would work. Trusting the advice he received, new to his job, politically committed to the removal of Castro, still in the process of building his administration and establishing its working procedures, the president deferred to the CIA. Kennedy felt that, while he had the presidential power to veto the plan, he lacked the personal authority to challenge the convictions of Bissell and the Agency. The military backed the plan, and despite the reservations of the State Department, Kennedy gave the go-ahead for its execution. Kennedy was perhaps blinded by a certain romanticism. The idea of Cubans landing on home shores to liberate their fellow nationals from the evil tyranny of communism would give practical expression to Kennedy's New Frontier rhetoric. The precise details of the invasion plan were to prove hopelessly romantic rather than shrewd, practical, and realistic. The landings on April 17, 1961, did not result in a mass uprising. The Bay of Pigs proved a perfect location at which to contain an invading force, and the landings were not combined with offensive operations by anti-Castro forces already inside Cuba. Faced with failure, Kennedy procrastinated. Most notably he refused to allow the United States Navy to intervene in the struggle. In part Kennedy wanted to limit the scale of the debacle that was unfolding, but he also wanted to prevent an escalation of the incident. In addition, he did not want to overstep his constitutional powers by appearing to wage war on a sovereign state in the western hemisphere. The result was that the majority of the anti-Castro Cubans were taken prisoner and Kennedy was humbled as he was eventually forced to take personal responsibility for what was seen as an act of aggression in many quarters.

The Bay of Pigs had important repercussions for Kennedy. His presidential credibility was called into question. Some wondered whether Nixon might have been right when he questioned whether one so young could possess the necessary experience to lead the nation effectively. This put pressure on Kennedy to demonstrate his leadership abilities. In the longer term this would manifest itself in an expansive foreign policy. In the shorter term it would mean firing

Allen Dulles, the Director of the CIA, and Richard Bissell. Kennedy was determined to rein back the power of an organization whose influence had grown steadily since 1947 to the point where some thought that it was a law unto itself.

Kennedy was not the only one to blame the Bay of Pigs on the intelligence community and the national security state. Norman Mailer, for example, openly pondered whether Kennedy was the victim of a set of illusions about Castro, Cuba, and the Cold War deliberately fostered by the intelligence agencies:

> The Bay of Pigs remains a mystery. One can doubt it will ever be found out how it came to pass, or who in fact was the real force behind it. But there is a tool of investigation for political mysteries. It is Lenin's formula: 'Whom?" Whom does this benefit? . . . Well whom? Kennedy and the liberal center did not gain honor from the Bay of Pigs. Castro most certainly did not gain an advantage for he was forced now finally to commit his hand altogether to Russia. The Left in America, that fine new Left of Pacifists and beatniks and Negro militants and college students who just knew something was bad – this Left certainly did not benefit from the Bay of Pigs. . . . No, the people who benefited from the Bay of Pigs were the people who wanted a serious Communist threat to exist within ninety miles of America's shore. They were the people who had taken the small and often absurd American Communist Party and had tried to exaggerate its menace to the point where the country could be pistol-whipped into silence at the mention of its name. They had infiltrated this party until even the *Saturday Evening Post* offered hints that a large part of the American Communist Party was by now made up of FBI men. . . . If there were no Communists, the FBI would be required by the logic of their virility to take on the next greatest danger to American life, the Mafia, and how were they ever to do that, how were they ever to investigate the Mafia without ripping the Republican and Democratic parties up from top to bottom? Because the Republican Party was supported by the Mafia, and the Democratic Party was supported by the Mafia (Mailer, 1976, pp. 78–9).

Whatever concerns Kennedy may have had about the national security state and the Mafia, his attack on the Central Intelligence Agency effectively meant boosting his own power and authority within the American government. The firing of Dulles also sent a clear signal to other branches of government about how they ought to serve the President in the future. Kennedy's desire for greater personal control was signaled by his instructions to Robert Kennedy to take operations against Cuba into his own control. From 1961 onwards it could be argued that the Kennedys pursued a personal vendetta against Castro. The fact that it was so personal a policy shows how far the Bay of Pigs convinced Kennedy to take greater charge of the presidency. May and Zellikow have recorded other, related, effects of the Bay of Pigs on Kennedy's "style of decision making":

> Afterward, he recognized that he had not only listened to too few advisers but that he had given the issue too little time. Eisenhower, before giving him the public backing he sorely needed, subjected him to a staff school quiz. "Mr President," Eisenhower asked, "before you approved this plan did you have everybody in front of you debating the thing so that you could get all the pros and cons yourself and then make the decision . . . ?" Kennedy had to confess that he had not. Bundy, whose offer to resign Kennedy refused, also counselled that he become more deliberative (May and Zellikow, 1997, p. 28).

Thus, after the Bay of Pigs Kennedy's power and authority as president increased as he took a firmer hold on the American government. Kennedy realized that he had been too reliant on the brilliance of his advisers, and that it would be necessary to make a clear mental distinction between foreign policy aspirations and foreign policy realities and their likely outcomes.

But, as with Eisenhower, under Kennedy the president's problems with Congress were to accentuate the importance of foreign affairs. Congress was controlled by a conservative coalition of Democratic and Republican Senators and members of the House of Representatives. Kennedy was unable to get key elements of his domestic program through Congress. The provision of health insurance for the elderly, the creation of a Department of Urban Affairs, and the increase in aid to education all foundered on Kennedy's inability to work with Congress, to the extent that he grew reluctant to ask them to approve new legislation. Thus, whereas he was a believer in the principle of civil rights, and during his presidency he showed that he was willing to use federal authority to further the cause in the same way that his predecessor had, he was wary about introducing a new civil rights bill. When he did, the broad coalition of southern conservatives in Congress immediately moved to block the proposals.

Only in the field of foreign affairs and defense could the White House count on the support of the legislature. Indeed, Congress generally voted bigger defense appropriations than the president asked for. The Senate refused to approve tax cuts in 1963, but they were willing to support a space program designed to put a man on the moon in order to demonstrate American superiority over the Russians. Likewise, Congress opposed moves designed to help unemployed migrant workers, but they supported the creation of a peace corps to supply educational and technical volunteers to assist in the development of the third world. This measure found favor because Congressmen appreciated that poverty in Latin America, Asia, and Africa would facilitate the spread of communism. By personal inclination and congressional pressure, the Kennedy presidency was set on a course whereby its success or failure would rest more heavily on foreign affairs than any previous administration.

In particular, East–West relations would be the focus of much of Kennedy's attention. In June 1961, in the aftermath of the Bay of Pigs, Kennedy met Krushchev in Vienna to discuss the problem of Germany, especially the thorny issue of Berlin. The two men took a mutually poor view of each other. In August 1961, under Krushchev's orders, the East German authorities began the erection of a security zone involving a wall, minefields, and barbed wire to stop the continuing outflow of Germans from East Berlin to a new life in the west. The outflow was a political embarrassment to the communist bloc and a threat to the stability of the East German regime. The wall was to be 103 miles long at an average of 12 feet in height, and was to bring the flood of refugees to a halt. The attempts of many of those Berliners who continued to try to escape even after the erection of the security zone were to end in tragedy. In the face of Krushchev's move Kennedy did very little, because there was, realistically, little that could be done. The wall was an offense against human rights, but there was no way to respond effectively to its construction without risking a nuclear war. In some quarters Kennedy was attacked for his lack of response. The episode also served as a further demonstration in Kennedy's mind of the inadequacies of the CIA who had failed to predict how the communist bloc would deal with the problem of a flood of refugees moving into West Berlin.

Berlin was a significant test of Kennedy's presidential mettle, but the greatest test of the administration's credibility came in mid-1962 as the Soviet and Cuban governments agreed to site nuclear missiles in Cuba. The Bay of Pigs had provided ample evidence of the extent of American hostility toward the Castro regime. In many ways that hostility had intensified as a consequence of the personal humiliation of Kennedy after the failure of the landings by the Cuban exile brigade. Covert action to undermine Castro continued and the Kremlin could not rule out the possibility of a direct American assault on the island. Krushchev wanted not only to continue developing the relationship between the communist bloc and its newest member, Castro having declared himself to be a Marxist-Leninist on December 2, 1961, but he was also aware that missiles in Cuba would provide a useful bargaining chip in negotiations over Berlin or over half a dozen other troublespots. In Cuba would be stationed Soviet intermediate-range ballistic missiles as well as short-range nuclear missiles for use against a potential invasion force. The missiles were to be under the command of, and would be launched by, Soviet forces stationed on the island.

By the end of July 1962 the CIA was monitoring an increasing Soviet build-up on the island. To the increase of conventional forces on Cuba was being added some sort of new program of military construction. By August 29 aerial reconnaissance had identified the construction of surface-to-air missile sites. The question was, what were they there to protect? On September 4 the Kremlin and the White House exchanged messages, Kennedy warning the Soviet

Union against the development of offensive military potential in Cuba, and Krushchev promising not to cause any incidents until after the November congressional mid-term elections. This was a tacit recognition of the political realities of presidential power. Foreign policy was a key area of US politics and on the president's handling of a particular crisis would depend his public approval rating and, in November, seats in Congress. On those would depend the level of the president's power and authority. With elections looming there would be a political imperative for any president to take a hard line with the Soviet Union in any crisis.

On October 14 the United States learned precisely what the surface-to-air missile sites identified in August were being set up to defend, as a further U-2 aerial reconnaissance flight pinpointed the location of launching areas for the intermediate-range ballistic missiles. Kennedy's response was interesting. He formed a special group to advise him and to talk out the issues: the Executive Committee of the National Security Council (Ex-Comm). After considerable deliberations the president was presented with three options ranging from covert negotiations through to an immediate air attack and possible invasion. Kennedy preferred a middle option: a naval blockade of Cuba. This would send a clear message to the Soviet Union that the United States was not about to let Cuba become a base for offensive weapons directed against the United States. It was thus a long way from private talks and the possibility of a compromise solution, nor was it guaranteed to lead to an immediate nuclear exchange which the air attack/invasion option threatened. It took until October 22 for Kennedy to go public with the news about what was happening on Cuba, and what the response of the United States would be. Congress was informed and then the President went on television to speak directly to the American public about the grave situation which was developing.

Kennedy's decision to go public is intriguing. By broadcasting to the American public, he was turning what was an already difficult situation into a major crisis. The naval blockade could have been implemented with appropriate messages sent to Moscow, but without informing the American public. Some figures in the administration such as Bundy have defended the move as being only right and proper. In a democracy the people needed to know about such a grave threat to the country, and with an active media there was an inevitable danger that a garbled version of the facts might find its way into the public arena. Moreover, if the public were to have time to take the necessary civil defense preparations for war they needed to be informed. However, such explanations have been challenged by historians such as Stone and Russell who have argued that the decision to go public had more to do with JFK trying to reinforce his presidential authority and image than with a desire for open government. The Bay of Pigs had dented Kennedy's reputation as a man of resolute and decisive action and the Berlin crisis had done yet more damage. The new crisis over Cuba would allow him to recover lost authority. Some historians have even gone so far as to suggest that Kennedy was deliberately escalating the crisis in order to bolster his presidential image. One of them, T. G. Paterson, has argued:

> The Cuban missile crisis provided an opportunity for exercising managerial skills and for establishing the . . . President's toughness. What is most telling about Kennedy's response to the reckless Soviet installation of missiles in Cuba is that he suspended diplomacy and chose a television address, rather than a direct approach to Moscow, to inform Krushchev that his flagrant intrusion in the Caribbean would not be tolerated. Kennedy practised public rather than private diplomacy, and thereby significantly increased the chances of war (Paterson, 1988, p. 203).

Paterson's charge is devastating: would a president deliberately risk the annihilation of his country, and possibly the extinction of all human life on the planet, for the sake of his opinion poll ratings and the possibility of a few more votes for the Democrats in the congressional mid-term elections? Demonized as Kennedy has been by some recent scholars, it is hard to believe that he would have consciously chosen such a course of action for the sake of reinforcing his public image as a man of action and determination.

It is perhaps worth raising questions about the amount of stress that Kennedy was under during the missile crisis, and whether that could in part provide some insight into his behavior. Almost all of the studies of the Cuban missile crisis approach their subject from the perspective that it was an interesting piece of international history, rather than a series of more personal dramas involving Kennedy, Krushchev, and Castro. Most of the biographies of Kennedy see the missile crisis as evidence of Kennedy's qualities as a statesman and thus as president. The picture of the missile crisis is either too big or too small and it is biased depending on the approach. This has meant that certain, unanswerable but significant, questions have not been asked. For example, given that Kennedy as a chronic adulterer constantly faced the threat of exposure and public ruin, how much more tension could he comfortably cope with? Did his relationship with the Mafia, which added a further threat of disgrace, prey on his mind during the crisis? Rather than an image of cold calculation, that victory in the missile crisis would eliminate memories of earlier troubles, did thoughts of the Bay of Pigs, and allegations of presidential mishandling and betrayal, haunt Kennedy in October 1962? Kennedy was an all too human figure in his fragility and flaws, but the standard western narrative of the Cuban missile crisis will not admit that such questions might have a bearing on this tale of American triumph. Presidents are, after all, people as well as holders of their office: and all their actions do not revolve around their conception of the presidency as distinct from their own troubled selves.

After raising the stakes by his public address on October 22 Kennedy tried to do everything he could to secure a peaceful settlement of the crisis. Diplomatic channels to the Soviet Union were opened. On October 24 five Russian ships bound for Cuba stopped rather than try to run the blockade. In the course of secret negotiations Krushchev demanded the removal of American Jupiter missiles from Turkey. Time and time again Kennedy's advisers in Ex-Comm came to the point of advising an attack on Cuba with all that that would mean in terms of a Soviet–American nuclear exchange. Throughout Kennedy remained committed to the path of peace, and he remained in complete charge of events. The Bay of Pigs had been a valuable lesson in the education of a president about when, and when not, to listen to advisers. As May and Zellikow have commented:

> Saturday, October 27, may well have been the finest hours of John F. Kennedy's public life. To us he seems more alive to the possibilities and consequences of each new development than anyone else. He remained calm, lucid, and constantly a step, or several steps, ahead of his advisers. He is the only one in the room determined not to go to war over obsolete missiles in Turkey. Yet he fully understands and is trying to work around the large consequences of appearing to sell out the Turks (May and Zellikow, 1997, pp. 691–2).

Sell out the Turks is precisely what he decided to do. On October 28 Krushchev agreed to remove Russian missiles from Cuba on the understanding that Kennedy would remove American missiles from Turkey. The deal was not made public in the United States, and the Jupiter missiles from Turkey were removed quietly in contrast to the very public withdrawal of the missiles from Cuba.

Kennedy had scored an apparent victory for the United States in his handling of the Cuban missile crisis. The public saw him standing up to the Soviet Union which was seemingly forced into a humiliating retreat. However, appearances sometimes mask deeper realities. Both sides had gained as a result of the crisis. Missiles had been withdrawn from both Cuba and Turkey and the episode ushered in a number of improvements in East–West relations. A telephone hotline between Washington and Moscow was established so that future crises could be dealt with more swiftly on a leader-to- leader basis. The episode had also demonstrated the danger of nuclear weapons, and in 1963 the Soviet Union and the United States would conclude an agreement banning atmospheric testing of nuclear missiles. This was a symbolic step on the road to a lessening of Cold War tensions and some people have speculated that if Kennedy had gone on to gain a second term he would have tried to bring the Cold War to an end. In effect, Kennedy may have hoped to cap his second term in the same way that Eisenhower had hoped to end his.

If the Cuban missile crisis had important repercussions for East–West relations then it also had important lessons in terms of the development of the presidency. What was particularly striking is that Kennedy was able to claim victory in October 1962 because of the nature of the deal which he had concluded with Krushchev. It could be that Kennedy was simply cleverer than Krushchev in defining what he was willing to agree to, but there is another possibility. Krushchev had promised before the crisis began that he would do nothing to upset East–West relations until after the congressional mid-term elections. Realizing that for various reasons (some concerning domestic politics), Kennedy had to take a tough line over the Cuban issue once it had arisen, Krushchev was willing to agree terms that recognized the realities facing both leaders. Kennedy's address to the nation was a powerful reminder to the Russians of the problems of power and authority facing the President of the United States. To Krushchev, leader of a one-party state with a captive media, the appearance of the deal done over missiles in Cuba mattered considerably less than it did to Kennedy facing all the vagaries of the democratic system. Thus in return for substantive concessions over Turkey and a commitment not to invade Cuba, Krushchev was willing to leave the cosmetics of the agreement to Kennedy. In effect, both leaders were recognizing the political realities of the presidency and were working around them in their search for a way out of a potentially devastating crisis.

The problem of a communist Cuba was one of a number of issues bequeathed to the Kennedy administration by its predecessor. A similar difficulty faced by both Presidents concerned what to do about the growth of communism in Southeast Asia. Following the Geneva accords of 1956 the situation in Vietnam and neighboring Laos had continued to deteriorate. In Laos war raged between the Royal Army and the communist guerrillas of the Pathet Lao. Kennedy was warned by both Eisenhower and the Chairman of the Joint Chiefs that direct intervention might be the only way to prevent communist victory. Kennedy preferred an alternative policy: covert action to support the Royal Army coupled with negotiation to create a neutralized Laos in which the various factions would share power. In 1961 talks opened in Geneva, which led to an agreement in the following year, based on the principles of neutrality and power sharing. However, both the United States and Soviet Union continued covert assistance to their respective allies.

Covert action in Laos and in Cuba was a direct continuation of the practices of the Eisenhower administration. War was waged in secret and the possible implications kept from the American public. It was to be the same story in Vietnam. After the country had been divided in 1954 the leadership of the South had been entrusted to premier Ngo Dinh Diem. Diem had been elected in 1955 but support for him had declined rapidly after this. Diem was a Catholic like Kennedy, and their religion caused political problems for both men. Whereas Kennedy was able to overcome them to win the presidency in 1960, for Diem being the leader of a largely Buddhist country caused continuing difficulties. By 1960 Diem was facing a revolt against his rule which he had partly provoked by policies designed to consolidate his hold on power. As the elections to reunify Vietnam promised under the 1954 Geneva accords became ever less likely, the communist leadership of North Vietnam began to increase their aid to the forces in the South fighting against Diem. By 1961 Kennedy was becoming alarmed at the deterioration of the position in South Vietnam. According to Robert McNamara, the man Kennedy had brought in to reform the Department of Defense, Kennedy was in part motivated by a missionary zeal and was concerned in 1961 at his dented reputation for being a tough anti-communist. In Vietnam Kennedy could begin to recoup lost political ground. Kennedy's views on Vietnam also involved, according to McNamara, a belief that the fall of Vietnam would be a major blow to containment, and that American involvement should be distinctly limited. This was both interesting and important. Kennedy's identification of Vietnam with containment highlighted the way in which under John Foster Dulles, Eisenhower's Secretary of State, containment had been extended into Asia and the Middle East. But Kennedy's hope that containment could be maintained with limited American input also showed that the United States was hard pressed to maintain the global commitments that had been undertaken during the Eisenhower administration.

In May 1961 Kennedy affirmed that a stand would be made against communism in Vietnam. National Security Action Memorandum No. 52, dated May 11, stated that America's objective in Vietnam should be "to prevent Communist domination," to "create in that country a viable and increasingly democratic society, and to initiate, on an accelerated basis, a series of mutually supporting actions of a military, political, economic, psychological and covert character designed to achieve this objective." The CIA would engage in covert war against the enemies of the Diem regime which was regarded as the cornerstone of a successful US policy in Vietnam. The number of American advisers in Vietnam would be steadily increased to help the military forces of the Republic of Vietnam give a better account of themselves. At the end of 1961 there were 3,200 advisers in Vietnam: by the time of Kennedy's death there were 16,000, in clear contravention of the limits set down under the Geneva accords. They were not supposed to be directly engaged in the military struggle, for that might lead to awkward questions about whether or not Kennedy had the necessary power to commit them. Was this just another "police action" like Korea, in which the White House could rely on some rather dubious precedents to justify military operations? Would Congress support the use of advisers in such a significant and often dangerous role? The increasing number of advisers was essential if defeat was to be avoided. In October 1961 General Maxwell Taylor was sent to Vietnam to assess the situation, which was continuing to deteriorate. Taylor found that the South Vietnamese needed more help if they were to cope with increasing infiltration from the north. From 1961 to 1963 $400 million of military aid would be provided to prop up the Vietnamese military effort. The amount of aid proved insufficient, however, and within the Kennedy administration the corruption and inadequacies of the Diem regime were identified as a major part of the problem. Diem refused to change his regime in ways which would make it more popular. For example, in 1963 he displayed his suspicion of the Buddhist faith by having thousands of Buddhists arrested and the flying of the Buddhist flag prohibited.

By the last quarter of 1963 Kennedy was retreating from the problem of Vietnam. He seemed determined to avoid the commitment of still more troops to South Vietnam and was ready to reduce the number of advisers and let the Vietnamese stand on their own feet. Somehow he seemed to sense that Vietnam had the capacity to derail his presidency. In setting a new course for the United States in Vietnam, it helped that on November 1 Diem was removed from office and killed in an American backed *coup d'état*. The new leadership in South Vietnam offered the prospect of a change of fortunes for the anti-communist side in the developing civil war. The policy which Kennedy seemed to be favoring was similar to that which he had followed toward Laos: neutralization and de-escalation. Kennedy would not leave South Vietnam to fall to communism, nor would he commit the United States to the pursuit of some kind of military victory there. Kennedy realised that in the circumstances of the Cold War there was no such thing as military victory. Maintaining the status quo in Vietnam while working with Krushchev for an end to the Cold War offered the only realistic chance for peace in Southeast Asia or indeed anywhere else. Kennedy unfortunately did not have the opportunity to follow his policy through as, on November 22, he was murdered in Dallas.

Dallas was undoubtedly a turning point in the history of the presidency. The assassination both elevated and undermined the presidency. The martyrdom of Kennedy, the fourth American president to die at the hands of an assassin, elevated the institution to new heights. A brave man, who some saw as embodying the hopes of a generation, had been cut down in the service of his country. But there were other more insidious effects. In the conventional narrative of presidential history Kennedy exercised his powers freely. He continued to consolidate the power of the presidency while laying the foundations of the Vietnam War. Covert action against Cuba, the attempts to kill Castro, the escalation of the Cuban missile crisis, his misuse of the office to hide his personal misdeeds, complicity in the murder of the leader of a friendly power add up to a serious indictment of the Kennedy presidency. And yet, following the lesson of the Cuban missile crisis Kennedy appears to have grown cautious, striving for a lowering of Cold War tensions and for a way out of the Vietnam quagmire. One might suspect that the terrible possibilities he wrestled with during the Cuban missile crisis produced a change within him: New Frontier giving way to new caution. Even if one takes a less charitable view of Kennedy then, with the President's room for policy maneuver constrained by a looming election, it was entirely probable that his policies would become less hawkish and more reassuring to the US public. This is certainly one aspect of the speech which he would have given at the Dallas Trade Mart on November 22 if he had lived long enough. His message was to have been that the deficiencies in the American military system, which had developed under Eisenhower, had now been made good and that America's foreign policy objectives might now be reconsidered in the interests of an improvement in East–West relations. So the reader of American history is left with two images of Kennedy: the imperial president aggrandizing his office; and Kennedy the reformed hawk seeking to reduce the tensions of the Cold War.

This second image of a reformed Kennedy has been suggested as the reason for the plot which some people believe led to his assassination. Since 1963 there have been questions about whether or not Lee Harvey Oswald was the lone assassin responsible for Kennedy's murder. Strong evidence suggests that Oswald did not act alone, and that he may have been the "fall guy" for a well-planned conspiracy. That conspiracy covered up the facts of the assassination after Kennedy's death, and, some would argue, continues to hide the truth even today. During the 1960s a series of books were published suggesting that the real story of Kennedy's assassination had not been told, and during the 1970s, 1980s, and 1990s the volume of Kennedy assassination literature would continue to expand. In 1991 the most persuasive case yet was put forward to suggest that a conspiracy had murdered Kennedy. Oliver Stone's 1991 film *JFK* not only probed the identity or identities of the assassin, but also questioned the motives of the conspirators for killing Kennedy. Various possibilities were suggested from a revenge killing by anti-Castro Cubans dismayed at the shifts in American policy, a pre-emptive strike by elements in the intelligence community concerned at Kennedy's attempts to rein in the CIA, through to a political *coup d'etat* by senior military figures concerned by the president's hopes for détente and a withdrawal from Vietnam. In the course of the film Stone even dared to indict Lyndon Johnson as an accessory to the Kennedy murder, and in Johnson's reversal of Kennedy's policy of withdrawal from Vietnam the director identifies the central purpose of the assassination plot.

The views of Stone and other like-minded people could be considered unsurprising and unimportant. There will always be a range of opinions on an event as traumatic as the Kennedy killing. But what is remarkable and significant is the idea that Kennedy was killed by a conspiracy which has hidden the truth from the American public ever since. This is a view held not by a small band of eccentrics, but, by the 1990s, by a majority of ordinary Americans. The idea that Kennedy was the victim of a conspiracy involving elements of the politico-military-industrial complex is vastly significant, but its importance has been largely overlooked. So far as the student of presidential history is concerned it does not matter who killed Kennedy or why. What is important is that if a majority of the American public think that Kennedy was assassinated by elements within, or protected by, some branches of the government of the United States then a problem of confidence and legitimacy is created. When the switchboard of a San Diego television company is besieged by callers condemning a CIA plot which they blame for the delayed transmission of a program on the Kennedy Conspiracy then there is a real problem. As Noam Chomsky has argued:

> . . . the assassination is depicted either as bringing to a close an earlier age of innocence (at least political legitimacy), or as aborting JFK's plans to lead us toward that condition, in a radical departure from the historical norm. Under either interpretation, the legitimacy of authority was lost in fundamental ways with the assassination, never to be regained (Chomsky, 1993, p. 64).

If the president can be killed by other elements within the US government, and that crime can go unpunished, then what is the nature of American democracy? Did the murder of Kennedy provide a brutal and persuasive warning to his successors not to challenge the interests of the politico-military-industrial complex? Did the Kennedy killing demonstrate what amounted in effect to a captive presidency? In Stone's *JFK* the leading character District Attorney Jim Garrison sums up the situation perfectly: "We have all become Hamlets in our country, children of a slain father-leader whose killers still possess the throne." The questions arising from November 1963 all stem from the possibility that Kennedy was killed by a conspiracy. The fears may be entirely groundless because Lee Harvey Oswald perhaps was the lone gunman as indicated by the Warren Commission report into the assassination. Perhaps even at the moment of death John F. Kennedy was helping to create another of those illusory images that had masked important parts of his life. With the presidency appearance is often more important than reality and during the 1960s a growing number of Americans felt that they had some grounds to mistrust their own government on this key episode. The effects of the Kennedy assassination and the possibility of a conspiracy are incredibly hard to judge as they are so nebulous. Although the president is a kind of living personification of the federal government the increasing numbers of people who came to believe the conspiracy theories, and the malign nature of certain elements within the American government, rarely focused their suspicions on the presidency or presidential incumbents. But the growth of mistrust inevitably had certain collateral effects on perceptions of the presidency. Under Kennedy's successors that mistrust would spiral out of control.

The Kennedy assassination generated a sense of unease: later Watergate was to prove that it had been well founded. In some ways, the suspicions surrounding Kennedy's murder were more significant than evidence of wrongdoing in the Watergate scandal. Watergate was to show that a particular president had overstepped the mark: the Kennedy assassination suggested that the whole body politic of the United States might be rotten to the point of murder. Cynicism, voter apathy and a public willingness to believe that the US government was capable of almost anything were part of the fallout from the events in Dallas in 1963. The cultural effects of the shooting of John F. Kennedy were to continue to unfold over the next three decades and beyond. In April 1995 the Alfred P. Murrah building in Oklahoma City was blown up by a car bomb planted by a member of an organization which believed that the president was planning to hand over the running of the United States to the United Nations. The mistrust between the governed and the government was one of the preconditions for the loss of 168 innocent lives. With the death of Kennedy in 1963 hope and belief in the future of humanity slowly turned to cynicism and credulity.

Re-examinations of the Kennedy assassination during the 1960s and the 1970s only added fuel to the fires of suspicion. Particularly important was the United States Select Committee to Study Governmental Operations with Respect to Intelligence Activities whose investigations from 1975 to 1976 revealed links between the Kennedys, the CIA, and the Mafia in a joint quest to eliminate Castro. The committee found that the plots between the CIA and Mafia had not been reported to the Warren Commission by the CIA, FBI, or Robert Kennedy. This report of the committee helped to provide impetus for the setting up of the House Select Committee on Assassinations in 1976, to investigate the killings of John and Robert Kennedy and Martin Luther King. The formation of the committee was a dramatic indication of the level of public disquiet over the issue. When the committee reported on July 22, 1979, it found that John F. Kennedy probably was the victim of a conspiracy. That the conspirators were not subsequently identified and brought to trial further exacerbated public mistrust. When the United States Congress had found that the president was probably killed by a conspiracy, but that even they could not get at the truth, it was not entirely irrational for the public to be concerned.

Public reactions to Oliver Stone's *JFK* in 1991 raised those concerns to still greater heights, and led Congress to pass the President John F. Kennedy Assassination Records Collection Act of October 1992, despite the opposition of George Bush's administration. The Act involved the appointment of an Assassination Records Review Board which would examine whether or not government and other agencies should make public particular records relating to the assassination. The Review Board began its work in 1993 and concluded it, as it was required to do by the Act, in September 1998.

Thousands of pages of additional information were released in an attempt to reassure the public that the US government was not involved in a major cover-up over a conspiracy to kill its leader. However, lack of media attention on the work of the Review Board, and a willingness to dismiss the released documents as containing nothing new, has only added to the suspicions of many. Moreover, the final report of the board, which argued that "critical records may have been withheld" and that it had not managed to locate "all that was out there," added to the flames of suspicion. So vast is the gulf of mistrust that has opened up since 1963 that a broad section of the American public simply refuses to believe its own government despite its attempts to rebuild public confidence on this issue. Dallas was a massive turning-point in the history of the United States and the presidency: its importance would be confirmed only too fully during the Johnson presidency.

FIVE

LBJ: *Zenith of Presidential Power*

What we are witnessing, of course, is a flagrant attempt on the part of the communist dictatorship of Hanoi to overthrow, by means of armed aggression, the democratic regime in Saigon. . . . Now I know that the majority of you could give goddam about the welfare of these people or their problems; they live in a land twelve thousand miles away with habits and customs foreign to our own so you assume that their struggles are not yours. Believe me, this is a rather narrow shortsighted view. Consider the human body. What happens if an infection is allowed to go untreated? The bacteria spread, feeding on healthy tissue, until finally the individual dies. Physicians are bound by a moral oath which forbids them to ignore the presence of disease. They cannot callously turn their backs on illness and suffering and neither can we. A sore on the skin of a single democracy threatens the health of all. Need I remind you that four presidents – I can't emphasize this strongly enough – four presidents have recognized the danger signs and have seen fit to come to the aid of these afflicted people with massive doses of arms, troops and economic assistance to ensure their continued independence. . . . Certainly we seek no personal gain; we're just pumping in the penicillin, gentlemen, just pumping in the penicillin (Wright, 1985, pp. 9–10).

As the novelist and Vietnam veteran Stephen Wright explains, there were what were thought to be good reasons for US intervention in the Vietnam War. Vietnam was to see presidential power and authority reach new heights, but it was also to generate a revolution from below against what was identified as too much executive power. That war and that revolution were to crystallize in the presidency of Lyndon B. Johnson. "Hey! Hey! LBJ. How many kids did you kill today?" was to be the chant of the demonstrators outside the White House in 1968, the same year in which Johnson, recognizing that Vietnam had ruined his presidency, refused to seek or accept the nomination of the Democratic Party for a further term of office. The Johnson presidency involved so much more than the war in Vietnam, but his achievements were to be largely overshadowed by a war in a remote corner of the globe that would grow inexorably without any sign of an outcome favorable to American interests.

Following the assassination of Kennedy in Dallas on November 22, 1963, Lyndon Johnson was sworn in as president. The time was 2:38 p.m. and at the time Johnson was in the air heading back to Washington. Johnson was flanked by his wife, Lady Bird, and Jacqueline Kennedy, still covered with the blood of her late husband. Johnson had been traumatized by the day's events, and many questions remained unanswered. Were there other assassins ready to make an attempt on the life of the new president? Was the killing of Kennedy a precursor to a Soviet strike against the United States or a *coup d'état* by elements within the United States? These questions haunted Johnson on the night of November 22 and, throughout the rest of his presidency, the killing of Kennedy, and rumours of conspiracy, continued to trouble his mind. Only slowly did Johnson begin to understand the enormity of the job which he had just inherited. The country and the cabinet were in mourning and he faced the problem of how to establish his personal authority as president in particularly distressing and emotional circumstances. He did it through a combination of his personal qualities and by gently tapping into the sentiment surrounding Kennedy's death. By the evening of November 22 he had appeared on television to make a personal promise and appeal: "I will do my best. That is all I can do. I ask for your help, and God's." He would not move into the White House until December 7 out of respect for Mrs Kennedy. His image as president was that of white-collar America: hard-working, responsible, God-fearing; a complete contrast to the movie star glamour of his predecessor. If Kennedy was slick, a man to deal in illusions, then Johnson presented himself as honest, straightforward, and simple. With Kennedy his charm could conceal the deepest of secrets – Johnson wanted the American public to feel that with him it truly was a case of "what you see is what you get." Although Johnson's rugged image was to be complemented by the continued pursuit of an activist presidency, his goals were far more expansive than those of Kennedy. Johnson was one of the most radical presidents in American history, pursuing goals far beyond the liberalism of the New Deal, Fair Deal, and New Frontier.

Public approval of the Johnson style of presidency came on November 3, 1964, when Johnson was elected to a full term in his own right. Johnson ascribed his victory "to the program that was begun by our beloved president, John F. Kennedy." But it was also a tribute to a man who believed in the aspirations of Kennedy, and who also had the personal qualities and political skills to dominate Congress in a way which few presidents had previously managed. However, within Johnson's victory lay warning signs. The scale of Johnson's triumph: 43,129,566 popular votes to Barry Goldwater's 27,178,188, and a victory in the electoral college by 486 votes to 52, gave him an unprecedented mandate from the people. In the midst of the campaign Goldwater had complained, as part of a right-wing Republican agenda, against what he described as too powerful a presidency. Johnson, with an extensive domestic program, was not about to change course and retorted "Most Americans are not ready to trade the American eagle in for a plucked banty rooster." Underlying Johnson's rhetoric was an attitude toward power that seemed reminiscent of the famous retort by Louis XIV of France "I am the state" – scarcely an encouraging omen. However, in 1964 Johnson's victory seemed to confirm that most Americans were happy with the way in which the office of president was continuing to develop. With such an endorsement behind him, and with his ability to cajole and persuade Congress to his chosen point of view, Johnson after 1964 was in a massively strong position. As one historian has commented:

Lacking the intellectual quality of a Wilson, the brilliance in management of a Roosevelt, or the charm of a Kennedy, Johnson nevertheless brought some formidable strengths to the presidency.

98

No President has been equipped with a better understanding of the United States Congress or exhibited more drive and determination to be its master. These personal attributes, in conjunction with the considerable political advantages of high standing in public opinion polls, a stunning victory in 1964 and a massive following in Congress made Johnson virtually unstoppable, at least in the short run (Shaw, 1987, p. 102).

Johnson was a firm believer in strength and his background was one in which the virtues of the frontier had been emphasized. At his home on the LBJ Ranch, near Johnson City in Texas, were reminders of the early struggles of the Johnson family as they battled against the dangers of frontier life. Johnson's grandfather had defended his home against surprise raids by native Americans and had founded Johnson City. The father of the man who became president in November 1963 was both a farmer and a teacher, who had also served as a Democratic member of the state legislature. Pioneering, politics, and teaching were also in the background of his mother Rebekah Baines Johnson. Lyndon Johnson had been born into this forceful family on August 27, 1908. A brother and three sisters followed. In his youth Johnson did a variety of menial jobs, including acting as a shoe-shine boy and goat herder. After finishing high school in 1924 he went to California, earning his keep from odd jobs before deciding to return to Texas and go to college. Johnson eventually got his degree from the Southwest Texas State Teachers' College in San Marcos in 1930. He then went on to teach in a high school in Houston. His upbringing, and his training and experience as a teacher, gave Johnson a real insight into the underside of society. He knew what it was like to be exploited and to work for low pay. He knew all about social deprivation and the value of education in combating it.

Johnson's political education had begun at the age of twenty-four when he had gone to Washington as the secretary to Congressman Richard M. Kleberg. From 1932 to 1934 Johnson saw how politics worked from the inside. In 1934 he married Claudia Alta Taylor, later nicknamed Lady Bird. She was to have two children, and she combined child rearing with a successful career as a businesswoman. Lyndon earned the prestige, while she earned the money: controlling a bank, several radio and television stations and dealing in real-estate. Lady Bird Johnson was a vital component of an equal partnership. In 1935 Lyndon Johnson was elected to the House of Representatives on a platform of out-and-out support for Roosevelt's New Deal. He became an acolyte of Roosevelt who valued the young Texan's support. During the war Johnson served in the Navy – although he exhibited rather less panache than a certain John F. Kennedy – and in 1948 he was elected to the Senate, where he devoted his not inconsiderable energies to the Democratic cause. He learned every trick that could be played in Congress, and grew to understand the mechanics of the American legislative system as only a perceptive insider could. In 1953 he became minority leader of the Democrats in the Senate. In due course, as the voters turned against the Republicans, while maintaining Eisenhower in office, he became majority leader in the Senate. In between, in 1955, Johnson suffered a heart attack, but he recovered relatively quickly. Johnson's style of politics while he was majority leader was revealing. He believed in cooperation between all the elements in the government of the United States, whether they be Democrat or Republican. In this way the Republican Eisenhower was able to work with a Congress dominated by Democrats such as Johnson.

In 1960 Johnson was nominated as the Democratic candidate for the vice-presidency. He was a senior and respected figure within the party and he helped to balance the ticket. Kennedy was a Catholic: Johnson an Episcopalian. Kennedy was from New England: Johnson represented the South. Kennedy was the image of youth: Johnson that of experience. This was despite the fact that Kennedy and Johnson had been bitter rivals for the nomination, and Robert Kennedy personally disliked Johnson. During the Kennedy administration Johnson played a full and active part. For example, he was head of the National Advisory Council for the Peace Corps, and attended National Security Council meetings. He also acted as a goodwill ambassador for the United States. Therefore after the assassination he was plausibly able to suggest, notably in his first address to Congress on November 27, that there would be continuity from Kennedy's administration to his own.

In the first few months of his administration Johnson was able to be all things to all people. He would develop closer links with the business community while maintaining his sympathy for American labor. In April 1964 he intervened in a dispute in the railway industry and not only prevented a strike, but also led to a fair and equitable deal for both capital and labor. In addition, he would make pledges to wipe out hunger, disease, and poverty, while maintaining his commitment to the doctrine of containment. Nevertheless, in his state of the Union address to Congress on January 8, 1964, Johnson announced cuts in the federal budget. The secret of his success was that he was benefiting from the continued growth of the American economy. He also knew how to win over voters cheaply. In February 1964 he signed the Twenty-Fourth Amendment to the constitution, making it illegal to use payment of the poll tax as a condition of voter eligibility in federal elections. This made it easier for the poor and the dispossessed, who could be regarded as natural Democrat voters, to take part in elections.

But following his victory in the 1964 presidential elections, the Johnson presidency was steadily soured by events in Vietnam. In the popular mind Vietnam overshadows every aspect of his presidency. In the conventional narrative of American presidential history it was under Johnson that the White House turned truly imperial, and the consequences of an activist presidency became manifest. This is undoubtedly true, but the benefits of an activist presidency became just as manifest as the potential downside of involvement in costly foreign, and some might say unnecessary, wars. Before turning to these negative aspects, which came increasingly to dominate Johnson's presidency, it is important to appreciate the very real achievements which an activist president was able to make from 1963 to 1968. As one of Johnson's biographers, Irving Bernstein, has put it: "Lyndon Johnson was short-changed. He has been charged with what went wrong and has not been credited with what went right" (Bernstein, 1996, p. vii). And there was a great deal that "went right." His considerable achievements came under Johnson's broad promise to create a Great Society. Johnson explained what he meant by this in a speech at the University of Michigan on May 22, 1964:

In your time we have the opportunity to move not only toward the rich society and the powerful society, but upward to the Great Society. The Great Society rests on abundance and liberty for all. It demands an end to poverty and racial injustice, to which we are totally committed in our time. But that is just the beginning. The Great Society is a place where every child can find knowledge to enrich his mind and to enlarge his talents. It is a place where leisure is a welcome chance to build and reflect, not a feared cause of boredom and restlessness. It is a place where the city of man serves not only the needs of the body and the demands of commerce, but the desire for beauty and the hunger for community. It is a place where man can renew contact with nature. It is a place which honors creation for its own sake and for what it adds to the understanding of the race. It is a place where men are more concerned with the quality of their goals than the quantity of their goods. But most of all, the Great Society is not a safe harbor, a resting place, a final objective, a finished work. It is a challenge constantly renewed, beckoning us toward a destiny where the meaning of our lives matches the marvelous products of our labor.

In his drive toward a Great Society Johnson wanted to surpass the social reforms of Franklin Roosevelt, and in his first weeks of office Johnson formed a relationship with Congress that would have been the envy of most other presidents of the United States. Although that relationship would begin to break down in 1966 under the impact of Vietnam it initially allowed him to drive through a series of major pieces of legislation designed to reform America toward the goal of a Great Society. Whereas Kennedy had found the relationship between Congress and president a constant strain and source of frustration, Johnson thrived on it. To Johnson presidential performance could be measured by his ability to get Congress to agree to his domestic program, and by the subsequent effectiveness of the resultant legislation. The presidency would be as successful as the relationship between President and Congress would allow it to be.

The closeness of that relationship during the early years of the Johnson presidency is evidenced by the large number, and importance, of the statutes passed from 1963 to 1967. In 1965 he signed into law the Elementary and Secondary Education Act and the Higher Education Act. Building on earlier legislation such as the Higher Education Facilities Act of 1963 and the Vocational Education Act of 1963, the effects of Johnson's reforms were dramatic. As Johnson explained to Congress on February 28, 1967, the net result of the legislative changes was:

> that today appropriations for the Office of Education are nearly seven times greater than four years ago. Today we can point to at least one million college students who might not be in college except for government loans, grants and work-study programs, and to more than 17,500 school districts helping disadvantaged children under the Elementary and Secondary Education Act (MacGregor Burns, 1968, pp. 362–3).

Johnson's passionate belief in conservation and the environment was also reflected in his legislative agenda. The Wilderness Act of 1964 and the Water Conservation Act, passed in the same year, were designed to offer greater protection to the environment. In 1963 Johnson had signed into law a Clean Air Act which unfortunately proved to be stronger on rhetoric than on improving air quality but he continued to urge its importance, telling Congress on February 23, 1966: "Pollution touches us all. We are at the same time polluters and sufferers from pollution. Today, we are certain that pollution adversely affects the quality of our lives. In the future, it may affect their duration" (MacGregor Burns, 1968, p. 296). He was also responsible for some particularly popular legislation. The 1964 Revenue Act introduced a major tax cut to the American economy, designed to underpin the economic strength of the United States. The highest rate of tax was reduced from 91 to 77 percent and the lowest from 20 to 16 percent. At the same time, the Medicare Act of 1965 and the Economic Opportunity Act of 1964 addressed the problems of poverty and ill-health in the United States. Social security payments were raised and for those aged 65 or over there would be medical benefits to help in time of illness. On July 1, 1966, 20 million people became eligible for Medicare payments if they became ill. Johnson also strove to address the needs of youth. A Job Corps was founded to help people aged 16 to 21 to find work in the inner cities, and loans were provided for business to help the long-term unemployed. Johnson even went so far as to found a domestic American peace corps named Volunteers in Service to America, or VISTA for short. Johnson remembered what Kennedy seemed sometimes to forget: that poverty was just as endemic within the United States as it was in some foreign countries. In his program of reform Johnson adopted a broad approach to the problem of poverty. For example, the Head Start program aimed to secure immediate improvements for disadvantaged children by improving their quality of life, while enhancing their longer-term educational performance.

One further piece of landmark legislation that Johnson claimed credit for was the 1964 Civil Rights Act. The bill had been introduced in June 1963 in the midst of nationwide unrest and demonstrations about civil rights. After November 1963, with the demonstrations and disturbances continuing in cities such as New York and San Francisco, and with the tactics of the Civil Rights movement continuing to throw into sharp relief the discrepancies in the lives and rights of black and white Americans, Johnson threw his full weight behind the bill which went through the House of Representatives in February 1964 only to run into southern conservative opposition in the Senate. Despite dogged resistance, the bill was approved by Senate on June 10 by a massive majority. The new act was a sweeping effort to end discrimination in the South making it illegal to practise discrimination in public places and employment.

In short, Johnson enjoyed the most spectacular series of legislative successes of any American president. In part, he inherited the program from Kennedy. Reforms such as the 1964 Civil Rights Act and the 1964 Revenue Act had their origins in the Kennedy Administration. In part, Johnson's success stemmed too from his massive popular endorsement by the electorate. But the secret of his success lay in his ability to manipulate Congress in ways which made the passage of legislation very much quicker. Johnson knew who to talk to, and how to talk to them. His style was a mixture of charm and aggression depending on his audience and what he wanted from them. To serve as an example, on April 30, 1964, he rang Vice-President Hubert Humphrey to ask him about a press agency story which said that Humphrey had suggested that Johnson might compromise on the Civil Rights Bill that was being given such a rough ride in Congress. The conversation went:

> LBJ: Hubert, I don't believe you ought to be quoting me on what I'm ready to do on these amendments. Just go on and tell what you-all doing.
> HUMPHREY: [prickly] Mr. President, that was not my quote and I'm very sorry.
> LBJ: It's on all the tickers though and they're raising hell about it. Don't quote me unless . . . you know I want to say it (Beschloss, 1997, p. 336).

Johnson was capable of the most incredible arm twisting when he felt it necessary and that helped to propel his legislative program through Congress. "The Johnson treatment" when he was Senate majority leader was the stuff of legend in Congress. In making him their 1964 man of the year *Time* magazine noted:

> In cloakroom and corridor, in his baronial office or right out on the floor of the chamber, he would go to work on a colleague – squeezing his elbow, draping a huge paw over his shoulder, poking him in the chest, leaning so close as to be practically rubbing noses. On the phone (and he was seldom off it) he was equally effective. Hubert Humphrey once complained that the only way he could resist Johnson's hypnotic persuasiveness was by not answering the phone.

After Johnson became president in 1963 he continued to use the political skills honed to a fine edge by years of combat in Congress to get his own way. Even at the height of his success in 1965 he still had one major failure when Congress refused to repeal the Taft-Hartley Act that had placed important and significant limitations on the ability of organized labor to pursue their goals. But, his successes far outweighed such occasional setbacks.

In Johnson's drive toward a Great Society the enhanced power and authority of the modern presidency reaped its greatest rewards for the American people. Johnson dramatically expanded on Roosevelt's promise that the federal government would take continuous responsibility for the lives of ordinary Americans. Educational reform, Medicare, the war on poverty and the 1964 Civil Rights Act were massive achievements, made possible only by the power and authority enjoyed by Johnson, particularly after the 1964 election. In that election Johnson defended the principle of a powerful presidency, as his domestic program was showing the kind of benefits it could bestow. However, the other side of the coin, the dangers of a strong presidency were just as evident during the Johnson years. The triumphs of the war on poverty and ignorance would be balanced by the tragedy of war in Vietnam.

The deteriorating situation in Vietnam was one of a number of problems bequeathed to Johnson by Kennedy. The fall of Diem did not result in a significant improvement in the situation in South Vietnam where communist infiltration and effectiveness increased as the efficiency of the forces of South Vietnam declined under an increasing onslaught. Johnson faced a difficult choice. The Great Society required the spending of massive sums at home, but if South Vietnam were not to fall vast amounts would have to be spent there instead. Which was more important: social reform or maintenance of containment and America's international obligations? Containment had been a sacred cow ever since 1947 and to jeopardize it involved serious political risks. However, with social unrest manifest in a number of cities outside the Deep South, and with the South going through major social upheavals courtesy of the civil rights movement and the policies of a proactive president, Johnson had to press on with the Great Society. Instinctively, Johnson appreciated that building the Great Society and containing the communist threat in Asia were both essential for the well-being of the United States. His biographers often refer to the chaos of Vietnam that derailed the social revolution of the Great Society: a tragic tale of how war interrupted one man's search for justice and hope in the United States. This makes a nice dramatic narrative, but an alternative one might be how a powerful man facing an unpalatable choice between two courses of action, both of which he regarded as essential, lacked the wisdom of Solomon which might have enabled him to resolve the unsolvable conflicts of interest. The former narrative makes a better story, ending in failure, disillusionment and death. The latter is much more mundane and perhaps more damaging, because it supposes that Johnson did not expect to win the war in Vietnam – he only wanted to avoid losing it.

Johnson knew that he could not devote sufficient resources to the war and so 58,000 Americans were compelled to die in an unwinnable conflict. This narrative could make Johnson seem like a monster rather than the all-too-human, flawed figure which he was. But it fails to acknowledge the realities of the Cold War. Under Kennedy it had become obvious that there could be no such thing as victory in a Cold War conflict. A draw or a continuation of the conflict was the best that the statesmen on either side could hope for, because victory would probably involve nuclear weapons. That is why Kennedy made efforts after the Cuban missile crisis to decrease East–West tensions. Johnson was part of the same mind-set. In Vietnam there could be no victory: the war was unwinnable, as was the Cold War. Not losing was the only realistic goal.

Only if one accepts the second narrative does Johnson's handling of the Vietnam war after 1964 become explicable: the use of airpower to punish the North Vietnamese; limited troop deployments; failure to mobilize fully; the reluctance to invade North Vietnam or go into Cambodia to attack communist sanctuaries. One of the favorite stories told by Clark Clifford, Secretary of Defense from 1968 to 1969, was that after he took over at the Pentagon he asked the Joint Chiefs of Staff for their plan to secure victory in Vietnam, only to be told that there was no plan. Clifford expressed his astonishment at such an omission. However, the absence of a plan for victory in 1968 was simply an expression of the instinctive judgment of Johnson, and some of those who surrounded him, that avoiding defeat in Vietnam was the best that the United States could hope for. This was typical of Johnson: shrewd, pragmatic, and realistic. There would be a compromise between containment and the Great Society. Johnson probably did not recognize that this compromise would have to be made until he started making it. In that sense Vietnam was a personal quagmire for Johnson: each small step propelling him into deeper compromises so that he could maintain his two goals.

On becoming president, Johnson had very quickly affirmed that there would be no retreat in Southeast Asia. In national security memorandum 273, regarded by many as the foundation stone of the Vietnam war, the administration laid down that "The central role of the United States in South Vietnam [is] to assist the people and Government of that country to win their contest against the externally directed and supported Communist conspiracy." Even so, during late 1963 and early 1964 the Johnson administration increasingly agonized over what policy to pursue toward Vietnam. Secretary of State Dean Rusk explained the alternatives to the British Foreign Secretary in a letter dated March 2, 1964:

> As we see it there are three broad alternatives before us in South Viet-Nam. We could withdraw and leave Southeast Asia to the Communists. We could continue on our present course and do everything possible to assist the South Viet-Namese to win their own war. We could escalate the war by positive and direct military pressures on Hanoi. I can assure you that the second course is the one we greatly prefer. We cannot adopt the first course, with its calamitous results for the free world, and the third course is obviously one which would be turned to with the greatest reluctance (Rusk to British Foreign Secretary, March 2, 1964, British Public Record Office F0371/175494).

Increasingly, however, as South Vietnamese resistance continued to weaken, the third option became more and more likely.

Perhaps the key moment came in early August 1964 when two United States destroyers, the USS *Maddox* and USS *C. Turner Joy*, found themselves under what they believed was an attack by North Vietnamese torpedo boats. The two destroyers had been in the Gulf of Tonkin while South Vietnamese units launched attacks along the coast of North Vietnam. The events of August 2 and 4 are still shrouded in mystery, and it may be entirely possible that no attack was launched against the American naval vessels. In the excitement and danger of a war zone erroneous radar images may well have led the crews of the destroyers to believe that they were under attack. But confusion surrounding the engagement did not reach the ears of the president. He received a simple and categorical version of events. The first Johnson heard of the incident was in the form of the following memorandum from the duty office in the White House situation room:

Mr President:

1. Early this morning the USS *Maddox* was attacked by three DRV PT boats while on patrol 30 miles off the North Vietnamese coast in the Gulf of Tonkin.
2. The Captain of the *Maddox* returned the fire with 5-inch guns and requested air support from the carrier *Ticonderoga* on station nearby in connection with reconnaissance flights in that area.
3. *Ticonderoga* jets arrived shortly and made strafing attacks on the PT boats resulting in one enemy boat dead in the water, two others damaged and turned tail for home.
4. The *Maddox* reports no personnel or material damage (Glennon, 1992, p. 590).

The report was unambiguous and emphatic. There was no mention of South Vietnamese operations in the vicinity and similarly there was no doubt that an attack had taken place. Pressed by among others the American ambassador in Saigon to take a firm line with the north, Johnson knew that he could not back down. Determined to stand up to what he saw as unprovoked communist aggression, at 11:30 am on August 3 he held a short press conference to announce:

I have instructed the Navy:

1. to continue the patrols in the Gulf of Tonkin . . .
2. to double the force . . .
3. to provide a combat air patrol over the destroyers, and

4. to issue orders to the commanders of the combat aircraft and
   the two destroyers, (a) to attack any force which attacks them
   in international waters, and (b) to attack with the objective not
   only of driving off the force but of destroying it (Glennon,
   1992, p. 597).

Johnson's response to the initial attacks, couched in direct and
simple language to assure the audience of the power of the US and
her president, was measured and careful. If the North Vietnamese
chose to attack the US Navy in international waters then there would
be an effective but limited response. However, Johnson also signaled
his willingness to escalate the incident if the North Vietnamese
should fail to heed the warning by ordering the Navy not just to
drive off, but to destroy, any force which attacked its ships in the
Gulf of Tonkin. Unfortunately, at the meeting of the National
Security Council on August 4 at 6:15 p.m. Secretary of Defense
Robert McNamara was to report that further, again inconclusive
attacks, had been made on the *Maddox* and *C. Turner Joy*. Johnson
asked the members of the National Security Council, "Do they want
a war by attacking our ships in the middle of the Gulf of Tonkin?" to
which the Director of the CIA, John McCone, replied:

No. The North Vietnamese are reacting defensively to our attacks
on their off-shore islands. They are responding out of pride and on
the basis of defense considerations. The attack is a signal to us that
the North Vietnamese have the will and determination to continue
the war. They are raising the ante (Glennon, 1992, p. 611).

Johnson could see no alternative but to raise the ante in return. The
Tonkin Gulf incident helped to clarify the situation in his mind. South
Vietnam was slowly collapsing and without American assistance
communist victory was inevitable. To the imperative to intervene to
save the south was now added the need to punish an attack on the
forces of the United States. Given his background, Johnson was
acutely aware of the need to win congressional support for his
Vietnam policy. He was only too well aware of the difficulties Truman
had encountered as a result of his failure to enlist congressional

support for the intervention in Korea. Johnson was determined to avoid such difficulties over Vietnam. So after the "attacks" on the USS *Maddox* and USS *C. Turner Joy*, Johnson appeared on national television to describe the unprovoked aggression of North Vietnam. Then he submitted to Congress the Tonkin Gulf Resolution, giving the president the power to "take all necessary measures to repel any armed attack against the forces of the United States and to prevent further aggression." The House of Representatives passed the resolution unanimously, and in the Senate there were only two who voted against. Even some of those who voted in favor of the resolution, however, questioned its rather nebulous wording. Authorizing the president to take necessary steps to prevent aggression was all very well, but what were the precise limits on presidential authority? Those Congressmen who received "the Johnson treatment" to ensure the safe and swift passage of the resolution were assured that it was merely an expression of support for limited action to chastise the North and prop up the South. Certainly some, such as Senator William Fulbright, would argue that Johnson deliberately misled them. Either way, the purpose of the resolution was political rather than constitutional. Johnson knew that he had the power to take what he saw as the necessary course of action, but he wanted Congress fully behind the presidency. He did not want the kind of gap to open up between Executive and Legislature which had marred the last years of the Truman administration, and he was determined to ensure the backing of Congress for his foreign policy as well as for the drive toward a Great Society.

Johnson's concern to carry Congress with him was further demonstrated by his initial hesitation to draw on the authority afforded by the Gulf of Tonkin Resolution. Retaliatory attacks against North Vietnam followed the Tonkin Gulf incident, but throughout the rest of 1964 Johnson refused to punish the north further despite continuing Viet Cong attacks on American advisers in the south. Then on February 5, 1965, 8 Americans were killed and 126 wounded during an attack on Pleiku. Johnson felt that he had no option but to step up US efforts in Vietnam. Retaliatory attacks in late 1964 had failed to deter communist aggression and the situation in the south was going from bad to worse. During the Christmas period of 1964–5 the Viet Cong at Binh Gia had destroyed two battalions of the Army of the Republic of South Vietnam. It seemed as though, following the Maoist model of guerrilla warfare, the Viet Cong were moving toward conventional engagements with their enemy. This sent an important signal that the Viet Cong were increasingly confident and were ready to move to the next phase of their plan for military victory in South Vietnam. These developments, combined with the casualties at Pleiku, left Johnson with the conviction that he had to order stronger action. McGeorge Bundy, who had continued to serve as a special presidential assistant after the death of Kennedy, together with the State Department, urged Johnson to escalate the military effort in South Vietnam. The pressure was increased on February 10 when a further Viet Cong attack, this time in Qui Nhon, resulted in the deaths of 23 Americans. Johnson thus ordered retaliatory air strikes against the north. The President's explanation of the attacks implicitly invoked the Gulf of Tonkin Resolution. They were not the result of a single incident, but a calculated response to the "continued aggression" of North Vietnam. On February 13 Johnson extended the attacks into a sustained assault against North Vietnam from the air. The first attacks under Operation Rolling Thunder were launched on March 2, against a background of growing Viet Cong confidence and success in operations against the Army of the Republic of South Vietnam. The south meanwhile was undergoing yet another bout of chronic political instability. Johnson had to do something – the situation was increasingly grave and, quite apart from the domino principle or the doctrine of containment, the prestige of the United States and her President were increasingly at stake in Vietnam.

By March 1965 it seemed as though the defeat of South Vietnam was a matter of weeks away, despite the bombing of the north, unless the US effort was intensified yet further. It seemed as though North Vietnam had not been convinced that America would stand by its commitments under SEATO and the United Nations Charter, and thought that Johnson would fail to uphold the obligations inherent in the Gulf of Tonkin Resolution. The only way to convince the politburo in Hanoi that America would not allow the defeat of the south seemed to be to commit ground troops to the fighting. So on March 8, 1965, a battalion of Marines landed at Da Nang, South Vietnam. A second battalion arrived by air that same day. Their ostensible purpose was to protect the air base at Da Nang, but the commitment was to be momentous. From this point on the number of American combat troops in Vietnam would expand steadily until 1968, as would the range of their duties. Inevitably, defending the airfield involved patrolling great distances away from Da Nang to guard against the dangers of artillery and mortar attack. Increasing numbers of casualties across the whole of South Vietnam led the military to call for more men to secure the positions of those who were already there. Da Nang was not the only base facing a serious enemy threat, and as the military situation in South Vietnam continued to deteriorate, the US forces found themselves shouldering an ever larger share of the fighting and the dying. This was despite Johnson's promise in the 1964 election campaign not to let American boys do the job of Asian boys. Johnson explained his position in his memoirs, published shortly after he left office:

> In the summer of 1965 I came to the painful conclusion that an independent South Vietnam could survive only if the United States and other nations went to its aid with their own fighting forces. From then until I left the Presidency, we had three principal goals: to insure that aggression did not succeed; to make it possible for the South Vietnamese to build their country and their future in their own way; and to convince Hanoi that working out a peaceful settlement was to the advantage of all concerned. Those three main strands of action – defeating aggression, building a nation, and searching for peace – were tightly braided together in all that we, the other allies, and the Vietnamese tried to accomplish over the next three and a half years (Johnson, 1972, p. 232).

Johnson's recollections in his memoirs are borne out by an analysis of the advice reaching him from the Department of Defense and other government agencies in early 1965. In clipped sentences a paper prepared by the Assistant Secretary of Defense explained the thinking inside the Pentagon on March 10, 1965:

ACTION FOR SOUTH VIETNAM
1. *US aims*:
    70 percent – To avoid a humiliating US defeat . . .
    20 percent – To keep S[outh] V[iet] N[am] (and then adjacent territory) from Chinese hands.
    10 percent – To permit the people of SVN to enjoy a better, freer way of life. . . .
2. *Deteriorating situation*:
    (a) Politically, 50 percent chance of coup within 3 weeks
    (b) Militarily, SVN has been cut in two with G[overnment] V[iet] N[am] control in north reduced to enclaves.
3. *Prognosis*:
    (a) GVN officials will adjust their behavior to an eventual V[iet] C[ong] takeover.
    (b) Defections of significant military forces will take place.
    (c) Whole integrated regions of the country will be totally denied to GVN.
    (d) Neutral and/or left-wing elements will enter the government.
    (e) A popular front regime will emerge and will invite the US out.
    (f) Fundamental concessions will be made to the VC.
    (g) Accommodations to the D[emocratic] R[epublic]V[ietnam] will put SVN behind the Curtain (LaFantasie, 1996, p. 427).

Faced with such a stark prognosis the Johnson administration felt compelled to act. But Johnson perhaps made a mistake when intervening so heavily in the conflict in South Vietnam by relying on presidential prerogative for the constitutional basis of his actions. Although the Gulf of Tonkin Resolution gave him something which might be interpreted as *carte blanche* to do as he wished in Vietnam, Johnson did not invoke it in going to war in Asia. The resolution was a device to win the backing of Congress. It gave him some extra authority to deal with the crisis over Vietnam, but in terms of bestowing extra powers on Johnson its effects were limited. Johnson preferred to rely on presidential prerogative as the basis for his actions rather than try to expand the authority given to him by the Gulf of Tonkin Resolution. In so doing, Johnson was expanding the principle of presidential prerogative beyond any constitutional bounds. In effect, he was claiming the right to send troops into action simply because he was the President of the United States and in his opinion the interests of the United States merited it.

As US ground forces were being committed openly to the fighting in Vietnam in the spring of 1965, they were also being sent to the Dominican Republic. Again, presidential prerogative was invoked and Congress ignored as Johnson defended his action as necessary to protect American lives. As Arthur Schlesinger has argued, the number of troops, some 22,000, was disproportionate to the situation in the Dominican Republic. Johnson's purpose was to deliver a warning to the communist world that the United States would not tolerate the establishment of another Cuba in her Caribbean backyard. Johnson's actions in intervening in the Dominican Republic were constitutionally dubious, and they only served to highlight the still greater misdemeanor of the intervention in Vietnam.

The expansion of presidential prerogative to serve as a basis for intervention in Vietnam raised worrying questions about just how far the ability to make war had passed into the hands of the president. Johnson's decision, and his constitutional defense for that decision, were unprecedented. In Arthur Schlesinger's opinion:

Unlike Roosevelt's Atlantic policy in 1941, Johnson was ordering American troops into immediate and calculated combat. Unlike Truman's decision in Korea, there were no UN resolutions to confer international legality, nor had there been clear-cut invasion across frontiers. Unlike the Cuban missile crisis, there was no emergency threat to the United States itself to compel secret and unilateral presidential decision. Unlike the Dominican Republic, there were not American civilians to be rescued (Schlesinger, 1974, p. 179).

Johnson's expansion of presidential prerogative amounted to a power-grab by the White House, but for the most part Congress was willing to acquiesce as long as containment of communism was maintained in Vietnam.

Johnson's strategy for waging the war in Vietnam relied on gradual escalation. Pressure on the enemy would be intensified slowly, and there would always be further steps which the United States could take to bring the North Vietnamese to the negotiating table. Bombing operations were restricted to minimize the risks to the population centres in North Vietnam. Johnson wanted his intervention in Vietnam to be seen as a measured response to communist aggression. American ground forces were forbidden to strike at North Vietnam, or to cross into Cambodia to attack communist sanctuaries. The former, with memories of Korea still fresh in many minds, would make the Chinese feel uneasy, and the latter would lead to international condemnation. Johnson reassured the world that America's aims in Vietnam were distinctly limited and there was no question that the existence of the regime in Hanoi would be threatened. The build-up of ground forces continued slowly to the point where in 1968 there were over half a million Americans serving in Vietnam.

On the battlefield, US forces proved highly successful and, despite rising numbers of casualties, criticism of the war was muted throughout 1965. Even so, on November 2, Norman R. Morrison, a Quaker and a father of three, set fire to himself outside the White House. His death in protest at the war would be followed twenty-five days later by a mass rally of anti-war protesters in Washington. Vietnam was a war with which the American public found it hard to come to terms. A military doctrine based on rapid movement of friendly troops and massive firepower to degrade and destroy the enemy's human and other resources meant that this was not the kind of war which the American public had become used to. Instead of the landings at Iwo Jima during World War Two, or at Inchon during the Korean war, the public were told of search and destroy operations. Territory did not seem to matter in this new kind of war. There would be no repetition of World War Two heroics such as smashing through to Bastogne with Patton, or the drive to Berlin. Instead there would be the body count – the estimation of how many casualties had been inflicted on the enemy in a particular operation. This was a war of attrition in which the victor would be the power which proved most resilient in the face of the casualties inflicted by the enemy.

During 1966, as the nature of this new war became fully apparent, discontent began to mount within the United States. The bombing of North Vietnam intensified and so did public concern. During 1965 the first waves of protest had been felt as staff and students held anti-war teach-ins at some college campuses. The efforts of the Johnson administration to explain the war in Vietnam to an American public who could see just what the war involved on their television screens, proved largely ineffective. Johnson firmly believed that the anti-war protest movement, which continued to grow in numbers and importance, was simply a vocal minority. But while the majority did not join in vocal protest, their silence merely hid their growing doubts about the operations in Southeast Asia.

By 1966 Johnson was facing a revolt from below by people who questioned the morality and wisdom of the war. They also questioned the constitutional grounds on which they thought it was being waged – attacking the Gulf of Tonkin Resolution rather than presidential prerogative which Johnson regarded as giving him the power to wage war in Vietnam. Suddenly in some people's eyes the resolution had become a remarkable swindle by a president who wished to mislead Congress into granting him what amounted to a declaration of war. In 1966 Senator Fulbright of Arkansas, who had played a leading role in getting the Gulf of Tonkin Resolution through the Senate, turned against the war. He was chairman of the powerful Senate Foreign Relations Committee which began to investigate the policies being pursued toward Vietnam. Witnesses before the committee dealt Johnson's policies some damaging public blows. George F. Kennan, who had first suggested the principle of containing communism, came before the committee and argued that containment had only meant to apply to Europe, not Asia. A senior military figure came before the committee and claimed that the military strategy being pursued in Vietnam was the wrong one. Johnson found Congress increasingly less compliant over his domestic legislative program. Vietnam dominated the political agenda. Even the outbreak of the six day war between Israel and her Arab neighbors in June 1967 was only a temporary distraction involving Johnson in talks with the Soviet premier Aleksei N. Kosygin. There were riots in several US cities such as Detroit and Newark: in the previous year there had been over forty such riots. And in place of the toleration advocated by Martin Luther King, by 1967 the civil rights movement had been surpassed by that for black power. In 1966 the Black Panthers had been founded in California. Leaders such as Huey Newton and Stokely Carmichael advocated what amounted to a revolution. The penchant of the Black Panthers to parade openly with guns and some semblance of a paramilitary uniform terrified many white Americans. During 1966 and 1967 it appeared as though the United States was being ripped apart.

Two distinct fissures in American politics had opened up to an alarming extent: Vietnam and race. Vietnam was producing massive demonstrations against the war as well as more personal protests such as refusing to serve and others who followed the example of Norman R. Morrison. The President was blamed for the war – and the US system of government for allowing it to happen. On the issue of race limited presidential intervention gave rise to increasing black militancy in the late 1960s. Enough had been done to suggest that dramatic change was possible, but not enough to pacify northern urban blacks who saw that federal power could do little to ameliorate the conditions of poverty and discrimination which they faced. What many wanted, and even more needed, was for the Great Society to be expanded. But by 1966 the political emphasis had switched from the ideal of a Great Society to a war in which Black Americans were significantly more likely to be drafted: significantly more likely to end up in a combat unit; and significantly more likely to be killed. On April 4, in New York, Martin Luther King publicly condemned the war. Stressing the link between poverty and continued discrimination at home and the millions of dollars being spent on waging war in Vietnam, his speech was particularly impassioned:

> There is at the outset a very obvious and almost facile connection between the war in Vietnam and the struggle I, and others, have been waging in America. A few years ago there was a shining moment in that struggle. It seemed as if there was a real promise of

help for the poor – both black and white – through the Poverty Program. Then came the buildup in Vietnam, and I watched the program broken and eviscerated as if it were some idle plaything of a society gone mad on war, and I knew America would never invest the necessary funds or energies in rehabilitation of its poor so long as Vietnam continued to draw men and skills and money like some demonic, destructive suction tube. So I was increasingly compelled to see the war as an enemy of the poor and to attack it as such. Perhaps the more tragic recognition of reality took place when it became clear to me that the war was doing far more than devastating the hopes of the poor at home. It was sending their sons and their brothers and their husbands to fight and die in extraordinarily high proportions relative to the rest of the population. We were taking the young black men who had been crippled by our society and sending them 8,000 miles away to guarantee liberties in Southeast Asia which they had not found in Southwest Georgia and East Harlem (Ruane, 2000, pp. 152–3).

Dr King's speech sounded like an epitaph for the civil rights movement, and was an indication that discontent could not be contained for long.

Johnson realized that fighting a war in Southeast Asia was tearing the country apart. The presidency was beseiged by opponents ranging from hardcore black revolutionaries through to militant Christian pacifists. At least, though, he felt that he could rely on the military assessments which suggested that, slowly but surely, the war was being won. Then on January 31, 1968, the Viet Cong used the annual ceasefire and celebrations for the start of the Vietnamese Tet New Year to launch a major offensive. Although the communists were eventually defeated, the scenes of Marines having to fight their way into the old imperial capital, Hue, together with dramatic efforts to evict the Viet Cong from the American embassy in the middle of Saigon, resulted in a seismic shift in public opinion against the war. The Tet offensive was a military disaster for the Viet Cong, but it was an even bigger propaganda defeat for the Johnson administration in the eyes of the American public. Johnson felt increasingly alone and isolated even within his own party. In 1968 he would face re-election and there was every sign that his candidacy would be opposed by senior Democrats such as Robert Kennedy and Senator Eugene McCarthy. Both would use Vietnam against Johnson. In early 1968 he found himself a president lacking authority over broad sections of the American public, over Congress and over the party of which he was a member.

The decline of presidential authority was remarkable. In 1964 Johnson had been elected in a landslide: by 1968 he knew that if he stood for reelection he would almost certainly be heavily defeated. The change in public perception of Johnson and the war in Vietnam had undermined a president as never before. In the 1950s and the 1960s it had all been so different. Eisenhower's and Kennedy's support for Diem's corrupt regime had not troubled the American public. Nor had Kennedy's gradual escalation of the war from 1961 to 1963. Even Johnson's response to the Gulf of Tonkin incident had not aroused significant levels of public concern. With his customary acidity Noam Chomsky has argued:

> If the President wanted to send the US air force to bomb villages in some far-off land, to napalm people who were resisting the US attack or who happened to be in the way, to destroy crops and forests by chemical warfare, that was not our concern. . . . As late as 1964, even beyond, forums on the war were often – literally – in someone's living room, or in a church with half a dozen people, or a classroom where a scattered audience was assembled by advertising talks on the situation in Vietnam and several other countries (Chomsky, 1993, p. 2).

The deaths of American advisers in Vietnam had grieved the families of the deceased, but had not resulted in more widespread disquiet. But the landings at Da Nang in March 1965, and the start of a full-scale ground war with Americans carrying a heavy and escalating share of the fighting, followed by the final horror of the Tet offensive, produced a massive backlash among the US public.

By 1968 the presidency was facing a growing crisis of legitimacy. The Kennedy killing and fears of conspiracy continued to do their work. Indeed, investigations by Jim Garrison, the district attorney for

New Orleans, during 1967 and 1968, and the bringing to trial of Clay Shaw on conspiracy charges, served only to highlight the possibility that Kennedy had been removed in a *coup d'état*. Although Shaw was eventually acquitted, and Garrison was disregarded as something of a self-serving attention seeker by the establishment, there were many Americans who considered that Garrison really was *On the Trail of the Assassins*, as his bestselling book was later called. Johnson, however, did not dismiss Garrison as a fool. On the contrary, newly released audio tapes, which Johnson recorded while he was in the White House, show that he took a very great interest in the Garrison investigation, after he had earlier gone to considerable trouble to shape the outcome of the Warren Commission report. Johnson knew that Garrison's investigation threatened further to call into question the legitimacy of his presidency, which by 1968 was under attack in so many different ways as a result of the war in Vietnam. The war threw up a myriad of awkward questions from the American public. How could a president continue to wage what many thought was an immoral war? How could the will of one man, the president, result in the deaths of so many Americans? When demonstrations like that in Washington in October 1967 could number over 100,000 how could they be ignored? Many of the questions were politically naive, but in pondering their answers a good many gained a rather fuller understanding of the system of government in the United States. For example, in the minds of some members of the anti-war movement the willingness of Congress to pass the Gulf of Tonkin Resolution called into question the nature of American democracy. Parallels could perhaps be constructed between that resolution and the Enabling Act which had legitimately allowed Hitler to subvert the power of the Reichstag in the 1930s. Was it president Johnson or an American führer who was waging a brutal imperialist war in Indo- China? The analogy was entirely bogus, but the sentiments sometimes deeply felt. There were those who could remember that, even before Norman R. Morrison had burned himself to death outside the White House in 1966, an 82-year-old survivor of the Holocaust named Alice Herz had burned herself to death in Detroit in early 1965 in protest against the war. The moral authority of the presidency was called into question by growing numbers of Americans after 1965. Johnson retained the constitutional authority to carry on the war but, by 1968, he lacked democratic legitimacy. Johnson faced an immediate crisis, but so too did the presidency.

On March 31, 1968, Johnson appeared on television to announce steps to bring the war in Vietnam to an end. He had reluctantly come to the view that America could not win the war and that American escalation of the conflict would have to stop. The president was also at the end of his tether. His personality was extreme, embracing a series of selves that ranged from the bully of the "Johnson treatment" through to the sensitive and caring man responsible for the Great Society who would seek the plaudits of his contemporaries after any public performance. The attacks on Johnson as a result of the Vietnam war exacerbated his inner fragilities until he reached such a point in March 1968 that he could no longer contemplate further protracted exposure to them. In their psychological profile of Johnson, Muslin and Jobe have commented:

> Johnson's reaction [to the attacks on him] was predictably a self-collapse, an acute and chronic fragmentation reaction which continued over several years. He did go through the anxiety states, the self-breakdown . . . and regressive outpourings of rage, with transient delusional states of persecution, which characterize such a self-collapse. How could he continue to hide the evidence of so many deaths on both sides? How could he hide the evidence of this in the cities and countryside in the foreign countries of Southeast Asia resulting from the actions of the war machine? How could he continue to hide the fact that the United States economy was faltering under the financial pressure of paying for the war and the Great Society? . . . His fragmentation became more and more discernible to his staff (Muslin and Jobe, 1991, pp. 194–5).

No man, Johnson included, could continue to withstand the public assault on his presidency. It was just too painful, and in his television broadcast of March 1968 came the time to draw the agony to an end.

Toward the end of the broadcast Johnson, who invariably conveyed his earnestness, became rather more grave than usual. He confided to the American public:

> For 37 years in the service of our Nation, first as a Congressman, as a Senator, and as vice-president, and now as your President, I have put the unity of the people first. I have put it ahead of any divisive partisanship. And in these times as in times before, it is true that a house divided against itself by the spirit of faction, or party, of region, of race, is a house that cannot stand. There is a division in the American house now. There is divisiveness among us all tonight. And holding the trust that is mine, as President of all the people, I cannot disregard the peril to the progress of the American people. . . . Fifty-two months and ten days ago, in a moment of tragedy and trauma, the duties of this office fell upon me. I asked then for your help and God's, that we might continue America on its course, binding up our wounds, healing our history, moving forward in new unity, to clear the American agenda. . . . Believing as I do, I have concluded that I should not permit the Presidency to become involved in the partisan divisions that are developing in this political year. With America's sons in the fields far away, with America's future under challenge right here at home, with our hopes and the world's hopes for peace in the balance every day, I do not believe that I should devote an hour or a day of my time to any personal partisan cause or to any duties other than the awesome duties of this office – the Presidency of your country. Accordingly, I shall not seek, and I will not accept the nomination of my party for another term as your President.

It was a historic moment in the history of the presidency. By resigning the chance to run for a second term Johnson had shown the increasing sensitivity of the modern White House to public opinion. He had underlined the fact that while a president might try to expand his powers beyond those stipulated by the Constitution the people remained the ultimate source of authority and power. Illusion might blind the people for a while, but in Johnson's case he had tried to be honest with the electorate from the outset. By 1968 he was still powerful but he had lost much of the moral authority which he had enjoyed since 1963. Johnson's action was personally necessary but it was also courageous: it took courage to face up to the fact that he could not withstand indefinitely the assault of the protesters over Vietnam. He also showed, in the rather humble way in which he resigned the chance to run for a second term instead of publicly attacking those that had made his job impossible, that for him the buck really did stop with the president. If the people were divided then it was because of his policies – he was responsible because he was the president. Johnson wanted to eliminate the divisiveness that had come to dog the United States since 1966 and if that meant an end to the Vietnam war, and the termination of his presidency, then so be it. From 1964 to 1966 Johnson (and with him the presidency) had been at a pinnacle of success and power. From 1966 to 1968 both had suffered a rapid decline. The momentum of decline had quickened appreciably in the months before his speech on March 31, 1968. Under his successor, Richard Milhous Nixon, the decline would become cataclysmic.

SIX

Tricky Dicky: The President as Villain

For the United States 1968 was a climactic year in many ways. The launch of the Tet offensive in Vietnam and Johnson's refusal to run again for the presidency were just the start of it. Four days after Johnson's speech withdrawing from the 1968 campaign, Martin Luther King was assassinated by James Earl Ray who, to further inflame public concerns, might well have been part of a larger conspiracy. There were riots in over sixty American cities and a great outpouring of grief besides. Johnson's fears about a house divided seemed only too real. Then on June 6 further tragedy followed as Robert Kennedy, whose victory in the California primary election had just made him the Democratic front-runner, was mortally wounded by a Palestinian assassin. America was being ripped apart by violence: the violence of Vietnam, the violence of intolerance, and the violence of the assassins of King and Kennedy. The trouble escalated as Democratic delegates gathered in Chicago in August 1968. Johnson's refusal to seek reelection, and Robert Kennedy's assassination, left Vice-President Hubert Humphrey as the leading Democratic contender and he was duly nominated. But the convention was besieged by demonstrators ranging from the Black Panthers to white middle-class intellectuals protesting the war in Vietnam and seeking to further their other political ends. The Mayor of Chicago, Richard Daley, decided to take a firm line against the protests and when a riot broke out in front of the Hilton Hotel the police used tear gas and clubs to quell the disturbance. Their response seemed out of proportion to the situation, and the resulting scenes of violence were televised across America. The "siege of Chicago" only served to undermine further the chances of the Democrats. Hubert Humphrey was no Bobby Kennedy, with all the mystique of his name and his personal charisma; he was seen by the electorate as a representative of the war party which had plunged America into the disaster of Vietnam.

To run against Humphrey the Republicans nominated Richard Nixon. Nixon was perhaps an unlikely choice of candidate even though his knowledge of the Republican Party machinery was reputed to be second to none. In 1960, after Nixon and Kennedy took part in four televised debates in Washington, New York, and Chicago in September and October that would change the course of American politics, Nixon was defeated by a narrow margin in the race for the White House. Trying to do too much, Nixon simply wore himself out during the course of the campaign. He also seemed not to appreciate the importance of the visual image on television even though by 1960 88 percent of American families had a television set, and the election debates were watched by 65 to 70 million Americans. Despite Nixon's defeat, among concerns that electoral fraud had won Illinois and Texas for Kennedy, the president-elect flew to see Nixon on December 14 to see if he was going to contest the result of the election. For the sake of the country, Nixon preferred to take his defeat stoically. Two years later, after a further failure in the 1962 California gubernatorial contest, he had bade national politics an emotional farewell. His attempt to create a political base in California from which to challenge Kennedy in 1964 had gone badly wrong. Blaming the media for conducting a vendetta against him Nixon railed: "For 16 years, ever since the Alger Hiss case, you've had a lot of fun . . . Just think how much you're going to be missing. You don't have Nixon to kick around anymore." His career had seemed to be over, but the depths of his ambitious nature propelled him back to the fore of Republican Party politics after Johnson's landslide victory in 1964.

Born into a poor family in California in 1913, Nixon's nomination in 1968 seemed to be yet another step in a remarkable career. His drive, ambition, and intelligence had propelled him forward through Whittier College and the Law School at Duke University. He entered politics after serving in the Navy during World War Two and, after a short spell in the House of Representatives, he was elected to the Senate in 1950. Nixon made a name for himself as an anti-red, especially during the Alger Hiss affair, and in 1952 he was selected as

Eisenhower's running mate. He proved particularly active as vice-president, but at the same time the public regarded him as the political equivalent of a used car salesman: the unnatural toothy grin and attempts at charm generating a sense of threat rather than reassurance. To many, Nixon seemed to be a man on the make – a hustler peddling falsehoods – an obvious dealer in illusions. Yet sometimes a president who deals in illusions is exactly what the electorate wants. It is important to appreciate that many people mistrusted Nixon in the run up to the 1968 presidential elections. It is not simply a post-Watergate reading of public opinion. In his study of the party conventions in the same year, Norman Mailer wrote: "There had never been anyone in American life so resolutely phoney as Richard Nixon, nor anyone so transcendentally successful by such means – small wonder that half the electorate had regarded him for years as equal to a disease. But he was less phoney now, *that was the miracle*" (Mailer, 1968, p. 45).

The 1968 campaign hinged on the perceptions of the electorate about which candidate could be trusted to bring about an end to the Vietnam war. But beneath the surface other, rather darker, issues lurked. The electorate wanted not just an end to the war in Vietnam but a return to stability at home: the combination of stability and peace that America had enjoyed during the Eisenhower years. There was a realization that the war was harming the American economy which, in turn, had detrimental effects on the standard of living at home, the effectiveness of federal programs aimed at reducing poverty, and the long-term ability of the United States to maintain its technological lead over the Soviet Union. Another important issue at the heart of the election was that of trust: which candidate could be trusted to be president; which candidate could be trusted to bring the agony of Vietnam to an end; which candidate would be willing in their actions to reflect the will of the people; which candidate would not betray the people as Johnson, in the eyes of his accusers, had managed to do? In effect, the electorate wanted to know which candidate would exercise restraint in the use of their presidential powers. This was a significant moment in the history of the presidency. Some sections of the American public no longer trusted the federal government. In 1968 they sought reassurance that trust between president and people could be restored. One perceptive watcher of the events of 1968 noted:

> I can recall when that recognition came to me – during the campaign of 1968, when, for the first time, Americans of our generation realized their government had lied to them and, also for the first time, young Americans refused to fight at the call of their government. It was Edmund Muskie, then running for Vice-President and later to become a superlative Secretary of State, who sounded the theme of "trust." His campaign had brought him in that year of bloody divisions to a rally in the coal-and-steel town of Washington, Pennsylvania, a center of primitive George Wallace blue-collar workers, and also of the home of Washington and Jefferson College. The students and the rowdies joined to boo him and to prevent him from speaking. Muskie offered to give any of their spokesmen ten minutes on the platform if they would then give him a ten-minute hearing too. And so he spoke of trust: without trust there was no community, no civility. No headlines picked up the theme that day. But a few days later, at a run-of-the-mill New York press conference of Broadway stars supporting Humphrey and Muskie, Muskie let go once more with the theme that had come to him at the Pennsylvania rally: "I believe that the great issue in America is whether or not, as in the past, Americans can trust each other. . . ." The theme caught. It became Humphrey's final thrust against Richard Nixon. . . . Every presidential year has its own catch phrases. But again and again since, in each succeeding campaign, I have heard the theme rising (White, 1983, pp. 430–1).

Rebuilding the trust between presidency and people was the key task for any incoming president in 1968. The events which had followed Johnson's speech refusing to seek reelection had widened rather than closed those gaps, and, with antiwar demonstrations continuing, it seemed as though broad sections of the American people were in revolt against presidential power. The perception that the president had too much power, and had used that power to fight an immoral war in Vietnam, was widespread. In view of the Gulf of Tonkin Resolution, and its perceived subsequent failure to bring the war back under some sort of control, Congress was seen as a body whose powers had been usurped by an activist presidency. In writing about these perceptions the American liberal academic establishment has had a tendency to underplay the seriousness of the situation. It seems to take the view that the history of the United States should be a source of unity rather than division. Thus the situation in 1968 is described as troubled or difficult. However, a historian from the Marxist or the European, particularly the French, historical tradition might describe the conditions prevailing in 1968 as a moment of crisis in American history. They might even go so far as to describe them as pre-revolutionary. Revolutionary conditions in America, except for the "good revolution" against that hated tyrant King George III in the eighteenth century, are not something that American historians feel entirely happy writing about. The point at which liberal becomes perceived as left wing remains difficult to determine, and one suspects that to be seen as left wing is perhaps still not wise even after the end of the Cold War. But some Americans, from outside the establishment, *have* captured the seriousness of the situation in 1968. Tom Hayden, reflecting on the events of 1968, wrote in 1970: "We live in a constitutional crisis. The ruling powers have usurped power not only from the people, but from their own Senators and Congressmen to a point where only the President and his military-industrial advisery board know where the next war will begin" (Hayden, 1971, pp. 150–1). Hayden was also prepared to make reference to the Third Reich in his description of the situation prevailing in America:

> They lack the consent of the governed in the ghettos, colleges and high schools. Losing control over the conscripted army, they turn increasingly to professional Gestapo-types at home and abroad. At best, they are ruling half a society – and the ageing half at that (Hayden, 1971, pp. 155–6).

In Hayden's eyes, the level of discontent in the late 1960s did indeed threaten the established order.

During the 1968 campaign the fractures within American society were emphasized as George Wallace, the pro-segregation governor of Alabama, entered the race as an independent third candidate. Wallace ran a right-wing campaign warning of the dangers of the federal government meddling in local affairs and showing his contempt for the antiwar movement and the counter-culture of the 1960s. With such a broad message Wallace was able to appeal to working-class whites in the North as well as the South. Although it was widely believed that Wallace could not win the election there were those who thought that he might just be popular enough to deny either Nixon or Humphrey an outright victory. In the event however, Nixon ran out the winner by 31,700,000 popular votes to Humphrey's 31,200,000. Wallace polled 10,000,000 popular votes, which was more than respectable. In the electoral college Nixon's victory was even bigger: 301 votes to Humphrey's 191 and Wallace's 46. A rejuvenated Nixon, back from the political wilderness, had been returned to the White House.

In the midst of the turmoil of 1968 just enough voters had been tempted to reach back into the past to elect Richard Nixon as President, by a very narrow margin. To them he seemed to represent, as the political heir of Eisenhower, some kind of stability: some kind of return to a lost golden age. It was an illusion, but a politically powerful one in a divided and bewildered society. His campaign promises also struck the right note. He seemed to understand the problems facing America and to see that a return to traditional values would solve them. In his speech accepting the Republican nomination he captured the mood perfectly:

America is in trouble today not because her people have failed but because her leaders have failed. When the strongest nation in the world can be tied down for four years in a war in Vietnam with no end in sight; when the richest nation in the world cannot manage its own economy; when the nation with the greatest tradition of the rule of law is plagued by unprecedented lawlessness; when a nation that has been known for a century for equality of opportunity is torn by unprecedented racial violence; and when the President of the United States cannot travel abroad or to any major city at home without fear of a hostile demonstration – then it's time for new leadership for the United States of America (Nixon, 1978, pp. 314–315).

The key objective of the Nixon administration was to bring about withdrawal from Vietnam: but it would be gradual. Nixon would search for peace with honor, rather than the immediate peace with dishonor and the abandonment of South Vietnam which many members of the antiwar movement wanted. In effect Nixon's policy was a compromise between what America wanted and what American pride could stomach. In his domestic policies Nixon tapped into the prevailing mood with exceptional success. He labeled his policies New Federalism. The emphasis would be on slimming down the federal government, trimming back the New Deal, and returning power to the local level. Nixon's New Federalism echoed the policies of Eisenhower, accepting the New Deal while reining it back. Henry Brandon writing in 1972, argued that the American public looked to Nixon "as it looked to other uncharismatic Presidents, to set a path to 'normalcy', to lower the temperature, to bring order into chaos" (Brandon, 1972, p. 23). The American public wanted a return to a safer era.

In many respects the administration which Nixon put together promised a return to exactly the kind of unexciting presidency that the American public craved. Nixon would not construct an administration full of the best academic brains that the East Coast had to offer. Instead he would go for people whom he trusted and who could be relied on to do a competent job. Richard E. Neustadt has described the Nixon appointees collectively as "loyal, emphatic, and ignorant" (Neustadt, 1976, p. 54). Subsequent events were also to raise grave questions about their honesty. For example, Nixon's running mate in 1968 was Spiro Agnew, the governor of Maryland since 1966. He served as Vice-President, taking a leading role in the fight back against the antiwar movement, until in 1973, facing charges of income tax evasion, he resigned his office. Subsequently he did not contest the charges. Other members of the administration created animosity in different ways. John Ehrlichman, for example, one of Nixon's presidential aides, was often referred to as the president's Nazi guard: a reflection of a manner which many regarded as offensively arrogant. Along with H.R. Haldeman, Ehrlichman formed a double-act that was regarded as an important influence on Nixon, contributing to the remoteness and detachment from reality of the presidency. Henry Kissinger, meanwhile, was thought to exercise a still greater influence on the presidency. In 1969, Kissinger, after a highly successful career at Harvard, was appointed National Security Adviser. In this post he became Nixon's right-hand man so far as the development and execution of foreign and military policy was concerned. On his appointment:

> The President immediately authorized Kissinger to recruit a staff of the best available experts to service his National Security Council. Under his intellectual leadership, backed by the obvious approval of the President, the "Kissinger Operation" became the most powerful foreign-policy instrument in presidential history. Both Mr. Nixon and Kissinger were preoccupied with the power and strength of the presidency and anxious to create an instrument that could enable them to make quick decisions. Very soon the NSC became the fountainhead in the making of foreign and military policies. Kissinger and his NSC staff superimposed themselves over the State Department, Defense Department, the Joint Chiefs of Staff and the Central Intelligence Agency – to mention only the most important arms of government – overriding and cutting into the authority of the heads of those august departments (Brandon, 1972, p. 46).

Nixon's appointment of Kissinger was an administrative innovation which meant a centralization of power within the US government. Kissinger played an important role in coordinating the efforts of different departments to create a more holistic approach to the foreign problems that America faced. However, as so often with departures from the commonplace, Kissinger's role aroused concerns. Too much power seemed to reside in the hands of one unelected man. People questioned who took the really big decisions – was it Nixon or Kissinger? Just who was really responsible and in control of the nation's foreign policy? The reality was that the two men had a remarkably close affinity and the main lines of policy to be pursued would emerge from a consensus between the two. People still questioned all the same. One member of the State Department commented in 1971: "People often see Kissinger as a Rasputin who is whispering into the President's ear and exercising an evil influence . . . but that is not so" (Brandon, 1972, p. 51).

Nevertheless, appearance counted for more than reality, and the reference to Rasputin was an unconscious recognition of a regime in crisis, a regime surrounded by enemies, and implied that the "imperial court" faced the prospect of revolution from below. In 1917 Nicholas II of Russia faced the problem of a peasantry desperate for land and bread, encouraged onward by social revolutionaries and Bolsheviks. The peasants also wanted an end to World War One. The masses in the United States in the early 1970s simply wanted an end to the spilling of American blood in Vietnam, and they also wanted a presidency that offered the chance of stability.

At least in his domestic policy Nixon lived up to his campaign promises of the New Federalism. There was a new emphasis on local solutions to local problems. Nixon believed that the federal government bureaucracy served itself rather better than it served the people, and that it needed to be cut back. Shortly before he had joined the Navy he had been employed by the Office of Price Administration where he became a passionate opponent of the federal bureaucracy:

In OPA . . . I learned respect for the thousands of hard-working government employees and an equal contempt for most of the political appointees at the top. I saw government overlapping and government empire-building at first hand. I was startled by the mediocrity of many of my fellow civil servants. But most important, I became more conservative as I realized that what I thought it was possible for government to do, government could not do. In OPA, too, I saw that there were people who weren't interested in carrying out the regulations, but who had a real passion for getting business and used the authority they had to that end (Toledano, 1969, p. 37).

Under Nixon there would be a shift away from federal solutions to the nation's problems. Instead there would be local answers to local difficulties. For example, despite the landmark legislation of the Great Society, in 1969 almost 70 percent of African-American children in the South still attended black-only schools. Instead of responding with yet another piece of heavyweight legislation Nixon developed the alternative of locally controlled desegregation. Biracial committees at state level were set up to oversee the move toward integration. That the federal government should step back and allow the local voice to be heard went against the concentration of power at the center which had been taking place ever since 1933. It was also a massive success, so much so that by the end of 1970 less than 20 percent of African-American children were still in segregated schools.

Other aspects of New Federalism were no less striking. There was, for example, Nixon's plan for revenue sharing between the federal and local levels. The federal government would collect the money only for a substantial proportion of it to be given to the local level for distribution. Nixon considered that people at the local level knew how best to deal with their problems rather than the bureaucrats in Washington. Revenue sharing was a practical alternative to overblown federal programs and it was coupled with further initiatives such as the State and Local Assistance Act of 1972 . In its fourteen-year life it delivered $83 billion to states and cities, providing matching funding for that raised at the local level. The emphasis on the local, as opposed to the federal, level was significant. It, and Nixon's drive for efficiency and cost effectiveness in the administration of federal programs, seemed to signal that the big government, and with it the activist presidency, was being reined back.

But at the same time other aspects of Nixon's domestic program seemed to indicate a strengthening of federal and presidential authority. In response to domestic poverty Nixon championed the Family Assistance Plan. Believing that the welfare system created a poverty trap in which the poor became dependent on the state, and that the system also penalized the working poor, Nixon sought to replace various federal handouts with a cash payment to those in need. Nixon suggested that a figure of $1600 per year could be paid to a family of four. The Family Assistance Plan was attacked from all sides: by conservatives who rejected such an extension of state responsibility; by liberals who considered the amounts proposed to be insufficient, and by federal workers whose jobs were threatened by the reform. Nixon was eventually forced to drop the idea in the run-up to the 1972 presidential election. However, his belief in the power of the federal government was demonstrated more successfully in other fields. He championed the cause of women by creating a presidential task force on Women's Rights and by bringing sex discrimination under the aegis of civil rights legislation. He also set an example by bringing into government a large number of women.

Championing women's rights and school desegregation was part and parcel of Nixon's pursuit of a populist program. The rhetoric of shifting power away from the center and out to the periphery was similarly intended to respond to the mood of the voters. Americans wanted a smaller, more restrained presidency and a cheaper federal government. Revenue sharing was one aspect of this but it was also politically useful in another way: the distribution of federal funds at the local level benefited the political ambitions of Congressmen who could claim credit for improvements in their districts. Nixon's political savvy was also demonstrated with the Family Assistance Plan. He believed passionately in the plan, his early years having provided him with an acute understanding of poverty, but when it became politically expedient to drop it he did. Nixon was also prepared to learn from the successes of his predecessor, sending numerous proposals about the environment to Congress. But even in the domestic field, and despite his desire to tap into conservative concerns about big government, he was occasionally forced to show just how powerful the presidency had now become. When Congress passed the Clean Water Act of 1972 he used his presidential veto to block it. When Congress carried the Act over his veto he used his powers to impound half of the $18 billion that Congress had voted. In Nixon's eyes it was a waste of money: federal squandermania that had to be stopped in the interest of the American taxpayer. But, at the same time, by impounding the money Nixon was being seen to thwart the democratic will.

It was small wonder that, with a president prepared to impound funds voted by Congress and the public skeptical and critical about the role of Congress in the government of the United States, there should have been a strong reaction among the Senators and members of the House of Representatives. They were essentially caught between presidential power and the populace who demanded more democratic accountability and control. As Henry Brandon observed, even under Johnson the reaction of members of the legislature to their predicament had been sometimes temperamental and sometimes incisive: "The Congress, in its rebellion against the Executive, became emotional and occasionally blindingly furious. It felt impotent, cheated and humiliated by the way President Johnson had treated it. Its anger and lust for revenge were building up" (Brandon, 1972, p. 20). When Nixon entered the White House he knew that he was going to have an even tougher job than Johnson in managing the relationship between president and Congress. With the Democrats holding a majority in both the House of Representatives and the Senate he would have been in for a difficult time anyway, but the state of public opinion and the continuing war in Vietnam made his presidential performance even more problematic. It also, as we have seen, set him on a course toward a presidency that was more active on the foreign than the domestic front. Foreign affairs, especially Vietnam, were the burning issue in more ways than one, and he could enjoy greater freedom of maneuver in an area where he did not have to work too closely with Congress.

Despite his campaign promises in 1968 the war in Vietnam continued to drag on until cease-fire accords were signed in January 1973. More Americans and more Vietnamese had to die in a war which few thought America could win and which most hoped would simply go away. The American army in Vietnam suffered a serious decline in quality with low morale, drug abuse and the murder of unpopular or gung ho officers. The continuation of the war only served to inflame the feelings of mistrust that many Americans had for their government and their president. In 1969 it became public knowledge that in the previous year a group of American soldiers under the command of Lieutenant William Calley had massacred around 200 Vietnamese civilians at the village of My Lai. Calley was convicted only for Nixon to parole him. This outrage was topped by another. On April 30, 1970, American troops invaded neutral Cambodia to eliminate the enemy staging areas which had been active there since the early 1960s. The operation made military sense. The bases had been secretly and illegally bombed, but the supply routes to the Viet Cong fighters in the south had not been seriously disrupted. However, public opinion considered that the incursion into Cambodia meant that Nixon was expanding the war: reneging on his campaign promises and doing the precise opposite of what the people wanted. In May 1970 campuses across the United States erupted into protest. Four students died at Kent State University in Ohio and two others at Jackson State College, Mississippi, as the protests got out of hand. The Kent State killings had a particularly dramatic effect:

> The events at Kent State galvanized America's youth. With almost no planning, a rally held on 9 May in Washington drew over 100,000 protesters. Nixon trying to show his rapport with young people, went to the Lincoln Memorial to meet with demonstrators. Instead of discussing the war, however, he talked about football. "He just kept rambling," one student said, "and he didn't make any sense." Nor did he do much to bring calm to the country. Amid the climate of anger and frustration, protests and violence continued (Buzzanco, 1999, p. 107).

The divisions in American society seemed to be growing with Nixon failing in his attempt to rebuild trust between the American government and its people. Indeed, Nixon's actions were, at times, ill-considered and provocative:

> When Nixon was told in May 1970 about the clubbing of dissenters [in the aftermath of the Kent State killings] by hard-hat laborers in New York's financial district, he reacted to the affair in his own way. He invited Peter Brennan, the head of the construction union, for a little ceremony in the Oval Office, and the president posed for cameras wearing one of their helmets, the new symbol of blue-collar hostility toward bourgeois radicals. Once again, the administration came under fire, not only from liberals

who were outraged that the chief executive had sanctioned violence. It was a time when discord had reached a new high, when, having made his "big play" in Cambodia and touched off the reaction at home, he was accused of insensitivity by using the word "bums" to denounce young radicals (Parmet, 1990, p. 594).

Still Nixon did not heed the warning signs, and in February 1971 the Army of the Republic of Vietnam, with US assistance and Nixon's agreement, staged operation Dewey Canyon, the invasion of Laos. Again the idea was to disrupt the enemy's supply lines down the Ho Chi Minh trail which stretched from North Vietnam through Laos and Cambodia into the border regions of South Vietnam. The operation made military sense, but it provoked criticism and concern that Nixon was expanding the war.

In fact, Nixon was pursuing a policy of gradual withdrawal from Vietnam. The American commitment was being scaled back as the South Vietnamese shouldered an ever heavier share of the burden themselves. Nixon's policy of Vietnamization has been attacked by historians and others as an attempt to provide a fig leaf of decency to cover a naked American abandonment of South Vietnam. In this analysis Nixon and Kissinger are condemned for allowing the ultimate defeat of South Vietnam, and by implication for ensuring that 58,000 Americans had, apparently, died for nothing. Yet the administration's critics have perhaps been too quick to conclude that without American ground troops South Vietnam was inevitably destined for defeat. The process of Vietnamization was drawn out over a long period to ensure that the South had time to prepare to rely on its own military resources. Vietnamization was not some speedy and reckless abandonment: rather it was a slow and careful withdrawal which Nixon hoped would lead the North to withdraw its forces from the south. That this was not made a precondition of the cease-fire accords eventually signed in January 1973 has been used as further grounds to attack Nixon. But he knew that the North Vietnamese would not agree to it, and probably reasoned that with the south thoroughly prepared it would in any case make little difference. Most analysts assumed that the south would be able to go on resisting indefinitely, and that sooner or later the North Vietnamese would see the sense in political compromise rather than allowing the war to drag on indefinitely.

However, there were two vital underpinnings for the strategy of Vietnamization. The first of these was that US aid would continue to be available on a massive scale. Operations such as Dewey Canyon in 1971 were intended to measure the success of Vietnamization, but instead they only demonstrated that the process had a long way to go and that massive quantities of aid would have to be given almost indefinitely. Unfortunately, Congress proved increasingly reluctant to bankroll a country which many saw as corrupt and others blamed for the deaths of 58,000 Americans. Continuing massive aid was vital if Vietnamization was to work: the Vietnamese both north and south knew it; Nixon and Kissinger knew it; but Congress had other concerns. The second major element necessary for Vietnamization to work was the continued prospect of the massive use of American air-power if there was a serious threat to the south. This was a vital strategic factor and also important politically. It would send a power-ful signal to Hanoi that South Vietnam had not been abandoned, and that there was the possibility that the United States might intervene once more on the ground rather than see the destruction of a close friend. The importance of American airpower was amply demon-strated in 1972. When a massive communist offensive was launched on March 30, 1972, the Army of the Republic of Vietnam threatened to fold entirely. Even before the offensive some 20,000 ARVN soldiers a month were deserting and, in the face of a determined onslaught, South Vietnam was being overwhelmed. In response to the danger Nixon launched Operation Linebacker: a sustained air offensive against North Vietnam and its forces in the south. In South Vietnam alone, B-52 bombers flew over 700 missions. In the face of Operation Linebacker the communist offensive wilted and the resistance of South Vietnam strengthened. Airpower had saved the south, but the political fallout was considerable. Again it seemed as though Nixon risked expanding the war. Whereas Johnson had done his best to limit the war while increasing the American commitment to Vietnam, Nixon seemed to be expanding the war even as American forces contracted and withdrew.

Airpower was also instrumental in making possible the "peace" of January 1973. Throughout 1972 as Nixon ran for reelection against George S. McGovern, the Democratic antiwar liberal from South Dakota, the negotiations between the United States and North Vietnam dragged on. Nixon hoped to conclude a cease-fire in time for the election, but it was not to be. McGovern's campaign was damaged by the fact that his out-and-out antiwar stance alienated right-wing Americans, while his vice-presidential running mate, Thomas Eagleton, had undergone electro-convulsive shock therapy for depression. Nixon was able to romp home by 46,000,000 votes to McGovern's 28,000,000 (520 electoral college votes to a mere 17 for McGovern). That peace seemed to be close, if not actually at hand, was enough to convince a majority of Americans to endorse Nixon once again, although one also had to recognize that the American public were not presented with a particularly compelling range of choices. At least Nixon, the man who had expanded the war, seemed, in some convoluted, hard to understand way, to be delivering on his promises about the war.

Once re-elected Nixon strove to conclude the peace and when the peace talks broke down in late 1972 the president ordered Operation Linebacker II – an air offensive against the north to bring them back to the negotiating table. Starting on December 18, and concluding on December 29, American tactical and strategic aircraft dropped over 40,000 tons of bombs on the enemy. Again, the man who posed as peacemaker seemed rather more eager to wage war, and just one month after reelection his approval rating fell to 39 percent. But the Christmas bombings did bring the North Vietnamese back to the table. Nixon was inaugurated on January 20, 1973, and three days later he announced that a peace agreement had been signed, although the threat of American airpower remained a vital underpinning to it. Without it, South Vietnam appeared vulnerable to any repeat of the communist Easter offensive of 1972. After the conclusion of the Paris Accords, however, Congress successfully moved to ensure that the administration would find it harder to become involved in other people's wars in the future.

The use of airpower to save South Vietnam became an ever more unlikely possibility. The mood in Congress during the Nixon administration had become steadily more critical, especially at the administration's resort to covert actions in Indo-China. Senate investigations in 1969 and 1970 found that the United States had reached covert agreements with Laos, Thailand, and a number of other countries. The scope of these agreements varied, but Congress was alarmed at the commitments being made to foreign governments. To curb covert presidential foreign policy, in 1972 Congress passed the Case-Zablocki Act. The Act meant that the Secretary of State was required to send details of all international agreements to Congress within sixty days of their signature. Treaties would be dealt with by the normal constitutional procedures. If the president considered that sending the details to Congress might compromise national security, he was allowed to limit the circulation of text of any agreement to the Foreign Relations Committees in the House and Senate with an appropriate warning. Nixon and those who followed him would later ignore or get round the act, despite Congress's attempt to strengthen it in 1974. For example, in September 1977 the American and Russian governments signaled their determination to stand by the gains of the Strategic Arms Limitation Talks (SALT 1) by issuing parallel policy statements. Since there was no agreement the matter did not fall under the Case-Zablocki Act. Despite its flaws Case-Zablocki at least indicated that Congress intended to limit presidential power.

The legacy of Nixon's policy toward Vietnam also took other forms. It was somehow symbolic that, on the day before Nixon announced that peace had been reached in Paris, Lyndon Johnson died at the LBJ Ranch in Texas. For some, the death of the man whom they blamed for the Vietnam war was almost an act of atonement for the deaths of so many other Americans. The Paris Peace Accords paved the way for a rapid withdrawal of American troops, the last of which, except for a token presence, left on March 29, 1973. On the same day the last known American prisoners held by the North Vietnamese left Hanoi.

However, that was far from the end of the war. The cease-fire between North and South Vietnam was relatively short lived. More important, in terms of presidential authority, were the concerns raised after March 29, 1973, that American prisoners in Southeast Asia had been abandoned by their own government. It was alleged that so desperate was the United States to conclude peace that some of her sons were forgotten about and then deliberately overlooked because they were a reminder of an embarrassing war. It was further alleged that the Vietnamese and communist forces elsewhere in Southeast Asia decided to hang on to some US prisoners as bargaining chips in future negotiations with the United States. When the US government refused to be blackmailed in this way the men were condemned to rot in prison camps, in Vietnam and elsewhere. The American government, with the full knowledge of Nixon's successors in the Oval Office, instituted a cover-up. Again this belief was symptomatic of a deep malaise within the American body politic. Not only did Americans believe that their president would send them to die in a needless war, but they also believed that the commander-in-chief would not care if all the boys did not come back home. The rumbling concerns of the early 1970s became a crescendo later in the decade after Nixon had left the White House. They permeated popular culture to such an extent that in the early 1980s a series of popular films took up the theme of which *Rambo II*, *Uncommon Valor*, and *Missing in Action* are among the best known. In the 1990s, as American–Vietnamese relations improved, teams of forensic experts began to roam the old battlefields to find the remains that would lay the ghosts of Nixon's abandoned Americans. Again, to the student of the presidency and American government and politics, it is in a sense irrelevant whether or not American soldiers were left to die in communist prisons. If a substantial minority of Americans believe that their president is capable of such actions then that is enough to generate a crisis of confidence. What was perhaps even more damaging than the allegations that Americans might have been held against their will in Vietnam after March 1973, was the firm evidence unearthed during investigations into that possibility which showed that Americans had most definitely remained in communist hands after World War Two and Korea. The burden of guilt and suspicion extended back to include Truman, the honest guy from Missouri, and Eisenhower, the distinguished general. Even the image of the golden age of the modern presidency suddenly seemed rather tarnished.

If Nixon's policies toward Vietnam continued to haunt the presidency, then still more important for its future was the Watergate scandal, which led to Nixon's ultimate downfall. The scandal involved revelations that Nixon had resorted to dirty tricks against those whom he perceived as the enemies of the administration. During the 1972 presidential campaign the Democratic nominee, George S. McGovern, had publicly referred to Nixon's underhand methods. In particular, McGovern had made mention of the attempted burglary of the headquarters of the Democratic National Committee in the Watergate building in Washington. Five men were arrested during the break-in. As investigations into the burglary continued, it became clear that the men were acting on the orders of some superior authority, but Nixon was reelected before the case came to trial on January 8, 1973. During the trial one of the accused, James W. McCord, the security chief for the Committee to Re-Elect the President, gave evidence that suggested to some observers, including reporters Carl Bernstein and Bob Woodward of the *Washington Post* newspaper, that the conspiracy to burgle the Watergate building might extend all the way to the White House. On February 7 the Senate voted by 70 votes to 0 to establish a committee to further investigate Watergate. What emerged through the committee and the investigations of Woodward and Bernstein, who were being fed evidence by a source codenamed Deep Throat (who was possibly Mark Felt, Deputy Director of the FBI), was a pattern of systematic dirty tricks being played against Nixon's enemies. The president was personally implicated in these tricks to varying degrees. For example, he did not order the Watergate break-in, which was intended to place surveillance equipment in the heart of the enemy camp, but he did try to cover up the affair. The Watergate scandal ended with the imprisonment of twenty-five members of Nixon's administration and the resignation of the president. In July 1974, after Nixon had been forced to hand over audio tapes that he had had made secretly to record his conversations in the White House, the Judiciary Committee of the House of Representatives voted three articles of impeachment against the president. They involved the payment of hush money to those who

143

could implicate the president in criminal wrongdoing, the abuse of his office through the illicit use of federal agencies such as the CIA to try to hinder the investigations, and the thwarting of Congress by refusing to hand over to Congress tapes of the President's personal conversations. Knowing that the tapes would establish his guilt and that there was nothing further he could legally do to prevent their release, Nixon handed over the tapes, and on August 9 he resigned his office in order to spare the country and his family the pain of a trial in Congress which he knew that he must lose. Two things had precipitated Nixon's descent into dirty tricks: firstly, there was a long tradition of it in American politics; secondly, Nixon and his closest advisers, like John Ehrlichman, perceived that the White House was under unprecedented siege from its enemies.

Political espionage and vote-rigging had a long history in the United States which embraced Al Capone's manipulation of Chicago politics in the 1920s, through to Mafia help for John F. Kennedy's run at the presidency in 1960. Meanwhile, during the early 1970s as the Vietnam war expanded to embrace Laos and Cambodia, with the consequent response from the antiwar movement, the White House more than ever before seemed to be under siege, and it perceived itself to be so. Then in June 1971 an employee of the Defense Department, Daniel Ellsberg, leaked to the *New York Times* a top secret report into the origins of the war in Vietnam. The leaking of the so-called Pentagon papers gave the antiwar movement more ammunition with which to attack the administration. Nixon reacted with fury to the leaking of state secrets. He tried to stop publication of the Pentagon papers but failed. Feeling himself beset by enemies, Nixon asked John Ehrlichman to form a team of "plumbers" to stop the leaks. Nixon had already stepped up domestic surveillance in order to protect himself. For example, on May 12, 1969, the White House began tapping the telephone lines of some seventeen aides and journalists after the bombing of Cambodia had been revealed to the press. In July 1970 the president had approved, and then rapidly rejected, a plan calling for a massive extension of domestic surveillance. With the release of the Pentagon papers Nixon decided that he had to strike back. The question was how. Using the FBI, CIA, NSA, or some other organ of the federal government risked exposure by congressional investigation. Ehrlichman's team of plumbers offered a more low-key, expendable and deniable solution to the problem. So, on the night of September 3/4, 1971, White House aides Howard Hunt and Gordon Liddy oversaw the burglary of the offices of Daniel Ellsberg's psychiatrist. This was part of a crude attempt to discredit Ellsberg. From this point onwards, John Ehrlichman ran a dirty tricks campaign against the enemies of the administration which culminated with the Watergate break-in on June 17, 1972.

The Watergate investigations highlighted many disturbing aspects of Nixon's administration. Nixon's descent into illegality was clearly a massive breach of trust between President and people, but in the course of the investigations Nixon, by way of defense, also let it be known that Johnson and Kennedy had been just as ready to use wiretaps for "national security." Thus Nixon spread the burden of wrongdoing as widely as he could. Just as worryingly, the Watergate tapes showed a president who might be described as paranoid and malevolent. For example, Nixon was furious at the *Washington Post*'s investigations of Watergate. In a telephone conversation with presidential aide Charles Colson on October 25, 1972, Nixon expressed his desire to get even with the *Post*: "PRESIDENT NIXON: We're going to screw them . . . another way. They don't really realize how rough I can play. I've been a nice guy around here a lot of times, and I always play . . . on a hard-hitting basis. But when I start, I will kill them. There's no question about it." Nixon said that the *Post* ought to think twice before "taking on the guy that went into Cambodia and Laos, ran the Cambodian bombing campaign" (Kutler, 1997, p. 173). At times Nixon seemed to regard the American people as the enemies of its government.

Watergate and Nixon's resignation have evoked a variety of responses from the academic community:

Fred Emery, author of *Watergate: The Corruption and Fall of Richard Nixon*: If it was a self-destruct tragedy for Richard Nixon, for the American people it was a drawn-out ordeal that tested the robustness of democratic processes. Despite some alarms, institutions held steady, law was upheld, and a chastened republic survived (Emery, 1994, p. xi).

Stephen Bull, former special assistant to President Nixon: You have to look at Watergate within the context of the times. The times were tumultuous: there was great unrest throughout the country – civil unrest; antiwar activity; people getting shot on campuses; political violence abounded; there was uncertainty about motivations. . . . Secret documents were being published with impunity in the major newspapers; you had to wonder what things were coming to (Strober and Strober, 1994, p. 300).

Bob Woodward, journalist on the *Washington Post*: Watergate was probably a good thing for the country; it was a good sobering lesson. Accountability to the law applies to everyone. The problem with kings, and prime ministers, and presidents, is that they think they are above it, and there is no accountability, and that they have some special rights, and privileges, and status . . . I happen to believe in the essentially conservative idea that concentrations of power are unsafe and that those concentrations of power need to be monitored and held to account regularly. Watergate did that like nothing else that ever happened in this country (Strober and Strober, 1994, p. 505).

Jonathan Aitken, British Conservative politician and biographer of Nixon: In the view of this author, the forcing of Nixon's resignation was a political overreaction, a human injustice, and a tragic mistake. That was the consensus of international opinion at the time, and one which has strengthened with the passing of the years. American opinion still leans the other way (Aitken, 1993, p. 528).

Herbert S. Parmet, author of *Nixon and His America*: Had Nixon made a clean breast of the Watergate break-in at the beginning and promised to take action against the intruders (an act that would have contradicted the hubris of the modern presidency), the scandal might have been contained (Parmet, 1990, p. 640).

James Cannon, presidential biographer: The ruin of Richard Nixon came all too close to destroying the public trust in the Presidency.

For the first time since Harding, Americans were ashamed of their President. A healthy skepticism about politicians has always been a part of American feelings about their leaders; but until 1974, no President was known to be a criminal. Since Nixon, no President has been free from accusations by press and prosecutors that he or his close advisers broke the law for a political end. And none is likely to be (Cannon, 1998, p. 414).

Arthur Schlesinger, American historian: A few scholars feared during the Watergate crisis that too zealous an investigation might cripple the presidential office. Some formed a committee in defense of the Presidency, its eminent members claiming that their interest lay in the preservation not of Richard Nixon but of an office indispensable to the republic. The Luce Professor of Jurisprudence at the Yale Law School actually argued that, if Nixon turned over his White House tapes to Congress and the courts, it would raise the "danger of degrading or even destroying the Presidency" and constitute a betrayal of his "successors for all time to come." After Congress began its mild post-Watergate effort to restore the constitutional balance, scholarly pessimism intensified. Some saw the once mighty Presidency tied down, like Gulliver, by a web of debilitating statutory restraints. A theory arose about the fragility of the American Presidency. . . . Scholars mobilized their colleagues to join in producing books under such titles as *The Tethered Presidency, The Post-Imperial Presidency, The Impossible Presidency* (Schlesinger, 1987, pp. 282-3).

These myriad reflections are interesting, but Watergate and Nixon's downfall have to be set in a wider context. They have to be set against the background of a growing revolt from below against what was seen as the excessive levels of presidential power which allowed the Vietnam war to take place and continue for so long. Nixon had done much to encourage the revolt by his actions over Cambodia and Laos, despite the fact that in his speech accepting the Republican nomination he had seemed acutely sensitive to the dangers.

Nixon's impact on the presidency through Watergate and Vietnam was considerable. Presidential wrongdoing had been exposed for all to see. Even the most ardent patriot had to accept after Watergate that not all was well with the US presidency – the illusions of presidential rectitude and sagacity had been dispelled, perhaps for ever. That someone capable of such wrongdoing could rise to the White House was an indictment of the political process. Watergate and the Vietnam War overshadowed some very genuine achievements on the part of the Nixon administration: bringing American participation in the war in Vietnam to an end; the first moon landing of 1969; the use of shuttle diplomacy to bring about an improvement in relations between Israel and her Arab neighbors; a marked improvement in Sino-American relations (having first considered a pre-emptive strike on China to prevent it from becoming a nuclear power), with Nixon's bridge-building visit to Beijing in 1972; a marked improvement in Russo-American relations leading to successful Strategic Arms Limitation Talks to limit nuclear weapons.

Overall, Nixon managed to secure a marked lessening of Cold War tensions but in the 1970s Watergate overshadowed this remarkable achievement. It did not matter that the Nixon presidency was in many ways a success. The key fact for most Americans was that their president was corrupt. Worse still, that Gerald Ford, Nixon's successor in 1974, could so quickly pardon the ex-president seemed to suggest that a deal had been struck: that the establishment would always seek to protect itself and its own. That Nixon could (almost) get away with illegal activities on a massive scale from break-ins in Washington to the bombing of Cambodia was a cause for serious concern. The father-like image of presidency had been shattered. There had been bad presidents in the past such as Grant and Harding, but Nixon's crimes raised more fundamental questions about the presidency and American politics. In retrospect men like Grant and Harding seemed like the wrong men in the wrong post at the wrong time. Nixon, however, generated concerns that he was not only a bad president, but that the presidency itself had somehow gone astray. Some blamed the rise of the modern presidency: the presidency was too big and too powerful and needed to be cut down to size. Others blamed the constitution: maybe it required updating.

The issues that had been raised by involvement in Vietnam and by Johnson's growing powers had come to a spectacular climax, and the American public could never quite perceive the presidency after Watergate in quite the same rosy way that many of them had done before. The media were now more vigilant than ever in their scrutiny of presidential policy, and presidential character. "Is this person trustworthy?" was the key question that presidential candidates after Nixon had to answer in the mind of the voters. Restoring trust between presidency and people would remain the central issue for the president from 1974 to 1980.

SEVEN

Gerry and Jimmy: An Unlikely Double Act

On July 4, 1976, the nation celebrated its bicentennial. The outward mood was one of defiance against perceptions of a weakening America. As Vice President Rockefeller reminded a large crowd at the Washington Monument that evening, "Like every generation we face today what seems like insurmountable problems . . . Every such challenge is an opportunity; it has been the creative response to such challenges of these 200 years that has brought America to greatness." The reality was something else. Opinion surveys confirmed the pervasiveness of drift and alienation, with a loss of confidence in key institutions. A Harris poll found that fully three-fifths of those queried also expressed dissatisfaction with their lives. . . . "Indeed," as Christopher Lach wrote, "Americans seem to wish to forget not only the sixties, the riots, the new left, the disruptions on college campuses, Vietnam, Watergate, and the Nixon presidency, but their entire collective past, even in the antiseptic form in which it was celebrated during the bicentennial" (Parmet, 1990, p. 643).

When Richard Nixon was re-elected in 1972 he expected the celebrations for the bicentennial in 1976 to be his presidential swan song. His final year of office would coincide with the two hundredth anniversary of the Declaration of Independence, making a fitting moment on which to bid the political scene farewell. Instead of the triumphal moment of celebration, however, Watergate ensured that the bicentennial celebrations would be rather melancholic, and that the occupant of the White House would be Gerald R. Ford rather than Richard M. Nixon. When Nixon resigned on August 9, 1974, Vice-President Ford was sworn in. It was a unique moment in presidential history. No President had ever resigned the office before,

150

and no vice-president had ever acceded to the top job without the popular endorsement of the electorate. The resignation of Vice-President Spiro Agnew in October 1973 following charges of tax evasion and other wrongdoing meant that Nixon had the opportunity to appoint a replacement for his disgraced running mate of 1972. Under the Johnson-inspired Twenty-Fifth Amendment to the Constitution ratified in 1967 the president could appoint a replacement vice-president if the position fell vacant. In October 1973 Nixon decided to appoint Gerald Ford to replace the disgraced Agnew.

Ford was immediately subject to an intense period of scrutiny, perhaps the most intense that any prospective president has had to endure. With Nixon beset by the Watergate scandal it was more than a remote possibility that Agnew's replacement as vice-president might shortly inherit the top job. When Ford was appointed by Nixon he was still serving as the minority leader in the House of Representatives. The provisions of the Twenty-Fifth Amendment meant that Nixon's choice had to be confirmed by a vote in both the Senate and the House of Representatives. Ford's background was subject to intense scrutiny. Eventually, after a full investigation by the FBI and hearings in Congress, Ford's appointment was approved by 387 votes to 35 in the House of Representatives and by 92 votes to 3 in the Senate. The simple fact of Gerald Ford was that he was a simple man. Political opponents would subsequently label him as the man who could not walk and chew gum at the same time, and quip that in his youth Gerald Ford had too often played football without a helmet, but this was to denigrate the qualities of a man who in many respects was an honest, unpretentious, uncomplicated citizen. He did not have the charm of a Kennedy or the tortured complexity of a Johnson or a Nixon. In that respect he was an atypical incumbent of the postwar White House. But Ford hailed from a longer tradition. His character and presidency seemed to hark back to the nineteenth-century model of presidency that many figures on the right wing of the Republican Party had been hankering after ever since the days of the New Deal. In the aftermath of Watergate a return to a less active model of presidency was regarded as desirable and was in many ways unavoidable. In some respects Ford's presidency was the essence of dullness, but in the circumstances of Nixon's resignation, and the final dramatic denouement in Vietnam, this was a virtue, but the American public did not recognize it as such. America needed a chance to regroup, rethink, and move on. After two hundred years of growth and advancement, a decade of turmoil and tragedy, and mounting concerns about the nature of the US government, America needed a rest. The presidency of Gerald Ford provided exactly this breathing space.

Ford had been born in Omaha, Nebraska, on July 14, 1913. Less than two years later his parents divorced and his mother was left to look after the future president. In 1916 Gerald Ford's mother remarried and it was from her second husband that he took his name. Ford's stepfather was a businessman whose paint and varnish business only just avoided bankruptcy during the Great Depression. At high school Ford won all-state honors in football. Playing center at the University of Michigan, Ford was a key part of the championship-winning teams of 1932 and 1933. When he graduated in 1935 with a liberal arts degree, a career as a professional football player lay before him. Both the Detroit Lions and the Green Bay Packers wanted him to play for them. The points that could be made about his football career could also be used to describe his presidency. Ford was the safe pair of hands, playing an unglamorous role in a quietly competent fashion. From 1935 until 1940 he was football and boxing coach at Yale University. He also studied law at Yale, graduating in the top third of his class in 1941. Ford was called to the bar in the same year but, shortly after the outbreak of war in December 1941, he found himself in the Navy. By 1945 Ford, who had served as an aviation operations officer on an aircraft carrier, had risen to the rank of lieutenant-commander. Although he returned to civilian life ready to take up the law again, he was also considering a career in politics. In 1948 he made a bid for election to the House of Representatives and was successful by a wide margin. That same year he married Elizabeth Warren. The marriage lasted for five years, producing three sons and a daughter.

Ford's career in Congress was impressive. He believed in an internationalist approach to foreign policy, and strong defense for the

United States, while wanting to see less government interference in domestic affairs. Like Nixon he believed that federal programs were invariably inefficient. Ford was so highly respected that, in 1963, he was appointed a member of the Warren Commission to investigate Kennedy's assassination. This in part helped him become a national figure in American politics and in the following year he contested the leadership of the Republican Party in the House of Representatives. He defeated Charles A. Halleck of Indiana. From this point on, Ford distinguished himself as a dedicated and hardworking member of Congress. His spotlessly clean reputation, as well as his personal loyalty to the party and president, explains why Nixon decided to appoint him after Agnew's resignation. By this stage of his career Ford was considering giving up politics, but Nixon's appointment was to further his career in several ways. Following his appointment Ford did his best to rally a party traumatized by Watergate. While supporting the President in public Ford maintained that Nixon should cooperate with the investigation. Following Nixon's resignation, and Ford's swearing in, the President appeared on television to ask the nation to put Watergate behind it. Knowing full well that Vietnam and Watergate had resulted in unparalleled anxiety about the extent of presidential power, Ford assured the viewers: "Our Constitution works. Our great republic is a government of laws and not of men." The point implicit in his speech was that the presidency was part of the wider system of checks and balances of the Constitution, and that Nixon's resignation showed that the system continued to work effectively. Wrongdoing had been decisively checked. Convincing the American public that they could again trust the White House was to be Ford's task over the course of the next eighteen months before he was voted out of office.

Interestingly, one of Ford's first moves as president was to meet the representatives of various foreign governments to convince them that there would be continuity rather than change in American foreign policy. He also asked all the members of the cabinet, as well as the heads of various federal agencies, to remain in their posts for the sake of stability. Instead of simply appointing a vice-president, Ford asked senior Republican and Democratic Congressmen to suggest a candidate for the post. Ford was acutely aware of the fact that, although he was president, he had not received the endorsement of the electorate even as the second name on the ticket to Nixon. He had become president as a result of a bizarre and unprecedented chain of events: a recent amendment to the constitution introduced by Johnson; Spiro Agnew's problems over tax; and the uncovering of Richard Nixon's resort to dirty political tricks in response to the revolt from below. On August 20, 1974, Ford announced that he had selected governor Nelson Rockefeller to serve as Vice-President. Like Ford, Rockefeller's career had suddenly embarked on a new path at the moment that he was considering retirement and a private life. Rockefeller was a strong believer in the notion of public duty, and if the country had need of his services he was quite prepared to serve it in any capacity he could. It would be up to Congress, however, to endorse the selection since under the terms of the 25th Amendment to the Constitution, the president's choice needed to be approved by Congress, as had happened when Ford himself had been appointed vice-president. Ford's decision to bring congressional leaders into the selection process proved to have been a sensible move as the gregarious Rockefeller received the endorsement of the Senate and the House of Representatives. The oath of office was administered on December 29, 1974. America now had a president and a vice-president, neither of whom had contested a presidential election. This in itself called for the projection of a rather softer, less abrasive, less imperial, presidency, but against the backdrop of Watergate it called for a great deal of presidential restraint. The presidency might remain committed to the activist principle, but the prevailing mood in the United States called for soft speaking and only limited resort to action. Kissinger, among others, has commented that Ford set great store by the projection of honesty and simplicity, even if it sometimes led the press to mock him:

Whereas in the age of mass media, highly developed verbal skills are among the distinctive attributes of national leaders, in Ford's congressional district in small-town, Midwestern America, a far higher premium was placed on sincerity and on substance than on facileness. Since Ford had never developed a capacity for quick repartee and sound bites, he was dismissed by many in the media as inadequate. In fact, Ford, a Yale Law School graduate, had a first class analytical mind. Since television rewards glibness rather than substance, the media delighted in making Ford squirm as he tried to distance himself from clumsy formulations, even when journalists knew quite well this did not reflect his real competence (Kissinger, 1999, p. 1066).

Even though in the early days of his administration Ford tried to maintain an image of stability if not dullness, there were to be many and frequent changes in his cabinet as he tried to make changes to the way presidential government was functioning. For example, when he came to office Ford was convinced that the Justice Department required a shake-up. During the Watergate investigation many criticisms were made of the department's handling of presidential wrongdoing, so Ford appointed Edward Levi, the president of the University of Chicago, as its new head. Developments at other departments were to be more dramatic. No less than three Secretaries of the Interior served under Ford during his short presidency. As with previous administrations, some appointments attracted attention for social reasons. William Coleman Jr., who served as Secretary of Transportation, was only the second African-American appointed to a cabinet post. Likewise, Carla Hills, the Secretary of Housing and Urban Development, was only the third woman to serve in the cabinet. Then in November 1975 Ford made the biggest change yet to his administration when he undertook a massive shake-up of the foreign and military spheres of the government. Henry Kissinger was dismissed as head of the National Security Council, Donald Rumsfield was appointed Secretary of Defense, and George Bush took over from William Colby as head of the CIA. Kissinger had become an increasingly controversial figure and there were many allegations that by being both head of the National Security Council and Secretary of State he wielded too much influence over government policy. The personnel changes reflected Ford's concern that American foreign and defense policy needed a thorough reassessment. He would eventually follow the personnel changes with National Security Study Memorandum 246 on September 2, 1976. In the memorandum he said:

> I would like a thorough review and analysis of our national defense policy and military posture. This review should consider in detail the security and foreign policy impact of a range of alternative strategies for our strategic and ground forces. The review should . . . not necessarily be limited to the following:
>
> – The current and projected threat to the United States, its allies and US security interests throughout the world.
> – Foreign policy objectives and definable trends which influence these objectives.
> – The overall defense posture necessary to assure US security and foreign policy interests, including the desired balance between strategic and general purpose forces, manpower objectives, and preparedness.

Ford may have felt that various manpower changes, especially the removal of Kissinger, would facilitate this fundamental review to find a military and foreign policy appropriate for an era of post-Vietnam détente and arms control between East and West. But Vice-President Rockefeller disapproved of the changes so strongly that he announced publicly, in protest, that he would not be Ford's running mate in the 1976 presidential election. In making such significant changes to his administration Ford was trying to signal that the past of Vietnam and Watergate really was behind the country. The president was also making fundamental alterations to the national security state, erected under Truman, which some blamed for the rise of the kind of presidency that Richard Nixon had come to personify. Ford was trying to shape for himself an administration that owed little to the one that had gone before and which might prove attractive to the voters when the nation went to the polls in 1976. His changes were gradual, to try to preserve the image of stability, but the reaction to them emphasized the danger of even limited dynamism.

As Ford attempted to move the country on beyond Watergate and Vietnam, he found that even relatively minor executive decisions were greeted with public suspicion. He made two important errors. Firstly, to save the nation the long-drawn-out agony of the trial of Richard Nixon, he pardoned the former president for all the crimes he might have committed while in office. In the dying days of the Nixon administration Ford had been offered a deal that Nixon would resign, making him president, if he would agree to pardon Nixon. Ford refused that offer, but once in office he had to reconsider the question of a pardon for Nixon. He decided that a pardon should be granted. To some, it seemed as though there was one law for ex-presidents, another for the rest of the citzenry of the United States. Ford's decision undoubtedly harmed his chances of re-election, but the granting of a pardon was statesmanlike in its selflessness. The damage which would have been done to the United States by a protracted trial would have been considerable. Support for the presidency would have sunk to a new low and Watergate would have continued to haunt the nation into the next presidential election. Ford explained his decision in a televised address on September 8, 1974:

> My conscience tells me clearly and certainly that I cannot prolong the bad dreams that continue to reopen a chapter that is closed. My conscience tells me that only I, as President, have the constitutional power to firmly shut and seal this book. My conscience tells me it is my duty, not merely to proclaim domestic tranquility but to use every means that I have to insure it. I do believe that the buck stops here.

The trial of Richard Nixon would undoubtedly have thrown into relief certain facts about the US political system that most Americans did not want to think about.

Ford's attempt to draw a line under Watergate may have been reasonably successful so far as the nation was concerned but it seriously damaged his own standing with the American public. His second miscalculation arose from his attempt to heal some of the scars of Vietnam. He developed a scheme to grant conditional amnesty to Vietnam war draft dodgers. In return they would be required to do two years of public service. The scheme came to a close in 1975 after only about 20 percent of eligible draft evaders had applied to it. During Ford's administration the agony of the Vietnam war was to live on, even as the pain, but not the legacy of Watergate, passed away.

Détente was to remain the cornerstone of American foreign policy under Ford, and from 1974 to 1977 he continued to pursue good relations with China and the Soviet Union. In November 1974 Ford held a meeting with the Soviet leader Leonid Brezhnev in South Korea during which they managed to sketch an outline agreement on arms control; but subsequent negotiations proved less productive. Ford also worked for continuing improvements in Middle East relations.

However, these developments were completely overshadowed by Vietnam. As the North Vietnamese launched a major spring offensive in 1975, South Vietnam threatened to collapse spectacularly and completely. The military forces of the south simply disintegrated under the weight of the communist onslaught. In April 1975, as the final agonies of the south were played out on television, Ford had to face the decision of whether or not to use American forces to intervene once more. Nixon's policy of Vietnamization had spectacularly failed but, even as the Republic of South Vietnam entered its death throes, Congress still refused Ford's appeal for more aid to Indo-China. Knowing that public opinion and Congress would simply not tolerate the use of US forces to save South Vietnam, all Ford could do was order an evacuation of American personnel. The operation was highly successful, but the operation to remove orphans and those Vietnamese who would be regarded as capitalist collaborators by the conquering North Vietnamese was handled much less successfully. Sensitive documents naming those Vietnamese who had acted as "collaborators" and "spies" for the Americans fell into communist hands.

Thus a chapter in American and Vietnamese history closed in rather ignominious circumstances. The collapse of the south meant that 58,000 Americans had died for nothing in the eyes of the majority of the American public. But at least the agony was over. The chapter was closed in a way in which some regarded as fitting and it was absolutely final. Realizing that there was simply no way that Congress would allow him to help South Vietnam in any meaningful way, Ford had done the only remaining thing – order the evacuation.

The determination of Congress to avoid foreign entanglements was further demonstrated the following year when they again refused a presidential request for aid to support anti-communist forces fighting in Angola. Congress tried to leave Ford with as little room as possible to exercise military force to secure the nation's objectives, but when an American merchant ship, the *Mayaguez* was seized by the Cambodians in May 1975 Ford ordered a rescue mission that liberated both crew and ship. Such actions showed that, while Ford was willing to exercise restraint, he was not willing to be bound by Congress. Perhaps typically in view of the success of US policy in Southeast Asia, after the rescue of the ship certain facts became known which took much of the gloss off the successful resolution of the crisis. The initial wave of Marines that had landed on Koh Tang island to cover the seizure of the ship had run into heavy opposition. All but one of the nine helicopters in the first wave had been shot down or disabled, and fifteen Marines had lost their lives. It also emerged that the Cambodians had decided to release the ship just as the helicopter assault was approaching the landing zone. Although the Ford administration could hardly be blamed for failing to see into the near future when the operation was authorized, it transpired that as a result of the decisions arrived at by the communist leadership of Cambodia the *Mayaguez* rescue operation had not been necessary. The apparently needless deaths of American Marines was the Vietnam War replayed in microcosm and that did nothing to assuage congressional hostility toward presidential power.

Rebuilding the trust between presidency and people was the underlying theme of the Ford administration, but it found concrete expression in different ways. The first of these involved the economy. Under Nixon the economy had suffered from stagflation. In 1967, partly as a result of the Vietnam War, the annual inflation rate had begun to rise. From 3 percent in 1967 it rose to 12 percent by the time Nixon left office. By the end of 1970 unemployment had reached 6 percent and there were many predictions that it would go on rising. Inflation was bad enough, but the rising unemployment rate was also a signal that the economy was in the midst of a general recession. The cost of the Great Society and the war in Vietnam was too great a burden for the economy to bear, and by the late 1960s US manufacturers were facing increasingly stiff competition. In addition, there had been the oil price shock of 1973 when, as a result of the Yom Kippur war, Arab oil-producing nations had increased the price of oil dramatically. Increased energy costs took a heavy toll on the profitability of many American businesses and by the early 1970s the number of postwar baby boomers entering the workforce exceeded the number of available jobs. Nixon had tried to address the situation by reducing the federal budget and raising taxes. When Congress refused to cooperate, he had tried to restrict the money supply through using the Federal Reserve Board to increase interest rates. This produced a dramatic fall in the stock market which only compounded matters. By 1971 Nixon had resorted to the use of economic controls, freezing prices and wages for a short period. He used the breathing space thus created to set down guidelines on wages and prices, but by the end of his presidency they had proved to be a clear failure. The economic situation which faced Gerald Ford as he was sworn in at the White House in 1974 was very grave indeed.

Congress attempted to pressure Ford into an increase in the federal budget and a reduction in taxes so that America could spend its way out of recession. Ford refused to be browbeaten into making such a move and the economy seemed to worsen. The President urged private restraint rather than state regulation. In September 1974 Ford held an economic summit at which he met with leaders of Congress, business, and labor. He proposed a "whip inflation now" (WIN) program which relied on voluntary restraint to address the problem of spiraling wages and prices. However, the WIN program, complete with little badges that the public could wear to show their support of it, became something of a running joke. When Ford refused to bail out New York City, which was facing bankruptcy, and to prevent any moves in Congress to do the same, the president's economic and financial policy was widely ridiculed. Public comparisons between the bold initiatives of the New Deal era in the 1930s and the WIN program forty years later did not help Gerald Ford's reputation. He eventually agreed to tax cuts and to channeling government expenditure to stimulate the economy. At the same time he was determined to limit federal spending and not indulge in a bout of artificial job creation that the taxpayer would have to pay for. The measures which Ford took were just enough to bring an end to the problems of depression and inflation. In May 1975 unemployment peaked at over 9 percent, but from this pinnacle it started a steady descent. Even so by the time of the bicentennial celebrations it still stood at over 7 percent. Ford also reversed his decision on aid to New York City. In November 1975 the President proposed federal loans to the city if it could balance its books.

Ford, and his successor in 1977, Carter, were beset by a Congress in full hue and cry against the perceived excesses of presidential power. Congressmen were determined to bring the presidency back under some sort of control. Even before the resignation of Nixon, Congress had taken significant steps to limit presidential power. The 1973 War Powers Act placed important restrictions on the ability of a president to send US troops into combat. Under the provisions of the act, when the president felt that such a deployment was necessary he had to inform Congress within 48 hours of the commitment of troops. Congress could then place restrictions on the continued use of American troops. Use of the presidential veto would not affect the decision of Congress. The intention of the Act was to prevent any repetition of the Vietnam situation. Congress considered that a president, in his role as commander-in-chief, had more than enough power to wage what amounted to war without asking the members of Senate and the House of Representatives for the formal declaration of war required by the Constitution. The War Powers Act was meant to restore the balance between president and Congress. Nixon, Ford, and their successors, however, have argued that the Act is unconstitutional and have largely chosen to ignore it in practice. However, its very existence has imposed a check on how successive presidents have conducted American foreign policy since 1973. For example, Ford faced a number of foreign policy crises which involved the commitment of troops. In a speech at Kansas State University on February 20, 1978, he argued:

In none of these instances did I believe the War Powers resolution applied. Many members of Congress also questioned its applicability in cases involving protection and evacuation of American citizens. Furthermore, I did not concede that the resolution itself was equally binding or legally binding on the president on constitutional grounds. Nevertheless, in each instance, I took note of its . . . reporting provisions and provided certain information on operations and strategies to key members of the House as well as the Senate.

The combination of public refusal to be bound by the Act with private acceptance of its spirit was significant. Even though many in Congress rather reluctantly came to the opinion that the Act might indeed be unconstitutional, it has still continued to exercise an influence over the thinking of successive presidents. The possibly unconstitutional nature of the Act is itself interesting because it shows the way that in the early 1970s, as Watergate was unfolding and defeat looming in Vietnam, Congress was determined to rein in presidential power. That they should pass an act that was rapidly suspected of being unconstitutional points to the scale of congressional panic about presidential power. The president had to be restrained, and the balance between the different elements in the Constitution restored, even if the Constitution had to be breached in order to effect the change.

The presidency was further shackled by the 1974 Budget Act through which Congress weakened the power of the president by expanding that of the House of Representatives and the Senate. The Budget Act gave Congress greater powers to dictate the policy of the nation. Gerald Ford, who was convinced that it was in the nation's interest that it should live within its means, subsequently struggled to develop an economic policy which would meet with congressional approval. Ford urged Congress to show more restraint in its readiness to dole out federal funds and he was ready to use the veto if Congress was too open-handed. However, with Congress in semi-revolt against presidential power, the best Ford could do was to slow the growth of the national debt. That was essentially the key to the Ford presidency: Ford was fighting a holding action, showing that the presidency could be virtuous, setting an example of restraint. The nation had to have time to put the past behind it, and Ford's relative impotence helped it to do that.

Watergate also prompted Ford to launch an investigation into the American intelligence-gathering agencies. Vice-President Rockefeller was put in charge of a commission to investigate the activities of the Central Intelligence Agency. The Agency and the Federal Bureau of Investigation were also the target of congressional investigations which revealed widespread illegal and unethical activities among the intelligence community. The reports from these congressional committees proved highly damaging to public confidence in the CIA and the FBI. In the lengthy executive order 11905, covering United States Foreign Intelligence Activities, Ford attempted to rein back the CIA and the FBI by imposing a new structure of reporting and responsibility on the intelligence agencies. Most importantly of all, in his executive order Ford firmly spelt out that:

> The senior officials of the CIA, Departments of State, Treasury and Defense . . . and the FBI shall ensure that, in discharging the[ir] duties and responsibilities . . . which relate to foreign intelligence, they are responsive to the needs of the President, the National Security Council and other elements of the Government. In carrying out their duties and responsibilities senior officials shall ensure that all policies and directives relating to intelligence activities are carried out in accordance with law and this Order.

That a president had been forced to tell the CIA and other intelligence-gathering bodies that they had to obey the Constitution and the law of the land was highly revealing of just how out of control they had been perceived to be. While the Rockefeller investigation into the CIA, the congressional investigations, and Ford's executive order 11905 were intended to restore confidence in the organs of government, and with it the presidency, the overall effect was rather different. The muckraking only served to highlight the reasons why investigations had proved necessary, and in the process there was a further undermining of trust between government and the governed.

While President Ford emphasized his simple honesty and showed a more restrained approach to presidential power, he continued to enrage Congress by his use of the veto. Faced with a Congress controlled by the Democrats, Ford resorted to using the veto on sixty occasions to block the passage of legislation, some of which was intended to spend large sums to pump-prime the economy. Congress was able to override the presidential veto occasionally, but the gulf between government and legislature over economic policy was starkly evident. Ford's own changes of heart on how to address the economic malaise affecting the United States only added to the American public's confusion. It seemed as though president and Congress were locked in a continuing and vicious struggle while the American economy continued to falter. The sense of confusion that had been generated by Vietnam and heightened by Watergate seemed to persist during the Ford years.

Ford had done much to make possible the rebuilding of public trust in the presidency but, as the 1976 presidential election loomed, he could not be sure of securing the Republican Party's nomination, let alone of being re-elected. Many within the party considered that Ford was an electoral liability. His handling of the economy had left much to be desired. In the primary elections Ford, who had announced his candidacy in July 1975, faced stiff competition from Ronald Reagan, a former governor of California. At the Republican Convention in Kansas City, Missouri, neither Ford nor Reagan had a majority of votes, and it had to go to a first ballot to determine that Ford was the winner by 1,187 votes to 1,070. Instead of choosing the popular Reagan as his vice-presidential running mate Ford selected Senator Robert Dole of Kansas. Ford and Dole went to the electorate on a strongly conservative platform, promising economic orthodoxy at home and a robust role for the United States abroad. Against Ford and Dole the Democrats ran Jimmy Carter, a one-term governor of Georgia. Carter possessed a certain charm and, in the event, the American electorate were glad of a chance to ditch Ford, whom they saw as bungling, and the Republicans whom they associated with the lies of Nixon. Ford went down to a narrow defeat polling 39 million popular votes to Carter's 41 million. Carter's victory in the electoral college was rather wider, by 297 votes to 241.

Although one president had gone and another had arrived in the White House, the dominant theme remained the same as back in 1968 – that of trust. It had mutated over time: trust in an ability to bring the war in Vietnam to an end had become trust in a basic desire to obey the law, but trust remained the key issue. Ford had done a useful job in shoring up the presidency after Nixon's resignation, but he was seen as no more than a temporary stopgap. It would be up to Carter to chart a new direction for the presidency. Carter's key promise in the 1976 presidential race was: "I will never tell a lie to the American people." Carter's background had been an essential part of his appeal. He was not tainted by long association with the American political system. He was not from the same mold as Johnson, Nixon, and Ford: men who had spent most of their adult lives learning politics the hard way from the inside. Carter had been born on October 1, 1924, in Plains, Georgia. His father, James Earl Carter Sr., farmed and also owned a general store. In the 1930s he moved into peanut farming and selling agricultural supplies. The future president was required to work on the family farm and attend the local Baptist church. His religious beliefs were to be one of the guiding forces of his life. They were also to be an important political asset. In the wake of Watergate the born-again Baptist from the South seemed like an ideal answer to the perceived ills and corruption of the American political system. In his youth Carter had also shown his father's financial acumen, wheeling and dealing from an early age. He completed his high school education and went on to Georgia Southwestern College. A brilliant student, in 1943 Carter entered the Naval Academy at Annapolis. He graduated in 1946 and played a distinguished role in the development of the submarine arm of the United States Navy. In particular he took a leading role in the development of the nuclear submarine program for the Navy, working on, among other things, power plant design. In 1947 Carter married Rosalynn Smith, from an old established Georgia family. Together they were to have three sons and a daughter. Then in 1953 James Earl Carter Sr. died. At the time of his death Carter Senior was a member of the Georgia House of Representatives. The tributes to his father convinced Carter Junior to turn away from his career in the Navy and pursue a life in politics as a Democrat. The Carter family returned to Georgia where the future president threw himself into the family business. In 1962 Carter, in a campaign beset by vote-rigging, eventually won a seat in the Georgia Senate after a protracted legal battle. After toying with the idea of running for the House of Representatives, and failing to win the primary election for the governorship of Georgia in 1966, he was eventually elected governor of Georgia in 1970. In that office he supported racial integration and social reform together with an administrative efficiency drive. He also began to make contacts within the Democratic Party that were a prerequisite for running for the presidency. In 1974, he declared himself a candidate for the presidential elections in 1976.

Although Carter was not very well known as he began his campaign for election, this proved to be an asset. The public wanted a man untainted by what was seen as the political excesses of the past twenty years. In the primaries Carter did very well, coming first in 17 out of the 26 primaries that he entered. He was shown to have broad voter appeal and outlasted his other Democratic rivals. The public saw him as a man whom they could indeed trust. The liberal wing of the Democratic Party, which had been rather uncertain of Carter's policies that sought to balance social reform with careful economic management, eventually chose to back him. At the Democratic Convention in July 1976 Carter won the nomination on the first ballot as the party came together in a show of unity. Although he led President Ford by 30 percentage points at the time of his nomination, during the campaign Carter's lead was steadily eroded. His eventual victory was by a comparatively slim margin. Throughout the election campaign, coinciding with the bicentennial celebrations, the extent of the damage done to the presidency by Vietnam and Watergate was only too apparent:

The presidential election, like the nation's bicentennial celebration of the year, was by most accounts anticlimactic. Only 54 percent of the voting-age public ultimately cast ballots in the November election, the lowest turnout for a presidential election in twenty-eight years. Of those who were registered, but chose not to vote, significant increases were found among those who explained that they either

166

did not like any of the candidates or were simply uninterested in politics. As for the nation's bicentennial celebration, a reporter noted that on July 4 plenty of hotel rooms remained empty in the historic cities of Washington and Philadelphia (Morris, 1996, p. 224).

The nation was in no mood to celebrate, and the electoral turnout seemed to indicate a sharp decrease of support for the American political system. The opinion polls showed the same thing even more graphically. By 1976 the scale of cynicism among the American public about the executive branch of government had reached crisis proportions. In 1972, 53 percent of Americans had expressed faith in their government. By 1973 this figure had dropped to 37 percent, and by March 1974 it had sunk to a die-hard patriotic rump of 14 percent. The Ford presidency had slowed the process of decline. Nevertheless, by 1976 only 10 percent of Americans expressed faith in their government. Everywhere one turned there were manifestations of the collapse of support for a presidency which some blamed for what they saw as the corruption of American life. The film of the year in 1976 was Martin Scorsese's *Taxi Driver* in which a troubled Vietnam veteran finds himself in an America which has lost its way and which is beset by crime, vice and corruption. Travis Bickle, the Vietnam veteran played by Robert De Niro, eventually resolves to assassinate Senator Palantine, a self-serving presidential hopeful. In 1976 Bickle's inability to come to terms with the America he saw before him seemed to mirror the public mood. The public's dismay at the nature of the American political system found perfect expression in Bickle's desire to kill Palantine. The television viewing habits of the American public also spoke volumes about the malaise affecting American life:

The number one show in that election and inauguration year was the light-hearted situation comedy about life in an America before the crises of the 1960s, *Happy Days*, which was followed by its almost as nostalgic spin-off *Laverne & Shirley*. Even the most socially poignant popular show of the period, *M*A*S*H*, which ranked fourth in the season's ratings, was ostensibly set in the more quiescent 1950s (Morris, 1996, p. 207).

Throughout the campaign Carter sought to tap into the nation's spiritual mood by seeming to suggest that from his personal morality would emerge the necessary moral leadership as president that America was in desperate search for. One veteran British left-wing politician commented in his diary on November 3, 1976:

> It was clear that Jimmy Carter had won the American elections though it wasn't confirmed until later. I felt absolutely uncommitted and neutral about it. Better the Democrats than the Republicans, better maybe for the economy, better in some ways because of the forces on each side, but I felt no sense of excitement after a campaign which had so lacked any fundamental examination of the problems facing America or the West. It was a campaign just full of language about peace, prosperity, justice, brotherhood and love (Benn, 1989, pp. 635–6).

The sense of anticlimax felt by this British observer resulted from the fact that issue-driven politics had given way to the politics of personality. This trend had arguably been developing for some time, but Watergate propelled a decisive shift in American politics. The question was no longer which president had the best policies for the United States. The question henceforth was to be which presidential candidate was least likely to be lying about the promises he was making: which candidate was going to be best able to live up to commonly held notions of what made a good president. The 1976 presidential election turned on personality and Jimmy Carter was able to cut the more saintly image. From now on presidential personality would matter rather more to the electorate than the hard politics of the presidency.

The task facing the new president was summed up by *Time* magazine on January 3, 1977:

> The new President takes over at a particularly challenging time, one of those turning points in US history that seem to be occurring at shorter and shorter intervals. After the banishment of Richard Nixon, the decent solid and forthright Gerald Ford – to his

everlasting credit – did much to restore faith and confidence in Government and to curb inflation. But he did little to grapple with the nation's other problems. The US is still moving into the post-Viet Nam and post-Watergate era, still struggling to recover from a deep recession. Revitalizing the economy, of course, will be Carter's immediate problem, but there are others – racial relations, Government reorganization, energy, welfare, health care – demanding fresh and strong leadership.

Carter had come to power on a promise of honest, moral presidency. What *Time* reminded him on January 3, 1977, was that this was not enough to satisfy the aspirations of the American people. The presidency also had to be activist and successful.

After his election Carter made still greater efforts to address the national mood. During his inauguration he stressed the importance of traditional values. He also suggested a humbler presidency by walking the mile and a half to the White House. In office Carter continued to make symbolic gestures to allay public concerns about the presidency. His preference for a cardigan over a suit and his willingness to conduct a fireside television chat, and take part in an "Ask the President" radio phone-in, suggested a presidency more in touch with the people and the national mood. The presidential yacht was sold and the White House limousine fleet used sparingly. In a society conscious of presidential status and acutely aware of the energy problem, the limousine was to be dispensed with where possible. However, Carter was later to comment that in "reducing the imperial presidency" he

> overreacted at first. We began to receive complaints that I had gone too far in cutting back the pomp and ceremony, so after a few months I authorized the band to play "Hail to the Chief" on special occasions. I found it to be impressive and enjoyed it (Carter, 1995, p. 29).

Carter's quest for an ethical White House extended to members of the cabinet. He established ethics guidelines for members of the cabinet, in which a number of women and black Americans were appointed to high-profile positions. Among other things cabinet members had to put their financial assets into blind trusts for the duration of their appointment. Even so, the Carter administration was not immune from controversy. When in August 1979 it was revealed that Andrew Young, a black American appointed by Carter as ambassador to the United Nations, had held unauthorized discussions with members of the Palestine Liberation Organization, he was forced to resign. In the previous year, Bert Lance, director of the Office of Management and Budget, had to resign following allegations of improper conduct while he was a banker. Then in 1980 President Carter was criticized over his brother Billy's business links to the Libyan government. A Senate subcommittee held that the President should have prevented his brother's business activities in the Middle East. These trials and tribulations were comparatively minor compared to the prevailing standards of US political life, but with a president consciously trying to project an image of a trustworthy, ethical, restrained presidency they were disproportionately damaging.

What was perhaps still worse in political terms was that the forces which had propelled Carter into the White House began to dissipate very quickly after his election:

The marriage of convenience contrived between the Carter campaign and the majority liberal wing of the party began to break down the day he was elected. In their eagerness to win back the White House, liberals had been willing to suppress the ambiguity they felt toward Carter, believing that once in the White House he would follow traditional Democratic policies with a return to heavy government spending . . . Eight months into the administration, as it became clear this was not what Carter intended to do, liberal groups became increasingly angry, claiming that Carter had betrayed them. It could be argued that Carter had skillfully used titillating and misleading rhetoric to get the liberal vote, but it was equally true that liberals, so eager to recapture the White House, had failed to discern the careful precision with which Carter had made his promises (Bourne, 1997, p. 417).

The Carter coalition would probably have lasted longer if the United States had not continued to face serious internal difficulties. The nation was beset by the continuing problem of energy shortages. The winter of 1976/7 was particularly severe, causing a shortage of natural gas for heating. The president sought and obtained from Congress temporary powers to control the natural gas industry and he also used the hated Taft-Hartley Act to break up a strike by coal miners. That a Democratic president should resort to such measures was quite a shock. Less controversially, Carter proposed energy conservation measures, the deregulation of the price of natural gas, and government support for the development of synthetic fuels. The energy problem continued to hinder an improvement in the economic fortunes of the United States. Inflation also continued to harm the economy and Carter was forced to try a series of measures to control it. Finally, in March 1980, he responded to an increase in the cost of living by 13 percent during 1979 with the imposition of credit controls. They produced a slump in the purchase of cars and houses, which in turn resulted in a short, sharp recession. Carter also tried to strengthen the economy by deregulation of the transport industries and by reforming the banking system but the economic performance of the United States during his presidency was far from impressive.

More damagingly, in his conduct of American foreign policy Carter made a number of decisions that were to have a detrimental effect on public perceptions of his competency to govern. Granting pardons to the majority of draft-dodgers from the Vietnam War was his first official act as president, although the measure was resented by many who had served there and the families of those who had died there. In his refusal to go ahead with building programs for the B-1 bomber and neutron bomb he left himself open to the charge that he was neglecting America's defense. This was despite the fact that he eventually gave the go-ahead for the MX missile system to increase the survival chances of America's land-based nuclear missiles in the event of a Soviet attack. As former president Nixon publicly lamented:

Now the B-1 bomber has been canceled, deployment of the MX missile has been delayed by at least three years, the Trident

171

[nuclear missile carrying submarine] has been slowed. . . . and cruise missile development has encountered unforeseen problems. The backbone of our strategic deterrent force is still the land based Minuteman III. By comparison, the warheads on the Soviet SS-17 are twelve times as powerful, those on the SS-19 six to twelve times as powerful, and those on the SS-18 – the Soviet's supermissile – sixteen to forty times as powerful a those on Minuteman III (Nixon, 1980, p. 185).

Although Carter took a hardline stance on the issue of Soviet political prisoners, his overall foreign policy left him wide open to the charge of being soft on communism, especially after he gave China full diplomatic recognition in 1979. Nixon and other Republicans were only too happy to exploit the opportunity. Carter's conclusion of a Strategic Arms Limitation Treaty (SALT II) with the Soviet Union further raised concerns about the military balance between Russia and America.

When Carter's only response to the Soviet invasion of Afghanistan in 1979 was to impose bans on the export of high technology goods and grain to the Soviet Union, and to organize a boycott of the 1980 Olympics in Moscow, the critics of the administration had a field day. The measures were not only ineffective, but some commented at the time that withdrawing from the Olympics only guaranteed the communist bloc a better haul of medals than they would otherwise have got. It looked as though America's athletes, farmers, and businessmen were the ones being punished for the Soviet invasion of Afghanistan. Carter's actions looked ethical, but ineffective.

Closer to home he was charged by the Republicans with betraying America's interests by concluding two treaties with Panama by which control of the Canal Zone would revert to her in the year 2000. The treaties were passed by the Senate with only narrow majorities. At least the Carter administration scored one major diplomatic success when it helped the negotiations between Israel and Egypt which culminated in a peace deal between the two nations in 1979.

This success in the Middle East, however, was to be entirely overshadowed by ignominious humiliation in the same region. On

November 4, 1979, Iranian revolutionaries, who had just overthrown the Shah of Iran, seized more than fifty staff at the American embassy in Tehran. They were publicly paraded in a spectacle designed to humiliate the United States. Attempts to negotiate the release of the hostages were protracted and in April 1980 Carter called off a bungled attempt to rescue them in a military operation. Eight members of the American Delta Force lost their lives in the operation that was dogged by helicopter breakdown and misfortune as one helicopter collided with a C-130 transport aircraft. Carter's Secretary of State Cyrus Vance resigned over the risky gamble. The whole episode seemed to sum up a new national malaise. By his personal integrity Carter had restored some belief in the presidential system, but the issue of the Iranian hostages again raised the question of competency. America's inability to respond to the taking of hostages by Muslim fundamentalists suggested national impotency in foreign affairs. The perceived weak response of the administration to Soviet expansionism and the development of Russia's conventional and nuclear arsenals exacerbated these feelings of national humiliation. After continuing negotiations, the final American hostages would be released on January 20, 1981: the same day that Carter left office following his defeat at the polls in the 1980 presidential elections.

By the start of 1980 it was clear that Carter was in trouble so far as his bid for reelection was concerned. As Colin Seymour-Ure has observed:

By the 1980 election, Carter's record was widely regarded as exemplifying vacillation and ineptitude. An AP-NBC News poll in mid-September 1979 recorded the lowest approval rating – 19 per cent – for any president since such polls began in the 1930s (including the 24 per cent for Nixon just before his resignation) (Seymour-Ure, 1982, p. 157).

The American electorate had rediscovered an old crime which a president could be accused of – incompetency. The Iranian hostages affair and the disastrous rescue attempt suggested an image of military inadequacy and weak leadership that was highly damaging to

Carter. Within the ranks of the Democratic Party, Edward Kennedy made a dramatic challenge for the nomination. That the voters would not re-elect Carter was highlighted in the 1980 primaries as Kennedy beat Carter in a number of crucial states. If Carter could not win in states such as California and New York, a victory for the Democratic Party in the forthcoming presidential election campaign seemed highly unlikely. By the middle of the year Carter's approval rating as president had sunk to a level never before experienced by any president since 1945. Nevertheless, the Democratic Party still picked Carter as their nominee, although Kennedy was able to determine the economic programs on which his party would go to the country. In November 1980 Carter went down to one of the heaviest defeats ever experienced by a sitting president. His Republican opponent Ronald Reagan received a popular vote of 44,000,000 to Carter's 35,000,000, but in the electoral college Carter received a mere 49 votes to Reagan's 489. Carter had managed to prove that being a good, honest, and rather likeable man were not necessarily the best credentials for the job of President of the United States. One British observer recorded the final agony of the Carter administration on January 20, 1981: "The hostages were released from Iran thirty-two minutes after president Carter had seen his successor President Ronald Reagan sworn in. A bitter pill for Carter, a deliberate punishment by Khomeini" (Benn, 1994, p. 67).

Ford and Carter occupy a unique position in the history of the American presidency. Ford was a stop-gap president who did much to rebuild the relationship between the people and the White House. As one of his biographers has commented: "To Ford it was given to be a transitional President, a Constitutional bridge that carried an angry and frightened America back to a measure of accord and confidence in Constitutional government" (Cannon, 1998, p. 415). His achievement was certainly underrated. Like the newly appointed head of a failing business Ford came in and began to turn the company around. This was no mean task. The majority of the American people were alienated from the presidency and Congress was determined to shackle it as far as possible. Ford managed to draw a line under the Vietnam War, albeit very painfully, and also to draw a line under the Watergate scandal. In both cases he knew that America had to move on. Pardoning Nixon was the right thing for the country, but it probably cost Ford the 1976 election. His successor in January 1977, Jimmy Carter, continued to build on the foundations erected by his predecessor. Carter hoped to change public perceptions of the presidency and the government of the United States. The federal bureaucracy was reformed and rewards became available for successful civil servants. More importantly, he also wanted to alter the Constitution to create a popularly elected presidency. He wished to see the electoral college eliminated to permit the people to elect their president by a simple majority. Carter, however, lacked the necessary support to make progress with his fundamental reform of the American Constitution. Thus he had to concentrate on matters of style rather than real political substance in his desire to continue the rebuilding of public trust in the presidency. Carter was a virtuous man whose personal qualities as president perhaps changed how future potential holders of that office would be assessed by the electorate. Like Ford, Carter was a man of considerable intelligence who preferred to project an illusory image of himself of plodding respectability. The country had reason to fear quick-witted, slick Washington insiders – so Ford and Carter tried to show that they were something else. Carter was also willing to encourage the people to see his personal morality as the key to a moral presidency. Unfortunately for him, by the end of the Carter administration the American public wanted to be convinced that the presidency could not only remain virtuous but also that it could be powerful in projecting American strength. The public looked to Carter's successor to be both an activist and a moral president.

EIGHT

Ronnie: B-Movie Presidency at its Best

"Who would have thought five years ago that we would today be calling for new measures to strengthen the presidency?" That is how not one but two activist friends of mine put it in some meetings a year ago in Washington DC. A mere seven years after Watergate there is again an intensified call for vigorous presidential leadership. If our two most recent presidents have been a welcome relief from the profound tragedies of the Watergate period, they have nonetheless not regularly lived up to our expectation of presidential leadership. Plainly, our expectations were always too high. No doubt we give presidents more than they can do, more pressure than they can bear (Cronin, in Davis, 1980, p. 137).

Made in 1980, these observations of Thomas E. Cronin, professor of political science at the University of Delaware, vividly captured the mood of the American people at the start of a new decade. Watergate had brought an end to the excesses of the imperial presidency, but seemingly it had also marked the end of competence in the execution of the business of the federal government. The restrictions placed on the presidency as a result of Vietnam, Watergate, a cynical public, and an active media had produced a situation in which presidents were afraid to take action. When they did take action, as with Ford and the *Mayaguez* or Carter and the attempt to rescue the hostages in Iran, fortune rarely smiled upon them. Americans wanted to be given back their sense of national pride, and belief in American abilities, that had been lost in Vietnam and further tarnished by the disaster on a desert airstrip in Iran. By the late 1970s, even the belief of Americans in the strength of their economy was being steadily eroded by the problem of the price of energy and competition from Japanese

176

manufacturing. General Motors, Ford, and Chrysler faced a growing threat from the likes of Honda; and Harley Davidson, that icon of postwar US manufacturing, saw its wares being undercut by Far-Eastern competition. In the global confrontation with communism America also saw itself losing out to the competition. Growing Soviet military strength meant a rising threat to American interests. The invasion of Afghanistan in 1979 appeared to signal that Soviet communism was on the march once more. Carter seemed to have no answer to this problem. One joke going the rounds in 1979-80 accurately captured the American public's despair:

> The President's working late one night when T[heodore] R[oosevelt]'s ghost drifts into the Oval Office. Jimmy turns down Das Rheingold, jumps up, and offers him his chair. "No,"says TR, "you're the President now, I'm just haunting the place. How's it going?" he says. "Not too good," says Jimmy, "th' Iranians have imprisoned fifty-two of our diplomatic personnel." "So you sent in the Marines, right?" says TR. "Uh, no, but Ah registered a strong protest at th' United Nations." TR says in a cold voice, "Anything else?" "Well, uh, th' Russians just invaded Afghanistan." TR says, "And of course you retaliated with every weapon in our arsenal." Jimmy says, "No, but Ah've withdrawn our ath-eletes from th' Olympic Games." TR blows his top and shouts, "The next thing you're going to tell me is you've given back the Panama Canal!" (Morris, 1999, p. 407).

As Carter neared the end of his four years in office the American public began to look for a presidential hopeful who could offer a solution to the ills facing America, from the growing Soviet menace through to her economic problems and perceived moral drift. America was once again in search of strong leadership.

The man that they turned to in the presidential election of 1980 was Ronald Reagan. Born in 1911, Reagan had made his third run at gaining the Republican Party nomination for the presidency in 1980. In May of that year he secured it, having been opposed by some senior figures within the party. This had not, however, been sufficient to prevent Reagan from making a strong showing in the primaries and from winning considerable support among party delegates from the various states. The drift of opinion within the Republican Party, which came to favor tax cuts and other encouragements for wealth creators, a stronger foreign policy, together with a reduction in the level of federal expenditure, preferred Reagan who was an enthusiastic champion of right-wing Republicanism. To strengthen the Republican Party ticket Reagan selected George Bush, whom he had defeated in the race to the nomination, as his vice-presidential running mate. As the 1980 presidential election entered its final days Reagan found that he had lost the lead which he had held over President Carter for much of the campaign. At times Reagan appeared vague and elusive in his campaign speeches, but his oratorical abilities and well-chosen sound-bite phrases were sufficient to win over a majority of floating voters in the last week of the campaign. Reagan promised a revitalization of American politics, the American economy, and American foreign policy. His call for reconstruction was as potent at that made by Franklin D. Roosevelt in 1932.

Other, deeper, more long-term factors were also at work. Demographic change, and the growing disenchantment of American youth with mainstream political culture, meant that the elderly were an increasing political force. Together with a religious revival, this produced an electorate increasingly supportive of Reagan's brand of conservatism tinged with nostalgia. Bizarrely, in the 1980 presidential election the religious right would prefer Reagan, a divorcee who rarely attended church, to President Carter, a born-again Christian and man of sincere and pious beliefs. This state of affairs owed a great deal to Reagan's skills of presentation, and to his innate political abilities. Reagan instinctively knew what was necessary in politics. Patterns of migration which saw a rapid increase in the population of the southwest of the United States also improved Reagan's position. California was the power base from which Reagan launched his run for the White House in 1980.

Reagan knew that he had won the election on November 4, even before the polls closed. Carter did so too and conceded the election. Reagan received 44,000,000 popular votes to Carter's 35,000,000, but in the electoral college Reagan's victory was crushing. While Carter had received 49 votes, Reagan had received almost ten times that number with 489. Carter only managed to carry the District of Columbia and six states, including his home state of Georgia. Reagan's victory was massive, but also deeply worrying. Only 53 percent of the electorate had bothered to vote in the 1980 presidential election. Thanks to the intervention of a third party candidate (John Anderson), Reagan had only just managed to secure a bare majority of the popular vote and he had, in effect, been elected by less than a third of those entitled to vote. Low turnout was becoming a significant part of the political landscape of the United States, but in the euphoria of victory in 1980 Reagan and few others recognized its significance and dangers. In particular, it was noteworthy that the majority of those who had not voted were from the working classes. In some parts of New York voter participation fell below 20 percent.

The kind of policies being pursued by the Democratic Party were in part to blame. Increasingly wedded to economic conservatism, the Democratic Party no longer seemed interested in championing the people at the bottom of the social scale. This perception further undermined support for the federal government among the working classes, on whom the burdens of the Vietnam War had fallen most heavily, and who had been disillusioned by Watergate. To a broad section of the electorate it no longer seemed to matter which party one voted for – to the poorest sections of society it would make little difference. Consequently the job of voting in a President, members of the House of Representatives and Senators was increasingly the preserve of the American middle classes. As this process continued over the coming years American democracy was steadily undermined. However, few were concerned by this problem as Reagan was inaugurated in January 1981.

Reagan's path to power had been long and winding. He grew up in Illinois. He and his elder brother John were the sons of Jack and Nelle Reagan. Jack was a shoe-salesman, a Democrat and a passionate believer in equal rights for black Americans. During the depression, after a move into shoe retailing had failed, Jack helped to distribute poor relief while his wife worked in a dress shop. Meanwhile, at the age of fourteen Ronald Reagan began the first in a long line of jobs working as a laborer on a building site and as a lifeguard. This latter job owed much to Reagan's physique – he was strong and well built, and when he went to high school he rapidly demonstrated athletic prowess. At Eureka College he was partly able to support himself thanks to a football scholarship. Even at this early stage of his life Reagan exhibited a keen interest in politics, and he played a leading role in organizing a strike at Eureka College to protest at cuts in the curriculum. Reagan eventually graduated in 1932 with a degree in economics and sociology. By the end of that year he had become an announcer on a radio station in Iowa. Working for two radio stations in Iowa from 1932 until 1937, Reagan began his career in show business as a sports commentator. In 1937, he broke into Hollywood. Over the course of the next twenty-seven years he would make over fifty feature films such as *Knute Rockne – All American*, a film about a football coach in which Reagan was cast in the role of a celebrated player. Reagan was usually the co-star rather than the star, and with his clean-cut image he was seldom cast in the role of villain. He did not make great films, but in many ways they were reassuring. Good generally triumphed over evil. On the set of *Brother Rat* in 1938 Reagan met actress Jane Wyman, and two years later they were married. A daughter was born in 1941, and they adopted a boy in 1945, only for them to divorce three years later.

Throughout the war years Reagan made training films. Despite his physique and undoubted wish to fight, poor eyesight kept him out of military service. Reagan again chafed at being forced to take the supporting role, while some of his fellow actors in Hollywood, such as Jimmy Stewart, played a rather more glamorous and dangerous role in the big production. After the war Reagan's career became more political in nature. While still making feature films, he served as president of the Screen Actors Guild from 1947 to 1952, and again from 1959 to 1960. In this role he tried to secure better working conditions for actors, and in 1947 he appeared before the House Committee on Un-American Activities. Reagan cooperated with the Committee's efforts to try and identify communists in the motion picture industry, but he also did his best to clear those actors who had been wrongly accused. In 1948 Reagan supported Harry S. Truman in his successful re-election bid, and became increasingly identified with the Democratic Party.

Reagan remarried in 1952. His new wife was another actress, Nancy Davis, with whom he would co-star in *Hellcats of the Navy*. A daughter was born in the same year that Ronald and Nancy were married and they would have a son six years later. In the early 1950s Reagan became increasingly involved with television and in 1954 he became the front man for the series *General Electric Theater*. His contract also stipulated that he had to spend several weeks each year speaking at the different General Electric plants around the country. It was during these talks that Reagan emerged as a powerful advocate of free enterprise and reducing the role of the state. Reagan slowly drifted away from the Democrats and toward the Republicans. While still nominally a Democrat, Reagan supported Eisenhower in 1952 and 1956, and Richard Nixon in 1960. This was in spite of the fact that, ten years earlier in California, he had supported the Democrat candidate against Nixon in the election to the US Senate. Finally, in 1962 Reagan formally switched his allegiance to the Republican Party, supporting Barry Goldwater in the 1964 presidential elections. Despite Goldwater's defeat in 1964, Reagan established his own position within the party as his televised appeal for funds for the Goldwater campaign proved wildly successful. On the strength of this, in 1966 Reagan ran for the governorship of California and won it convincingly. He was re-elected in 1970.

Despite his Republican rhetoric during his period as governor, Reagan oversaw tax increases and higher levels of spending. There was significantly greater spending on California's schools, and mental health programs. At the same time, welfare reform was undertaken, cutting down on the number of recipients, but increasing the amount of aid for those remaining on welfare. From his base in California, Reagan began to plan a run for the presidency in the late 1960s. In the tumultuous atmosphere of 1968 he lost the nomination to Nixon. In the 1976 election Reagan made a strong showing, beating Gerald Ford in some of the primaries, but in the event he failed to win the nomination by the comparatively narrow margin of 117 votes. In 1980 his chance came at last.

That the winner of the 1980 Republican nomination, and eventual winner of the race for the White House, should be a former B-movie actor was a source of amusement in some quarters. Reagan's acting career had been less than distinguished and some observers mused that his presidency might be similarly unremarkable. However, in his straight-talking simplicity lay the origins of his attraction to the electorate. In politics, both international and domestic, Reagan saw things very simply, there were good choices and there were bad choices, right versus wrong, good versus evil. For Reagan policy choices were almost always stark: black and white – no confusing shades of grey. The simplicity of the political script which confronted Reagan in 1980 suited his Hollywood background and, in presenting the choices which America had to make as being essentially simple, he was in some ways a reassuring figure to a nation which felt that it had lost its way in the complexities of Vietnam and Watergate. America wanted a new set of illusions to believe in: that the world was essentially simple and international politics a battle of good versus evil; that the president would be both honest and competent. Who better to create the new illusions than a former professional actor? *Time* magazine, in making Reagan their man of the year in 1980, caught the mood precisely:

> If one were to take all of Reagan's qualities – the detachment, the self-knowledge, the great voice, and good looks – and project them into the White House, he would have a first-class B-movie presidency. That is no insult. The best B-movies, while not artistically exquisite, are often the ones that have moved us most because they move us directly, through straightforward characters, simple moral conflicts and idealized talk. . . . The President who remains above the fray yet is also capable of stirring people is the kind of President of whose life B-movies are made. After several years of *The Deer Hunter* and *All the President's Men*, perhaps the Ronald Reagan Story is just what the country ordered.

While the simplicity of Reagan's outlook was attractive to many Americans, there were some who were worried. One observer commented at the time of his election: "The new President approaches the world with a basic philosophical outlook which is a throwback to the 1950s when American power was paramount and which may founder on the more complex realities of the 1980s" (Smith, 1980, p. 99). Time would tell whether in Reagan's case simplicity would be a virtue or a vice.

Reagan continued the straight, simple talking in his inaugural address which set the tone for the rest of his presidency. In it he reiterated many of the themes of his campaign. In particular he told the people:

> It is my intention to curb the size and influence of the Federal establishment and to demand recognition of the distinction between the powers granted to the federal government and those reserved to the States or to the people. All of us need to be reminded that the federal government did not create the States; the States created the federal government. Now, so there will be no misunderstanding, it is not my intention to do away with government. It is, rather, to make it work – work with us, not over us; to stand by our side, not ride on our back. Government can and must provide opportunity, not smother it; foster productivity, not stifle it.

Reagan's rhetoric was what many Americans wanted to hear. It suggested that although there would be a new emphasis on a foreign policy and defense there would be no return to the days of imperial presidency. America would be respected in world affairs, but restraint would be shown in the exercise of American power overseas, while at home the federal bureaucracy would be further slimmed down.

To carry forward this bold agenda Reagan needed a strong cabinet. The team which he put together in his first few days of office included some notable figures. Reagan's first Secretary of State was to be Alexander Haig, whose career had blossomed under Richard M. Nixon. Before he left the White House in 1982, making way for George Shultz, Haig was a dominating figure. Contemporary views

183

on Haig varied widely: "To some, he is brilliant, diplomatic, an organizational wizard. To others, he is manipulative and ruthless. But all agree on three adjectives: Haig is ambitious, hardworking and loyal" (Smith, 1980, p. 188). As a member of Nixon's team during Watergate, Haig had excited the anger of some members of Congress by refusing to testify before congressional committees. After Nixon's resignation, Ford appointed Haig as Commander of NATO. In June 1979 he resigned his post and embarked on a tour of the United States which raised considerable sums for the Republican cause. Reagan's selection of Haig as his Secretary of State showed the way in which the new president intended to surround himself with experienced and able cabinet ministers to take as large a share as possible of the burden of executive government. This priority was also evident in his appointment of Caspar Weinberger as Secretary of Defense. During World War Two, Weinberger had seen action in the Pacific, after failing the medical to join the Royal Canadian Airforce at the height of the Battle of Britain in 1940. Like Haig, Weinberger was a Nixon appointee. Serving as Nixon's deputy director of the Office of Management and Budget, Weinberger had long experience of the defense budget, and, under Carter, Weinberger had urged bigger defense appropriations to meet the threat from the Soviet Union. Another former member of the Nixon administration, William Casey, was appointed Director of the CIA. During Reagan's run for the presidency, Casey played a key role in managing the campaign, but he also acquired a reputation for a certain lack of diplomatic skills in dealing with people. He was also involved in the attempt to persuade former president Gerald Ford to run as Reagan's vice-presidential running mate in the 1980 presidential elections. Yet another Nixon man could be found in the post of National Security Adviser to the president. Richard Allen had acted as Nixon's foreign policy adviser before the latter became president and replaced Allen with Henry Kissinger. Allen had the reputation for being a hard-line right winger in his views on foreign policy and defense.

Some of Reagan's other appointees were rather lower profile. For example, William French, the Attorney-General, was a close friend of the President. French had been one of Reagan's supporters since the

1960s. Donald Regan, initially appointed as Secretary to the Treasury, was a Wall Street insider, rather than a Washington insider, and Jeanne Kirkpatrick, the American ambassador to the United Nations, was a Democrat-supporting professor of political science from Georgetown University until Ronald Reagan, impressed by her views on foreign policy, worked his charms on her. The first Reagan cabinet contained several interesting selections, and it also suggested something of how Reagan intended to run the White House. His subordinates were trusted to control their own particular spheres and to carry into practice the broad themes that Reagan had outlined in his election campaign. Reagan was intent on carrying forward what in effect amounted to a mini-revolution and for that he needed dedicated, experienced, and committed people. Events were to show that Reagan had indeed selected the right people for the job at hand.

Reagan's image as president seldom reflected his approach to managing the affairs of government. Despite his willingness to let the members of the cabinet look after their respective spheres, Reagan still projected the image that he was very much in control of events. While Eisenhower with his "four-star generalities" tried to give the image of being above and beyond the fine detail of government business, Reagan tried to maintain an image of dynamism and of being in control. In order to do this he used various deception techniques. Anecdotes and witticisms could be used to deflect probing questions and indeed the fund of Reagan stories is almost limitless. One Reagan intimate later recounted:

> He used to tell a story about a family with two children. One was very pessimistic about everything; the other child saw everything as being bright and happy. So the parents took the children to a psychiatrist. He put the children in separate rooms. The pessimist was in a room filled with brand new toys; the optimist was put in a room filled with horse manure. After a few hours the doctor took the parents to each room. They found the pessimistic child crying and complaining that this or that toy wouldn't work. When they opened the door to the room where the other child was, they found him laughing and moving the manure around. So they said,

"What are you doing?" and the child said, "Well, there must be a pony in here somewhere" (Strober and Strober, 1998, p. 58).

At times the public Reagan could seem like an endless stream of one-liners and anecdotes, yet they endeared him to the American people and could be relied upon to charm a hostile journalist. In addition, his oratorical abilities could suggest a breathtaking vision and strength of purpose that could captivate any audience. He was also a genuinely nice man which meant that he could be forgiven for quite a lot in the eyes of the voters. If Reagan wished to maintain the image of being in charge, then he was a more than good enough performer to carry it through. On those occasions when the performance was not as polished as it might be, and the public could sense that Reagan was merely the front guy, the US people were quite prepared to forgive him for it.

The early months of the Reagan administration were over-shadowed by the attempted assassination of the president on March 30, 1981. Reagan was shot in the chest outside a hotel in Washington, before his would-be assassin was wrestled to the ground and disarmed. His assailant was John Hinckley, an ardent fan of the 1976 film *Taxi Driver*. However, the assassination attempt was quickly turned into yet another anecdote to embellish the Reagan myth. A story rapidly did the rounds in the capital that on being rushed to the hospital Reagan had expressed his hope to the surgeons that they were all good Republicans. Further stories followed, including that the thoracic surgeon who had operated on Reagan had sworn that Reagan's physique remained truly remarkable and that he had the chest of man twenty years younger. That after surgery Reagan healed quickly and made a fast return to public life further set the seal on the assassination story. However, the anecdotes and happy ending to Hinckley's attempted murder of the president deliberately minimize the seriousness of Reagan's injuries in March 1981. He very nearly died, and the stories were intended to reassure the American public that the business of government would continue and that they would not be left with a lame duck president. There was perhaps also a certain political sensitivity over the president's age. The need to understate the seriousness of the situation and to reassure the American people about the president's state of health was to be one of the continuing features of his presidency, especially when he later required further and repeated surgery for cancer, a blockage in his urinary tract and intestinal polyps. In March 1981 the White House staff handled a potentially disastrous situation extremely cleverly, and during the rest of his presidency they would continue to manage news about the president's health with an eye to the political consequences.

So efficient and effective was the handling of the media aspects of Hinckley's assassination attempt that public attention was deflected away from some of the pain being caused by Reagan's domestic policies. The American economy had been in difficulties for a decade when Reagan took office. The efforts of Ford and Carter to tackle the problem of economic stagnation combined with inflation had been ridiculed in the 1970s. Reagan decided to tackle the problem in a different way. Like his Conservative counterpart Margaret Thatcher, who had been elected as Prime Minister of Great Britain in 1979, Reagan thought that the economy had to be liberated from too much interference by government. Reagan considered that the entrepreneurs, the wealth creators, were the driving force of the American economy and they had to be able to reap the highest rewards for their endeavors. Thus he set about cutting taxes and domestic expenditure. He believed that the shortfall in federal revenues would be short-lived because greater prosperity would follow greater economic freedom, and with increased prosperity would come increasing government revenue. Reagan, like Thatcher, was influenced by the Nobel-Prize-winning American economist Milton Friedman, who thought that the best way of managing an economy was through the supply side, rather than the demand side favored by the doctrines developed by the British economist John Maynard Keynes. The Keynesian doctrine, that government should be prepared to intervene when an economy was in difficulty by borrowing in order to pump money into it, had been a significant influence on presidential management of the economy since Franklin Roosevelt used federal money to create millions of jobs at the height of the depression. Reagan's adoption of Friedman's monetarist principles signaled an important shift in the underlying doctrines governing presidential action.

In the first months of the Reagan administration oil price controls were abandoned and plans were drawn up for a fundamental reform of the tax system. So radical were the reforms which Reagan proposed that many doubted whether Congress could be induced to accept them. Then came Hinckley's attempt on the life of the President, which saw Reagan's popularity rise to new heights. This persuaded enough Democrats in Congress to vote with the Republicans for Reagan to get his tax reforms through. The Economic Recovery Tax Act, signed into law by Reagan on August 4, 1981, was designed to cut federal revenues by $737 million over a five-year period. Taxes on personal income were reduced by a dramatic 25 percent overall. The higher rate tax, which Reagan regarded as a disincentive to the wealth creators, was reduced from 70 to 50 percent. However, while taxes were reduced federal expenditure was not. The Reagan campaign team had overestimated the amount which could be pruned from budgets by insisting on efficiency gains and by stamping out corruption. In addition, military spending increased dramatically as Reagan pursued a bold foreign policy. This resulted in increased government borrowing which led some to christen Reagan the credit card president, running up a huge bill in pursuit of his policies which future generations would have to pay. Reagan's economic policy helped to produce a deep recession in 1982, but by the following year, as thoughts began to turn to re-election, the economy recovered strongly.

This was a piece of luck because the social effects of Reagan's domestic policy were quite severe. After a short slump from 1982 to 1983 which required Reagan to raise taxes under the Tax Equity and Fiscal Responsibility Bill of 1982, the economy began to take off. But, as the rich benefited from Reagan's tax cutting, fuelling a rising stock market, the poor grew worse off. The wealthy indulged in an orgy of spending and greed, fuelled by easy credit, and Wall Street appeared to go from strength to strength with a welter of leveraged buyouts of corporations, while the poorest sections of society were penalized to help to pay for it all. The welfare state was cut back and over

400,000 people were excluded from the aid for dependent children program designed to help poor families. Hundreds of thousands of American citizens also found that they were no longer entitled to Medicaid. The number of homeless people living rough on America's streets began to rise fueling, together with the emergence of the AIDS epidemic, and a continuing escalation of the drug problem, a steady deterioration of urban life in the United States. Although Reagan argued that his reforms were designed to return to the original concept of the welfare state, as created by Franklin Roosevelt, denying aid to families sat ill with the conspicuous consumption of the American middle classes. Economically Reagan's policies were successful, but the morality of rewarding the rich and penalizing the poor created unease in some quarters. In addition, excessive spending, helped by the increasing computerization of Wall Street, culminated in a stock market crash on October 19, 1987, that was reminiscent of October 1929. Indeed, in terms of the fall on the Dow Jones index of the stock values of America's top companies, 1987 was far worse than 1929. The wisdom of Reagan's economic policies, just like those of his hero Calvin Coolidge, was called into question by an economic blizzard that made millions poorer. However, for better or worse, Reagan had actually managed to achieve what he wanted, to get his legislation past Congress and to effect change. That was his real achievement, because in 1980 there were many who thought that the days of effective presidency were long over. One distinguished presidential scholar paid tribute to Reagan's achievement in an early examination of his presidency: "The Reagan presidency stands out by virtue of the chief executive's ideological closure, his propensity to act on his principles, his success in doing so, and the consequences of his success in transforming ideology into policy" (Greenstein, 1983, p. 4).

If Reagan's domestic achievements were to be called into question by the passage of time, few Americans would question the success of his foreign policy. Domestic policy was undoubtedly important to Reagan, but it was foreign policy which perhaps mattered to him more. In foreign policy, especially in his relations with the Soviet Union, the President saw the chance to pursue a simple, unambiguous policy, akin to the script of a B-movie. By the late 1970s the

Russians were perceived to be gaining a significant advantage over the United States, especially by those on the right wing of American politics. Richard Nixon, continuing to rehabilitate himself as an elder statesman, wrote in 1980 in *The Real War*:

> The Soviet Union today is the most powerfully armed expansionist nation the world has ever known, and its arms buildup continues at nearly twice that of the United States. There is no mystery about Soviet intentions. The Kremlin leaders do not want war, but they do want the world. And they are rapidly moving into position to get what they want (Nixon, 1980, p. 3).

For Reagan the Soviets could be unambiguously presented as the bad guys and the Americans as the good guys. It was one area of policy where things could be presented in the most stark terms: black and white – good versus evil. In a speech to the British House of Commons on June 8, 1982, Reagan described the Soviet Union as the "evil empire". He pulled few punches:

> In an ironic sense Karl Marx was right. We are witnessing today a great revolutionary crisis, a crisis where the demands of the economic order are conflicting directly with those of the political order. But the crisis is happening not in the free, non-Marxist West but in the home of Marxism–Leninism, the Soviet Union. It is the Soviet Union that runs against the tide of history by denying human freedom and human dignity to its citizens. It is also in deep economic difficulty. The rate of growth in the national product has been steadily declining since the fifties and is less than half of what it was then. The dimensions of this failure are astounding: a country which employs one-fifth of its population in agriculture is unable to feed its own people. Were it not for the private sector, the tiny private sector tolerated in Soviet agriculture, the country might be on the brink of famine.

Reagan was determined to end the Cold War, but not by the kind of negotiations that Eisenhower and Kennedy had had in mind. Reagan wanted to win the Cold War. In military terms this had been regarded

190

as unthinkable for at least the past fifteen years, but Reagan thought that victory could be achieved in another way. The US economy could be used to wage the Cold War, engaging the Soviet Union in an arms race that strategically it could not afford to lose, and economically could not afford to win. Thus, under Reagan the United States started a major build-up of its conventional and nuclear forces. Then in March 1983 Reagan announced the Strategic Defense Initiative (SDI). Labeled "Star Wars," SDI aimed at the creation of an antiballistic missile system using lasers and rockets based in space, together with air- and ground-launched munitions. With the completion of such a system the United States might be able to win a nuclear confrontation with the Soviets. This threatened to undermine the whole basis of nuclear deterrence and give the United States a decisive strategic advantage. The Soviet Union had to respond to the threat. Economically and politically they were not well placed to make such a response. The Soviet economy was in difficulties as the war in Afghanistan dragged on and the regime suffered from ineffective leadership after the deaths of Leonid I. Brezhnev on November 10, 1982, and his replacement Yuri Andropov on February 9, 1984. Steadily Reagan built up the pressure on the Soviet Union.

In his policy toward the Soviet Union Reagan had the opportunity to use strong rhetoric; in his policy toward other parts of the globe he seemed to display a propensity for strong action. When in 1981 the government of El Salvador was threatened by communist guerrillas, Reagan sent in aid and advisers to help the regime. Reagan also supported anti-Communist contra guerrillas fighting the Cuban-backed Sandinista regime in Nicaragua. The Central Intelligence Agency took a leading role in organizing the resistance. Aiding the contras caused diplomatic complications in central America as various other countries in the region feared that American meddling might produce a wider conflict. Many Congressmen were also fearful that the United States might be in danger of getting itself stuck in another jungle conflict.

More dramatic still was Reagan's authorization of American military force to deal with problems in the Caribbean and the Mediterranean. In 1983 Reagan decided to invade the island of Grenada after a radical left-wing, Cuban-backed, military government had taken office. Considering the new government a threat to US security, and concerned about the welfare of American students studying there, Reagan ordered a marine task force to seize the island. The United Nations, the British Commonwealth and Latin America were appalled at the use of force against a tiny island state. The American public meanwhile were ecstatic in their approval of Reagan. Grenada showed Reagan's decisiveness, and victory showed that America could once again be proud of its military. Likewise, Reagan's decision to bomb Libya, regarded as a sponsor of international terrorism, was a military and a political success. Wrongdoing had been punished in a display of US military strength. These incidents, combined with Reagan's strong rhetoric, and a desire to put the failures of the 1970s firmly behind America, produced a patriotic upsurge which amplified the true extent of the resurgence of American power. That America could celebrate the successful invasion of a small Caribbean island as though it were a rerun of the Normandy landings had more to do with the impact of Vietnam and the hostage humiliation of 1979 than the actual nature of the achievement of the United States Marine Corps. Likewise bombing a third world country, even one armed with up-to-date Soviet weaponry, was easily in the compass of the forces of a superpower. Such actions helped to create an illusion of a successful American military to redress the blows to American self-confidence struck in Vietnam. Outside of the United States there was sharp criticism of the operation. A United Nations resolution condemning the invasion of Grenada was only prevented from being carried by the United States using its veto in the Security Council, and in Great Britain there was condemnation that the United States should choose to invade an independent member of the British Commonwealth without even having the courtesy to inform the British government beforehand.

In fact, Grenada and Libya were a welcome distraction from the humiliation of American military power elsewhere on the globe. In 1982, the Israeli armed forces invaded the Lebanon in an attempt to end its use by the guerrillas of the Palestine Liberation Organization. Militarily it was a successful operation, but politically it was a disaster. The PLO were driven out only for the Lebanon to become home to a variety of Islamic fundamentalist groups which were Iranian and Syrian backed, anti-Israeli and anti-American. Terrorist activity increased dramatically and America became a target for the new generation of terrorists. Following the partial withdrawal of Israeli forces and the insertion of American, French, and Italian peace keepers, the Marine base in Beirut was targeted by Islamic fundamentalists. A suicide bomber drove into the building housing Marine headquarters on October 23, 1983, killing over 240 Marines. A few months later Reagan announced that the Marines would leave Beirut, which descended into anarchy. Islamic groups turned Beirut into the headquarters of world terrorism, and on the streets of the city Americans were kidnapped and held in solitary confinement as a means of exerting influence on the United States. Strong rhetoric and American military might could do nothing to help the hostages.

In 1984 the American public had their opportunity to pass judgment on Reagan. In his campaign for a second term Reagan promised to continue the same kind of policies which he had pursued from 1981 to 1984. However, the underlying tensions between Reagan's policies were increasingly manifest, even as former Vice-President Walter Mondale was nominated as the Democratic challenger for the presidency. While Reagan maintained the rhetoric against big government and high taxes, his spending on the military meant that the start of his reelection campaign coincided with his being forced to sign into law the 1984 Deficit Reduction Act raising taxes substantially. It was, however, the Democratic Party which continued to be viewed as the party of higher taxation, partly because in his acceptance speech Mondale told the American public that higher taxes would be necessary no matter who was in the White House. Having already signed into law tax increases of over $50 billion, Reagan promised that he would not approve of any further tax increase. He maintained a steady lead over Mondale throughout the campaign. Even though Mondale selected a woman, Geraldine Ferraro, as his running mate partly to attract the women's vote, on polling day it became clear that Reagan and his style of big talking presidency had received, with 59 percent of the vote, the overwhelming endorsement of the electorate. Reagan's victory in 1980 in the electoral college had been crushing, but the result in 1984 was still more emphatic, 525 votes to Mondale's 13. Such was Reagan's popularity that there was even a slight rise, to 53 percent, in the number of people who had bothered to vote. It seemed as though Reagan's policies were good for the country and good for American democracy.

In Reagan's second term he began to take an even bigger interest in foreign policy. On March 10, 1985, the Soviet leader Konstantin Chernenko died. Chernenko had replaced Andropov in February 1984, and by 1985 the Soviet Union was facing a crisis of leadership. The rapid succession of Soviet leaders after the death of Brezhnev in 1982 had meant that the mounting problems facing the regime had not been tackled. On top of an economic crisis which meant that the Soviet Union was ill-placed to respond to Reagan's build-up of American military forces, the subjugated peoples of Eastern Europe were once more growing restive under communism. Even within the very conservative hierarchy of the Soviet Union there was a recognition that something had to be done. The first thing was to signal a break with the past by appointing a relatively young man to replace Chernenko. The communist leadership appointed Mikhail Gorbachev, who very quickly announced his intention to reform the Soviet system. Part of that process of reform involved trying to end the ruinous expense of the Cold War. After an initial meeting in Geneva in November 1985, Reagan and Gorbachev continued to meet sporadically to discuss arms limitation. In 1986 the two men met again in Iceland where they talked about sweeping cuts in the nuclear arsenals of the two nations. Unfortunately, the cuts foundered on Reagan's unwillingness to sacrifice the Strategic Defense Initiative as part of any agreement. Reagan reasoned that SDI had brought the Soviets to the table and he could not afford to sign away the influence it enabled him to exert. Despite the collapse of the talks, in 1987 Reagan and Gorbachev agreed cuts in the intermediate-range nuclear arsenals of both countries. One year later they began exploratory talks about reductions in the numbers of intercontinental ballistic missiles. The two men had achieved much in the field of arms control, but what was still more important was that Gorbachev's program of reform, in part forced on the Soviet Union by Reagan's hard-line stance against communism, slowly produced its internal collapse. As this gathered pace, the Soviet leadership was forced to allow a rising tide of change in the communist bloc. By 1988 Soviet troops were evacuating Afghanistan, and in Eastern Europe the process of change was gathering pace. In true B-movie style the enemy had been vanquished.

Whereas in Russo-American relations success seemed increasingly evident, in other areas of the world tension increased. It was in the Middle East that Reagan would face his greatest challenge, and the failure of his policy toward the region would lead to the exposure of the nature of his presidency. Even after the release of the hostages in Tehran, Middle Eastern terrorism had continued to expose the weakness of American power. In June 1985 a Trans World Airlines flight had been hijacked between Athens and Rome. The aircraft was landed at Beirut and the American public were forced to watch helplessly as an American passenger on the aircraft was murdered and the rest of the passengers held hostage. America appeared impotent, even though the passengers were eventually released. The hijackers melted into the suburbs of Beirut where other Americans were still held captive by Islamic terrorists. Then in October 1985 Leon Klinghoffer, an American passenger, was brutally murdered when the Italian liner *Achille Lauro* was hijacked off the coast of Egypt. Eventually the ship was surrendered to the Egyptian authorities in return for safe passage from Egypt. The Egyptians allowed the terrorists to fly from Egypt to Tunis, only for the aircraft to be forced to land at Sigonella airforce base in Italy by jets from an American carrier. At Sigonella they were taken into custody. Events in the Mediterranean meant that there was a continuing focus on American policy toward the Middle East, especially on the matter of terrorism.

Then from Beirut in 1986 emanated allegations that the administration had been involved in secret arms sales to Iran. In return the Americans hoped that the Iranians would persuade fundamentalist Islamic groups in the Lebanon to release American hostages. Those hostages had been taken off the streets of Beirut and held in appalling conditions in secret locations throughout the city. Selling arms to the Iranians, who badly needed to build up their military after the end of the Iran–Iraq war, was in direct contravention of the public policy of the administration which had pledged never to negotiate with the kidnappers. It subsequently emerged that this was only half the story and that arms sales to the Iranians had been used to fund Contra rebels aiming to overthrow the communist regime in Nicaragua. At the center of these events lay Marine Corps Officer Lieutenant-Colonel Oliver North.

North, an aide to the National Security Council had run a network of covert operations from the White House. North believed that in channeling aid to the Contras he was carrying out the president's wishes to support anti-communist forces around the globe. From experience in the field in Vietnam, North knew what it was like to be let down by the politicians, and was determined not to sell out men whom he regarded as freedom fighters. In his memoirs he reflected:

> From 1984 on, I did my best to keep faith with two groups whom I cared about deeply, and whose fate President Reagan had put at the top of his agenda: our hostages in Lebanon and the Contras. While I worked frantically on behalf of both groups, I can see now that I was also motivated by my own pride and ambition. No matter how difficult or demanding the job was, I was sure I could handle it. I knew that if these missions were successful, only a very small handful of people would ever know what I had achieved. Paradoxically, I took pride in that, too. (North, 1991, pp. 405–6).

There was, however, a problem with aiding the Contras. Congress had been opposed to the administration's support for the Contras and the Boland Amendments, passed between 1982 and 1986, had steadily restricted the giving of aid to the anti-communist guerrillas. Rather like the War Powers Act, the Boland Amendments owed much to the spectre of Vietnam, and by prohibiting presidential action in foreign policy they too were possibly unconstitutional. But by continuing to aid the Contras, North and the administration were ignoring the law and the wishes of Congress. North had not acted alone: the operation had been approved by National Security Adviser Robert MacFarlane, and Admiral John Poindexter who replaced him.

The Director of the Central Intelligence Agency, William Casey, also knew of the operation. In her memoirs Nancy Reagan explains that Casey was at the time suffering from a brain tumor which would kill him by May 1987. She wonders whether his judgment was perhaps affected by his illness, but equally Casey may well have been affected by the reports about the hostages which reached his desk. In particular, details of the torture and eventual death of Bill Colby, CIA station chief in Beirut, who had fallen into the hands of the terrorists, probably convinced Casey that it was right to try and get the hostages out by any means that presented themselves. The Secretary for Defense, Caspar Weinberger, and the Secretary of State, George Shultz, both knew of the arms sales and had voiced their disapproval, with Shultz threatening to resign. However, it was a rare moment when the State Department and Defense Department found themselves agreed on a policy matter. With Shultz and Weinberger at loggerheads on almost every other aspect of the country's external policies, the Iran-Contra deal was overshadowed by greater issues, and was allowed to go through unchecked.

As the scandal broke the American people feared that another Watergate was unfolding. The administration had broken the law, undermined Congress, and traded with the power responsible for the Tehran hostages humiliation of 1979. The presidency's new activism, whether illusory or not, looked suddenly dangerous again. Reagan had done so much to create the appearance of a revivified presidency that the scale of public reaction to the Iran-Contra affair, as it came to be labeled, was out of all proportion to the wrongdoing involved. Poindexter resigned his office and North was sacked. Robert McFarlane made an unsuccessful suicide attempt, and amid the unfolding episode the public waited for the evidence that would finally prove Reagan's hand had been in the operation. Rather like Watergate, the public reasoned that it was simply a matter of time before Reagan was unmasked as the instigator of the whole sorry episode. Yet that evidence never came.

There was instead a growing understanding that Reagan did not fully comprehend what was taking place in the basement of the White House. This was hard for a skeptical American public to accept:

Most Americans simply could not believe that a President, any President, could be so out of touch with the policies and actions of his own government. They could not understand how Reagan could have forgotten whether or not he authorized the first arms sales, or how he could have signed presidential findings without comprehending what they meant, or how he could not have known about Oliver North's plan to divert funds from the arms deal to the Contras. Their basic perception of the American presidency had been shaped by a tradition that extended back over half a century to the days of Franklin D. Roosevelt. . . . Every chief executive since FDR . . . had been, in varying degrees, an activist who personally guided the course of foreign policy and set down the legislative agenda for domestic affairs. But Ronald Reagan was a throwback to the pre-Roosevelt era. His model was Calvin Coolidge. . . . Reagan was in high school during Coolidge's reign, but the man's *laissez-faire* approach to the presidency made an enduring impression on him. It was an act of some significance when, shortly after he moved into the White House, he requested that Coolidge's portrait replace Harry Truman's in the Cabinet Room (Schieffer and Gates, 1989, p. 303).

If by instinct Reagan was a *laissez-faire* president who chose to disguise the fact in deference to the activist inclinations of the American public, then Iran-Contra revealed that in his second term he was increasingly disengaged from the work of government. Reagan's official biographer explains:

Reagan's character by 1986 had become so lacking in curiosity, and his life as President so repetitive (except for great moments such as Reykjavik, which called on all his faculties), that when I went in to interview him I was often reminded of that MP's snapshot taken at Metro in '43: the furrowed eyes, the what-am-I-doing-here look of a screen actor between takes. At times like this, a National Security Adviser would truthfully tell him that there was another "undercover thing going" to the benefit of the "freedom fighters," and that an eyes-only, unquotable annex to Boland II granted him full power to authorize it as Commander in Chief. He would be uncapping his fountain pen halfway through the speech, and asking him where to sign. That's the way he was. Six years before, Mitterand's man had elegantly summed him up: "Formidable will, based on mediocre understanding of the facts. As often in politics, ignorance sustained strength" (Morris, 1999, pp. 615–16).

Morris has also speculated whether the president, perhaps suffering the first symptoms of what would eventually be diagnosed as Alzheimer's disease, was pursuing a policy of conserving his mental energies. Thus his involvement in the Iran-Contra scandal took place while the President was on mental auto-pilot. In his memoirs North said that, while the president must have been told of the covert operation to help the hostages and the Contras, this did not necessarily mean that the President was "aware" of what was taking place. Press conferences at the height of the crisis were deeply painful as it was obvious that the President had not been fully in charge of the White House, or indeed his own faculties. The American public could see that Reagan was not the superman his public image suggested him to be. His popularity declined dramatically as the frailties of the myth were exposed.

In early 1987 a joint Senate–House committee began investigating the Iran-Contra affair. The televised hearings revealed a web of deceit, but Oliver North managed such an effective defense of his actions that increasingly the public began to side with the Marine Corps Colonel, who frequently invoked patriotism as the guiding principle of his actions. North turned the tables for himself and indeed the administration, although Reagan struck a pitiful note, repeatedly saying "I don't recall." Six members of the administration were eventually convicted as a result of Iran–Contra. Oliver North was convicted of only three comparatively minor charges, having also been indicted on nine other, more serious counts. North appealed against his conviction and subsequently the charges were overturned. Throughout his trial and subsequently North continued to believe that the arms for hostages swap had been the right thing to do:

It ended in failure, but that's not to say it wasn't worth trying. Had we succeeded, not only would all the hostages have come home, but we would have opened a new relationship with a country that it still important to our national security. But we didn't succeed. Not only were we unable to establish a connection to the moderates in Iran, but we also undermined a valid and well established policy of not making concessions to terrorists. . . . While I recognize the liabilities of the Iran initiative, I continue to feel that saving a life – or trying to – is even more important than preserving a policy. . . . Our Nicaraguan initiative was more straightforward, and for me, at least presented no great moral quandary. Until Congress decided to resume its funding for the Contras, we succeeded in fulfilling the mission assigned by the President: to keep the resistance alive, body and soul (North, 1991, p. 406).

North's passionate defense of the Iran-Contra exchange meant that he avoided prison. Only Admiral Poindexter, who had obstructed justice and lied to Congress, served a jail sentence and even that was a relatively short six months. As the crisis unfolded many speculated on how Reagan could possibly survive it, but survive it he did, and the dip in his popularity was only short lived. This was in part a result of how Reagan had handled the crisis, confessing quite openly that he simply did not remember, and the realization that his crimes were those of omission rather than commission. He had not controled the White House as rigorously as he should have, but had not committed any crime.

The electorate was left confused by the episode. Reagan appeared at the same time strong but also weak – smart but yet confused. The public's confusion was an inevitable result of the contrast between the illusion and the reality of the Reagan presidency. But at least the story of his presidency continued to follow the plot of a B-movie. In the finest traditions of the genre, the plucky Marine had launched a desperate attack to rescue his wounded chief just as the enemy had moved in for the kill. It was exciting cinema, but perhaps not so great government.

It would perhaps be easy to dismiss the Iran-Contra episode as a minor blemish on Reagan's record. It could be argued that the politicians, public, and press overreacted to the affair. That overreaction was itself testament to Reagan's success at rebuilding the prestige and authority of the presidency. Fred Greenstein commented as early as 1983:

> By 1980 presidency-curbing statutes and extralegal changes in institutions and practices appeared to have significantly sapped the president's ability to exercise influence. Reagan and company [have] reversed the notion that presidents were becoming increasingly powerless (Greenstein, 1983, p. 6).

Early in his administration Reagan had managed to break out of the seemingly inevitable pattern of dwindling presidential power and authority. The Iran-Contra scandal threatened to undo Reagan's rehabilitation of presidential power, even though some members of the administration have attempted to play down the importance of the arms for hostages saga. For example, George Shultz has commented:

> Iran-Contra, of course, got a huge amount of attention – I think overattention. It wasn't like Watergate; Watergate had a rancid element. The things people did – even the things Casey and company did – they did for what they thought were the best interests of the United States (Strober and Strober, 1998, p. 575).

It was true that the Iran–Contra affair was not on the scale of Watergate, but Shultz was perhaps a little too quick to dismiss the episode. For one thing, there was a certain commonality in motives in the Watergate scandal and the Iran-Contra affair. Nixon believed that he was acting in the best interests of the state when he went down the line of law breaking. Oliver North did not have a monopoly on patriotism as a motive for wrongdoing. In addition, such was the lasting damage of the Watergate affair to the American body politic that the Iran-Contra affair reopened the old wounds, and the very real fears about executive power generated by the Nixon years. From 1981 onward Reagan had worked a political miracle, healing some of the scars of the 1960s and 1970s and making the American people realize that the presidency could be made to work despite the doubters in the American academic establishment. But the arms for hostages affair demonstrated that miracles are sometimes just a well-executed illusion. As one commentator noted in the aftermath of the scandal:

> John F. Kennedy was assassinated. Lyndon B. Johnson was shouldered into retirement by massive disenchantment with the war in Vietnam. Richard M. Nixon was sunk by Watergate, resigning in the face of probable impeachment. Gerald R. Ford was doomed by his pardon of his predecessor. Jimmy Carter ran aground on the shoals of Iran. Five Presidents. Five presidencies prematurely terminated. For almost six years, Ronald Wilson Reagan seemed destined to break the string, seemed, indeed to be one of those rare politicians blessed with the ability, so admired by Machiavelli, to identify himself with the national purpose. But then came the series of events for which no one has been able to devise a more euphonious name than the Iran-Contra affair (Apple, 1987, p. x).

The Iran-Contra affair once again focused attention on the weakness of the presidential system. Waging covert warfare behind the back of Congress harked back to the days of imperial presidency, but this time it was actually worse. Instead of presidential usurpation of the right of Congress to declare and wage war, an independently minded Marine Corps Lieutenant-Colonel had taken it upon himself to maintain the fight against communism. In effect, the military had determined how foreign policy objectives should be pursued, and in the face of such activity an indolent civilian presidency had connived at substantial wrongdoing.

Like any actor, Reagan was distressed by public criticism of his role. The president became withdrawn and depressed as the public turned against him. By February 1987 some members of the White House staff wondered whether he might have to be replaced by Vice-President George Bush, because Reagan seemed unable or unwilling to carry on the business of government. Indeed, one member of Reagan's staff drew up an emergency transition paper preparatory to invoking the Twenty-Fifth Amendment, section four, covering presidential disability. Reagan was watched closely during the month of March, but as the president did not appear to deteriorate further the concerns were temporarily alleviated. As the political storm passed, and Reagan's political fortunes improved, so did his outlook and ability to handle affairs of state. He resumed his part in national life, but his presidency had suffered a blow from which it could never fully recover.

The Iran-Contra affair merely highlighted the fact that the presidency remained under siege and that the manifest mistrust of the American public for their government could be reawakened at almost any time. The fundamental weakness of American government in the aftermath of Watergate and Vietnam was demonstrated once again, and indeed Congress used the Iran-Contra scandal as an opportunity to further erode the power of the presidency. In 1987 Congress passed a measure to strengthen the 1972 Case-Zablocki Act which had required any president to notify Congress of the signature of any international agreement. Having seen the Act evaded or ignored over the previous fifteen years Congress voted to cut off funding for any agreement which did not conform to the requirements of Case-Zablocki.

While this had limited impact, since international agreements falling short of the status of treaties had become an entrenched part of diplomatic life, the move to strengthen the Case-Zablocki Act had a symbolic importance that outweighed its value as a check on presidential power. It showed that Congress remained determined to keep the presidency firmly in check, even when the occupant was as tough talking and apparently dynamic as Reagan.

The months after the Iran-Contra scandal broke saw the low point of the Reagan administration which ended, in contrast to the bang with which it had had begun, on a whimper, with Reagan's retirement at the end of two terms. With the economy in trouble after the fall in share prices on black Monday, October 19, 1987, financial gloom was added to the feeling that Reagan had not delivered all he had promised. For so long he had maintained the illusion that he was a superman: a man who could make the post-Watergate presidency work in a way of which the voters could approve. But the invasion of

Grenada and the bombing of Libya had shown that America was once again willing and able to assert successfully its military power. Iran-Contra exposed a side of the Reagan administration that was deeply unattractive. It showed, in contrast to his stage rhetoric and image, a president who was not in charge of the White House. In public one got tough with terrorists: in private one talked to them and rewarded them, albeit indirectly. In some ways Iran-Contra showed that Reagan's achievements had been a triumph of rhetoric and style over substance – illusion over reality. Taxes were cut, but they were also raised, and the cuts were at the expense of a massively expanding federal deficit. Many of Reagan's achievements were little more than mirages constructed by the President's media team. Reagan was just the front guy who delivered the lines. And yet, for all that, in a nation built on myths, Reagan did achieve much. He gave back to the people of the United States a sense of self-belief and a confidence that Vietnam and Watergate were firmly in the past. He also helped to destabilize the Soviet Union and to propel change in Eastern Europe. For his achievements, both actual and imagined, Reagan was truly a great president. In Oliver North's opinion:

> It will probably take one hundred years for Reagan to be regarded as one of the greatest presidents this country has ever had because of what he accomplished. He set out to reduce the size and cost of government in our lives, and to free up the entrepreneurial spirit of this country, and to bring down the Evil Empire. And he darn well did it (Strober and Strober, 1998, p. 578).

Reagan had found a way to make the post-Watergate presidency work. A president needed to project the decisiveness of Truman, the gravitas of Eisenhower, the charm and wit of Kennedy, the legislative success of Johnson and the honesty and morality of Carter. Reagan had managed to combine all these different features into a near perfect performance. He was a hard act to follow.

NINE

George: The Unloved Success as President

When George Bush took over as president in 1989 he faced a particularly difficult problem. Ronald Reagan had been a fantastically popular president and had done much to restore the belief of Americans in themselves and in the institution of the presidency. He had demonstrated that restraint in the use of presidential power could apparently be coupled with effective management of the nation's affairs, especially in the prosecution of American foreign policy. Reagan had been a radical president pursuing a right-wing program of reform in domestic policy while standing up to the Soviet Union. In many ways he had been remarkably successful, barring the Iran-Contra scandal, and yet to many Reagan's presidency had seemed like a triumph of style over substance. The actor turned politician always had the snappy one-liner or anecdote to drive home a particular point, while the White House staff could be relied on to do the work of framing detailed policy. Reagan was the front man for the administration, but at the same time he did much to set the tone and direction of presidential policy, while trusting his subordinates to play their particular roles in the grand production. And yet, for all his success, Reagan's apparent power to control events had been at times an illusion rather than a reality. The Iran-Contra affair had shown the weaknesses of Reagan's method of leadership: that subordinates were sometimes allowed to do what they assumed the president wanted done, rather than what he had actually authorized them to do. The Reagan system was a source of strength as well as weakness.

George Bush, Reagan's Vice-President and heir apparent at the end of his second term, was determined that if he became president he would operate in a much more traditional way. This would involve a powerful, but self-restrained, presidency. Presidential policy would be

205

limited in its scope, but decisively effective in practise. Effectiveness of policy would be combined with honesty and transparency. Yet herein lay a potential problem. Bush's instincts called for a move away from the kind of presidency of illusion that had been part of Reagan's success. This would risk political failure – there was no doubt about the success of the Reagan formula. The presidency that eventually emerged from the conflicts between these different forces was a series of confusing paradoxes. Bush's achievements were considerable, but he did not have the ability or the inclination to weave them into the kind of illusions that would win the adulation of the public. Although Bush was to become president after the end of the imperial presidency he was in many respects the quintessential imperial president and Cold War warrior. His record on domestic affairs – indeed, his interest in them – was completely overshadowed by his concerns about foreign policy. In domestic affairs he strove to maintain Reagan's policies but to give them a kinder, gentler edge. He was not interested in major initiatives, simply in fine-tuning the Republican policies of the 1980s. But in foreign affairs he was remarkably proactive. The United States twice went to war during his four years in office. Bush oversaw the collapse of communism in Eastern Europe and scored a brilliant military victory in operation Desert Storm. Despite this, the American people remained supremely indifferent to the style and content of his presidency and he would be defeated in the 1992 presidential elections. It was another reminder, if one were needed, that the American public would not accept what had been labeled imperial presidency no matter how successfully it was prosecuted. They preferred the illusion of strong foreign policy to the reality of war, and the illusion of success to its actuality.

George Bush had been born in a suburb of Boston in June 1924. He was the son of Prescott Sheldon Bush, a banker who represented Connecticut in the Senate from 1952 to 1963. George Bush came from a privileged background and was educated privately before volunteering in 1942 for service in the United States Navy as a pilot. He flew 58 missions in the Pacific and on one occasion he was shot down. In 1945 he married Barbara Pierce with whom he was to have six children. After the war Bush went to Yale, graduating three years later in 1948 with a degree in economics. It took him some time to settle into a career but, after working as a warehouseman and a salesman, in 1950 he helped to found the Bush-Overby Company in Texas. The company dealt in oil and gas properties, and in 1953 Bush went on to become a cofounder of the Zapata Petroleum Company. Zapata took over the Bush-Overby Company. In 1954 a subsidiary of Zapata was formed, the Zapata Offshore Company, to manufacture drilling equipment. Bush served as president of the company from 1956 to 1964, and later as chairman of the board. Zapata Offshore became completely independent in 1958 and Bush sold his share of the company about a decade later. The significance of his business success was that Bush could have chosen to follow in the footsteps of his father Prescott Bush, who was a partner in a large investment house. Yet George chose his own route. He was a self-made man, despite his privileged start in life.

However, Bush did follow his father's career in one important respect: as a Congressman. In 1964 George Bush gained the Republican nomination to seek election in Texas for the United States Senate. Although Bush lost, it was thought significant that he had managed to gain 43.5 percent of the vote in the backyard of Democratic President Lyndon Baines Johnson. In his first run for Congress Bush showed himself to be a right-wing Republican opposing civil rights legislation and advocating withdrawal from the United Nations if communist China was admitted as a member. After 1964 Bush switched his attention from the Senate to the House of Representatives and in 1966 he was elected for Houston. In 1970 he left the House of Representatives to have another go at getting elected to the Senate. However, finding himself up against the conservative Democrat Lloyd Bentsen, Bush failed to win even though he had the personal support of Richard Nixon.

Despite this setback, Bush's political career took off as Nixon appointed him the top American delegate to the United Nations. There Bush scored a major victory when he was able to secure a reduction in the level of financial support given to the UN by the United States. Bush's job was especially difficult, given the importance of foreign policy to the Nixon administration and the complication that Nixon and Kissinger both played starring roles in that policy. Nixon clearly felt that Bush was one of his most loyal and trustworthy subordinates for in 1973 Bush was appointed chairman of the Republican National Committee. In the midst of the Watergate scandal Bush demonstrated his loyalty, but also his sense of honor and propriety. By the summer of 1974 Bush was convinced that Nixon had misled Congress and the American people, and that he had not cooperated with the investigations. So on August 7 he asked the president to resign and Nixon, realizing the game was up, complied the following day. After Nixon, Bush's political rise continued. From October 1974 until December 1975 Bush, at his own request, headed the United States liaison office in China. Following this, from January 1976 until 1977 he headed the Central Intelligence Agency, helping to restore confidence in the Agency after congressional investigations into allegations of abuse of power.

By the late 1970s Bush was actively considering running for the presidency. He felt ready and able to challenge for the top job, for which much of his life seemed an admirable preparation. Heading the CIA, and his role at the United Nations and in China had equipped him with considerable foreign policy experience. His background in the oil industry and his success as a businessman gave him the necessary expertise on economic questions. He was wealthy enough and fit enough to stand up to the rigours of a presidential campaign. In January 1977 Bush resigned as head of the CIA to prepare for the 1980 election. From 1977 until May 1979, when he announced his candidacy, Bush built up his campaign organization. In the primary elections in 1980 he made a good showing, but Ronald Reagan made a better one. One year after announcing his candidacy, in May 1980, Bush withdrew from the race for the White House, and at the Republican National Convention in 1980 he was taken onto the ticket as vice-presidential candidate. There was simply no getting away from the fact that Bush's background meant that he was more than up to the job. Whereas Reagan had the rhetoric and the snappy one-liners, Bush had the expertise to understand and execute the intricacies of policy.

After the Reagan–Bush team defeated Jimmy Carter in 1980, Bush repeatedly demonstrated his own qualifications for the top job while serving very loyally as Vice-President. One consequence of John Hinckley's attempt on the life of the president on March 30, 1981, was that Bush temporarily took over the presidential role. Reagan relied on his Vice-President to a considerable extent, appointing him head of the special situations group of the National Security Council. After the assassination attempt Bush increasingly ran the White House, and the Vice-President stood in for the President on numerous foreign trips. So loyal was Bush that he was accused in some quarters of changing his views to match the harder-line views of Reagan, but Bush ignored the critics. Reagan and Bush were a true political team, their strengths complemented each other. The American public realized this and in 1984 the double act was re-elected for a second term of office in a landslide. In July 1985, as Reagan had to undergo surgery, Bush was officially designated acting president. Despite Iran-Contra, the Reagan–Bush team was so successful that there was no surprise in October 1987 when Bush announced that he would be running for the presidency in 1988. The tail-end of Reagan's second term saw Bush steadily building a campaign fund of over $11 million.

In the 1988 presidential election Bush had to struggle hard firstly to secure the nomination of the Republican Party, and then to best the Democratic Party candidate. In the run-up to the election he was unfairly charged by the media with lacking a separate identity from the outgoing president, and also with being deficient in charisma and moral strength. As a presidential candidate Bush suffered from a number of other political disadvantages. He could rely on no natural power base, since he enjoyed no affinity with any particular geographical area and he was not seen as the representative or champion of any particular section of American society. He could also appear rather wooden and awkward on the platform and, more importantly, on television. He had the contacts in the media and the campaign team to redress the balance – former president Nixon was on hand to give his advice to the Bush campaign, and Kissinger could also be turned to for help – but Bush's early showing in the primary elections was weak and Reagan, exhibiting a certain ambivalence toward his vice-president, waited for almost the last possible moment before endorsing Bush's candidature. In the Iowa caucus Bush came a disappointing third with 19 percent of the vote, behind Republican Party stalwart Robert Dole with 37 percent and televangelist Pat Robertson with 25 percent. But from this opening low point Bush's support began to grow as his campaign team started to get their act together. The American public also appreciated Bush's loyalty to Reagan. Bush was not about to take issue with the President simply because it was politically expedient. Instead Bush, while admitting that "things aren't perfect," held out the hope that he could couple continuing economic success with the development of a kinder, gentler America. The recognition that change was necessary, joined with continuing loyalty to Reagan, made a powerful electoral appeal. By the time of the New Hampshire primary Bush was able to emerge the winner with 38 percent of the vote, as veteran test pilot Chuck Yeager, Boston Red Sox baseball player Ted Williams, and the 1964 Republican Party presidential candidate Barry Goldwater were wheeled out onto the Bush platform to endorse the candidate. Dole and the other Republican hopefuls were left trailing in his wake.

In winning the Republican nomination for him and launching the campaign proper, the Bush team's tactics had begun to convince the American public that there were hidden depths to the Vice-President. Bush started to show some moral strength, a certain charisma, and to demonstrate his independence from Reagan. Even so, faced with a strong challenge from his Democratic rival Michael Dukakis, Bush resorted to negative campaigning. Dukakis was repeatedly referred to as a liberal and it was implied that he would be weak on crime and hard on the taxpayer. Bush's description of Dukakis as the "liberal Massachusetts governor" was repeated like a mantra. It was robotic, but it was also effective in emphasizing concerns about Dukakis's record on crime, and that he lacked experience of federal government, especially in the realm of foreign policy. Meanwhile, Bush told the American voters that he would not increase the tax burden, inventing the phrase "read my lips: no new taxes." In many ways the 1988 campaign summed up the state of American politics. Politics was no longer about issues: it was about personalities. Smear and inference were more important than political debate. Bush's background and preparation for the job did not matter: what mattered was which candidate had the campaign team which could do most damage to the opposition. In the event, Bush's victory in the 1988 presidential election was by a narrow margin. Bush won with 53 percent of the vote, but if a total of fewer than a million extra voters in certain key states had voted for Dukakis, the Democrats, not the Republicans, would have won the election. Bush carried states such as Illinois and Pennsylvannia with a wafer-thin 51 percent of the vote. More damagingly, only 49.1 percent of the American people had bothered to turn out at the polls. That effectively meant that just 26.8 percent of the total electorate had voted George Bush into the White House. American democracy was in decline. The deep disillusionment of the American voter was plain to see, but rather less obvious was the solution to this apathy. Broad sections of the US public had concluded that, however they voted, it would make very little difference to their lives. Many Americans felt excluded from the political process in their own country. Politics was someone else's game, and the political system was run for someone else's benefit.

Once elected, and despite a pledge to bring new faces into government and move beyond the Reagan years, Bush set about building an administration that contained little fresh blood from outside Washington circles. However, controversy was caused over Bush's choice of John Tower, a former Texas Senator, as Secretary of Defense. Tower was discredited because of various allegations relating to his public and professional life. His nomination was therefore rejected by Congress. Although the senior figures within the Bush administration were all too familiar, Bush did at least appoint significant numbers of women to federal posts, including Elizabeth Dole, who had served as Secretary of Transportation under Reagan.

The puzzle of the Bush presidency for future historians was cleverly summed up by *Time* magazine in January 1991 when it gave its man of the year award to the "two George Bushes." One was a decisive commander-in-chief and arbiter of national foreign policy moving to establish a new world order by interventions in Panama and the Gulf of Arabia: the other completely failed to address America's mounting domestic difficulties. To *Time* it seemed that the same man could not be responsible for such strength in one area, and such weakness in another.

In the domestic field Bush was to achieve little. Banking reform, clean air legislation, reform of the laws governing immigration, expansion of the Head Start pre-school program and, reluctantly, an increase in the minimum wage were scarcely great achievements. At least the Civil Rights Act of 1991, making it easier for workers to seek financial compensation in the event of job discrimination, was a significant step forward. Overshadowing the whole of Bush's domestic program, however, was the problem of the federal deficit. After tinkering with domestic programs, while maintaining spending on the military, Bush was eventually forced to concede in 1991 that taxation would have to increase, despite his election pledge of no new taxes. Reductions in federal programs had led to a deterioration of conditions in the inner cities and in April–May 1992 there were serious riots in Los Angeles. The images of looting and violence seemed to highlight the failure of the Bush administration to tackle domestic problems. To some Americans it seemed as though Bush was more interested in events overseas than in downtown Los Angeles.

It was certainly true that Bush's background and interests led him down the path to a presidency dominated by foreign policy, but he was drawn there also by the political situation in Washington and by world events. Bush came to the presidency at a time when communism was collapsing across Eastern Europe. He was to face challenges to American policy and power in South America and the Middle East. The end of the Cold War threw up an array of foreign policy problems that, if ignored or mishandled, had the potential to produce even more dangerous situations than the old conflict between East and West. Bush was compelled to devote much of his time to these momentous events on the world stage. But there were also other reasons why Bush sought success in foreign policy. For one thing, with something of a political impasse on domestic matters because of the strength of the Democratic Party in Congress, foreign policy offered the only area for unfettered activity and the chance of spectacular triumphs. While Bush sought ways around his domestic impotence he used foreign policy as the means by which to build a reputation as president. One policy analyst noted:

> The president overcame Democratic opposition in Congress more by clever positioning than by political pressure. Faced with certain defeat over aid to the Contras, he embraced the position of his opponents. On protecting the environment and federal support for child care, he moved to the political centre. On cuts in tax rates on capital gains, where victory seemed attainable, he picked a fight and nearly won. Strong presidential leadership was limited to the international arena where, in spite of an active and assertive Congress, the executive retains the capacity for initiative and influence (Wildavsky, 1991, p. 296).

Thus the success or failure of the Bush presidency was going to be determined by success in the field of foreign affairs for domestic political reasons, for personal reasons, and because of the end of the Cold War. Bush was undoubtedly happy to accept this challenge, and to have the opportunity to revive some elements of the image of the imperial presidency.

Europe was the center of the first wave of problems to face the Bush administration. By 1989 the Gorbachev revolution meant that the Russians were no longer willing or able to enforce communism in Eastern Europe at the point of a gun. Consequently, in 1989 a wave of revolutions swept through the countries that lay behind the old Iron Curtain. Bush could sit back and enjoy final American victory in the Cold War, but the process of change still required careful management. Recognition of new governments needed to be pondered as well as how America would respond to the emergent regimes. Above all, Bush needed to maintain a close working relationship with Gorbachev. In 1989 Bush and Gorbachev met off the coast of Malta for a summit meeting. Six months later they met again in Washington to discuss trade and a reunified Germany. When on August 18, 1991, Gorbachev was overthrown by a group of military and political figures opposed to continuing reform, Bush threw America's weight behind the restoration of the Soviet leader.

Reacting to the calls of Boris Yeltsin, the president of the Russian Republic, he refused to recognize the new Soviet government and by August 21 the coup collapsed. Even though it failed, it led most of the fifteen Russian republics to declare their independence. The Baltic republics of Latvia, Lithuania, and Estonia became independent nations while the majority of the Soviet Republics accepted membership of the loose Confederation of Independent States. The birth of the Confederation meant the effective end of the Soviet Union and the end of the Cold War, although the problem of how to respond to the economic, environmental, and military problems of the new republics continued to dog the Bush administration. Bush had been pushing for massive cuts in nuclear arsenals even before the coup. In July 1991 he had signed into effect the Strategic Arms Reduction Treaty (START I) and announced to the world that America would destroy its tactical nuclear weapons in the European and Asiatic theaters, and that strategic air command would be taken off its constant alert status. Reciprocal reductions in the Soviet arsenal had also been ordered by Gorbachev. The coup convinced Bush that he needed to continue the process of arms reduction, although with the federal budget massively in deficit, he was also motivated by the imperatives of national finance. Shortly before Bush left office in January 1993 he added to his considerable achievements in the field of East–West relations by signing into force START II, by which the United States and the Soviet Union promised to cut their arsenals of long-range nuclear weapons by two-thirds over the course of the next decade.

The second area of challenge to the Bush administration came in Latin America. On December 20, 1989, Bush authorized an American invasion of Panama after the Panamanian government had declared a state of war with the United States and begun to threaten American civilians and military personnel in the country. The American intervention in Panama in 1989 was unusual, but also seemingly typical. Unusual in that the aim of the intervention was to bring down General Manuel Noriega, head of the Panamanian government, who had been indicted on charges relating to drug trafficking by federal grand juries in Miami and Tampa in 1988: typical in that this kind of interference in the affairs of other American countries had been one of the hallmarks of US foreign policy since Theodore Roosevelt. But the presidency had come a long way since the days of Teddy Roosevelt. Viewing the US intervention in Panama against a background of the foreign policy excursions into Latin America and the Caribbean of Roosevelt, Taft, and Wilson creates a false image. The successful American invasion of Panama in December 1989, using 24,000 troops of whom 23 were killed, needs to be seen against the post-Vietnam background of Carter's failed attempt to rescue the hostages in Iran, and Reagan's actions against Libya and Grenada. Noriega was eventually captured during the operation, after hiding in the Vatican embassy, and in 1992 he was convicted in an American court on eight charges relating to drug trafficking and racketeering. The operation was widely welcomed, and it was taken as a demonstration that Bush would be forceful in his self-declared war on drugs. Bush followed the invasion of Panama with a summit meeting in Colombia on February 15, 1990, with the heads of the Peruvian, Bolivian, and Colombian governments. With the image of US troops invading Panama fresh in their minds, the heads of government of the largest drug-producing countries in Latin America signed an accord affirming that they would seek to reduce drug production in their territory. Bush again looked strong and successful.

Following on the heels on the invasion of Panama, Bush's role as commander-in-chief was further emphasized by events in the Middle East. On August 2, 1990, Iraq invaded Kuwait. Saddam Hussein, the Iraqi dictator, had grown increasingly desperate as his country had been virtually bankrupted by the cost of fighting a war against Iran from September 1980 to August 1988. Both sides had suffered approximately one million casualties and the damage done to their economic infrastructures was considerable. Iraq was almost totally dependent on its oil exports as the mainstay of its economy. During the war various regimes in the Gulf, including the Kuwaitis, had given Iraq large loans to help it fight the Iranians. Hussein was annoyed that after the war his creditors began to demand repayment of the loans. He felt that Iraq had fought a war on behalf of the entire region against the tide of Islamic fundamentalism that the mullahs in

Tehran hoped would sweep the globe. He was incensed that Iraq should now be forced to pay back the loans that had been needed to keep Iraq in the war. In addition, Kuwait angered him by failing to abide by restrictions on oil production imposed by the Organization of Oil Producing and Exporting Countries. This had the effect of depressing the price of oil, and thus the earning potential of the Iraqi economy. Increasingly, Hussein felt that western and other countries to whom Iraq owed large sums would band together to force Iraq to restructure its economy. Since this would undoubtedly mean a shift from spending on the military to the economic infrastructure of the economy, Hussein perceived the emergence of a threat to his continued hold on power. He owed his position to the military and any reduction in military spending might lead to his overthrow by the generals, or might weaken the ability of the military to resist a popular revolt or attack by Iran. Faced with some difficult choices, Hussein tried to bully Kuwait into restricting its oil exports and into addressing the issue of the bankruptcy of the Iraqi economy by canceling the repayment of existing loans and the granting of fresh financial assistance.

In July and early August 1990 the State Department and the Pentagon were fully aware of the military build-up in southern Iraq, but both concluded that Hussein would rattle the sabre rather than use it. American warnings to Saddam were carefully veiled so as not to offend the leader of a regime which was seen as a bulwark against Islamic fundamentalism sweeping the Middle East. Saddam was a tyrant and a butcher of his own people. His treatment of the Kurdish people in the north of Iraq had included the use of poison gas and systematic repression. However, Saddam showed signs of being pro-western, at least in his recent procurement of weapons, and he remained a heretic in the eyes of Tehran.

Hussein knew that his attack on Kuwait would raise all sorts of dilemmas for American foreign policy. On the one hand the threat to western oil supplies posed by the seizure of Kuwait could not be ignored: on the other, Saddam well understood his value to the West as a shield against Islamic fundamentalism. Similarly any attack on Kuwait was a flagrant breach of international law, but would the

216

United States care enough to risk taking heavy casualties to liberate Kuwait? In the aftermath of the Cold War might the United States prefer to sacrifice the principles of the United Nations for the sake of a peaceful resolution of the problem? Also, if the Iraqi regime was a dictatorship, then the rule of the Al Sabbahs in Kuwait also had its critics. Hussein thought this might condition the western response.

The conflicting attitudes arising from the Iraqi seizure of Kuwait on August 2, 1990, meant that it would inevitably be seen as a defining moment in the history of the international system. The world had faced similar moments in the past: Italy's attack on Abyssinia in 1935 and Germany's re-occupation of the Rhineland in 1936 had both raised similarly grave dilemmas for the western democracies. Failure to respond effectively to Hussein's challenges was perceived by the wartime generation, of whom Bush was one, as a chance missed to avoid World War Three. On August 2 Bush knew that he was faced with the defining moment of his presidency, and a defining moment in the history of the international system since 1945. The credibility of the United States, the western world, and the United Nations was on the line.

Bush's response was immediate and unequivocal. On the day of the invasion he publicly declared "this aggression will not stand." Despite his concerns about the costs involved in any military operation, and whether he could muster enough support in Congress, Bush had committed the United States to a course which could only end in the liberation of Kuwait or humiliation. If American diplomacy and intelligence before August 2 had been a failure in that it had failed to prevent the Iraqi invasion, then it was matchless after it. In the United Nations a rare degree of unanimity was achieved. The UN worked as its most ambitious proponents back in 1945 had hoped, in identifying and confronting aggression. This was a remarkable achievement of US diplomacy. In particular, James Baker, the Secretary of State, worked hard to ensure that the Soviet Union would not oppose an American-led intervention in the region. Baker and Bush forged a coalition to oppose Iraqi aggression. That the coalition included nations ranging from traditional allies such as Great Britain to Arab nations such as Syria and Egypt, despite

American ties to Israel, was similarly testament to Bush's powers of leadership. America led the world as it rarely had done. In 1988 Bush was at times criticized for being a wimp, and he was attacked for a lack of charisma. Yet in 1990 he was able to put forward a case for intervention that enjoyed remarkable levels of support not just in the United States, but around the globe.

By August 6–7, some four days after the invasion, American advance forces began arriving in Saudi Arabia. Their first task was to take up positions near the border with Kuwait to prevent any Iraqi incursion into Saudi territory. On August 22 the President issued orders to mobilize US reserve forces. As the build-up of forces continued during September, and Bush became convinced that the Soviet Union would not oppose an invasion of occupied Kuwait, he proclaimed the existence of a new world order: a world in which nations could cooperate to meet common threats to their security; a world not riven by religious or ideological divisions to the point at which the international system would not operate effectively. In his state of the union address in 1991 Bush described the new world order as being one where diverse nations are drawn together in common cause to achieve the universal aspirations of mankind: peace and security, freedom, and the rule of law. Bush considered "such a world is worthy of our struggle and worthy of our children's future." In his new world order speech he was trying to shape the kind of vision of the future that Reagan had been so good at doing, but Bush lacked the messianic qualities of his predecessor really to enthuse his following. The American people were, at best, only half convinced by their leader's grand vision, and wondered what it might cost them in lives and money.

The months after the initial American reinforcement of Saudi Arabia were marked by a steady military build-up, the exhaustion of efforts to persuade the Iraqis to leave Kuwait voluntarily, and preparation of the political ground prior to an assault against Iraq. On November 29 the passing of United Nations resolution 678 gave Bush the authority to use force to remove Iraqi forces from Kuwait. The president gave Iraq until January 15, 1991, to comply with the wishes of the United Nations. In the meantime he had to ensure that a worried Congress would approve his actions. The outcome of a two-day debate from January 10–12 gave narrow approval to the use of force against Iraq. The House approved by 250 votes to 183, but the vote in the Senate was much narrower: 52 votes to 47. In the lead-up to the vote in Congress Bush had done much to anger congressional opinion. The military build-up in the Gulf had been undertaken with precious little congressional involvement. Although Bush was very much aware of the mistakes which Johnson had made over Vietnam, he was still prepared to interpret his powers as commander-in-chief liberally:

> Bush and his advisers pushed to the very outer limits, and beyond, the case for presidential primacy in war-making. They placed far more weight on the Commander-in-Chief clause in the Constitution than it could reasonably bear and argued spuriously that UN resolutions superseded congressional constitutional responsibilities. Furthermore, this crisis could hardly be said to fall within the President's constitutional right to "repel sudden attacks". The situation was not comparable to, say, the Cuban Missile Crisis where swift decision-making was, arguably, imperative. The war with Iraq did not begin until four and a half months after the invasion of Kuwait and there had, therefore, been ample time for extensive consultation with Congress. The administration rode roughshod over the rights of Congress and it is highly questionable whether the assault on Kuwait really represented the threat to American interests claimed by the President and his spokesmen (Mervin, 1998, p. 196).

Even though Congress was eventually asked to approve the president's decision to wage war against Iraq under United Nations resolutions, it was a marginal decision. There is evidence to suppose that Bush was quite prepared to authorize the liberation of Kuwait with or without congressional support. For one thing Bush believed that it was better to take action swiftly and decisively than to commit America to a longer-term struggle which would raise the spectre of Vietnam. He felt that he had to wage war and win it quickly and, if Congress stood in the way of that, then that was too bad. Bush's concerns were exacerbated when 56 members of Congress unsuccessfully tried to get the Supreme Court to rule that the President could not go to war against Iraq without a declaration of war under the Constitution.

The military assault on Iraq began on January 16 with the firing of cruise missiles against air defense, and command and control sites in Iraq. Over the next five weeks Iraq was subjected to round- the-clock bombing designed to degrade its military potential and, it was hoped, force Saddam to withdraw from Kuwait. The Iraqi dictator refused to comply, reasoning that American public support for the operation would collapse, as in Vietnam, when United States forces began taking losses in a ground assault. On February 24 that assault began but, in an operation that saw the American military machine operating with ruthless technological ingenuity and efficiency, the numerically formidable Iraqi forces were outflanked and annihilated. The land campaign lasted little more than one hundred hours and allied casualties were minimal. One hundred and thirty-seven Americans were killed, but that figure has to be contrasted with Iraqi losses of approximately 100,000. Kuwait was freed and Bush triumphant.

In the aftermath of the liberation of Kuwait two contradictory moods were apparent in the United States. The first was a sense of relief at the unexpectedly small cost of victory: the second was a sense of complacency. There was pride in the achievement of the US armed forces, but also a feeling that America expected nothing less. It was almost as though the rhetoric of the Reagan years, Hollywood's often bogus portrayal of American history, and burgeoning patriotic pride meant that the remarkableness of victory was not accurately appreciated. What America perceived was *"Gulf War: The Movie,"* rather than the realities of a stunning military and political success to rank with any other in the history of the world.

The one aspect of the Gulf War which did not stand to the administration's credit was its aftermath. Encouraged to revolt against Saddam's rule, the Kurds in northern Iraq and the marsh Arabs in the south rose against rule from Baghdad. In the resulting civil war, Saddam's regime proved unexpectedly resilient. The Kurds and the marsh Arabs were defeated, and all the West could do was establish defended safe havens in northern Iraq to protect Kurds, coupled with no-fly zones in the north and south to try to limit the activities of the Iraqi military against the hostile ethnic minorities opposed to Saddam. To many observers, it seemed as though the Kurds and the marsh Arabs had been betrayed by the West. More obvious still was the fact that Saddam continued in power, and continued to rule by violence and terror. Thus the nature of the victory in the Gulf was almost immediately called into question by political events.

Few recognized the complexity of the issues facing Bush as a result of the Gulf War. While the romanticized public ideal of America in war called for a glorious tank drive on Baghdad to bring the evil dictator to trial, create a democratic infrastructure, and otherwise make Iraq safe for redevelopment at the hands of corporate capitalists, the politics of the region had called for Bush to halt the war short of what could be considered complete victory. The dangers of ousting Saddam from power, involving a possible break-up of Iraq and the advance of militant Islam from Iran, had all been factors in how Bush had chosen to conduct the war. The dangers of inflaming Russian and Arab opinion, and exceeding the United Nations mandate, had added to his concerns, as had the fate of allied prisoners of war if Baghdad was threatened. Whereas at the height of the war the President's concerns were dangerously complex, in its aftermath the view taken by the American people was rather more simplistic – Bush had stopped short of total victory leaving an anti-American dictator in power. That perception was damaging, and rapidly after the end of the Gulf War euphoria gave way to a growing cynicism. To some observers it appeared that Bush had managed to snatch political failure out of the jaws of military success, and the contrast with the Reagan years was stark. During the 1980s small-scale actions over Libya and Grenada, combined with fine rhetoric, had allowed Reagan to create the illusion of the United States successfully battling evil. In the 1990s, Bush had successfully fought the evil tyranny of Saddam Hussein, but Middle Eastern reality was inevitably less perfect than Reaganite illusion.

While Bush proved adept at handling the grave issues thrown up by a rapidly changing world, but weak at exploiting them politically, he also demonstrated a singular lack of vision. His new world order was a rhetorical flourish that he did not have the imagination to make real. He could deal with the crises but he could not shape the international environment to bring about fundamental change. Daniel Franklin and Robert Shepard summed up Bush's difficulty while he was still in office:

> George Bush has devoted the greater part of his energy in the presidency to foreign affairs issues. He has made little secret of his preference for the challenges of international relations to those of domestic policy. His tenure in office has been marked by two epic international events: the disintegration of the Soviet empire and the multilateral effort to evict Iraq from Kuwait. Both events have led to increased US stature in the world, and both have shown the president to have an excellent talent for guiding the United States through complex situations. Bush proved himself masterful at encouraging the spread of democracy in Eastern Europe and in the states that once composed the Soviet Union without unduly antagonizing the Kremlin . . . And in the Persian Gulf War he demonstrated a remarkable talent for coalition-building as well as the ability to manage a complex military operation. Despite these formidable successes, Bush has yet to develop a clear-cut strategy for dealing with the new international order. He has yet to articulate what sort of order would be amenable to the United States or what US interests will be in the post-Cold War era (Barilleaux and Stuckey, 1992, pp. 165–6).

In the aftermath of the Cold War, however, it was perhaps too much to expect that Bush should have been capable of establishing a grand vision. Dealing with the various crises thrown up by the collapse of the Cold War was achievement enough. In the midst of the collapse of an ideology, the break-up of a superpower, and the downfall of its client regimes in Eastern Europe, US foreign policy was a resounding success. Bush handled the transition from Cold War to peace with the consummate skill of a man who had been at the political center for the majority of his adult life. In the Middle

East he gained a remarkable military and diplomatic victory, but for the American public it was still disappointing. At the end of the war Saddam remained in power in Baghdad and the need to save the Kurds and to do something to help the marsh Arabs, meant that the departure of American forces could be neither swift nor heroic. Bush did not understand that the American public wanted the political and military reality of the Gulf War to follow the plot of some potential Hollywood blockbuster. The script needed to be simple – decisive victory and a triumphant homecoming. Bush would go into the 1992 election campaign confident that America could not fail to re-elect him. All he need do was remind them of the success of his foreign policy and the victory in the Gulf. However, for most Americans *Gulf War: The Movie* was a good film spoiled by an indifferent end. Maybe even more importantly, by the time of the 1992 election that movie was doing ever less business at the voter box-office. What the electorate now wanted to see was the White House taking an interest in what they cared about most: their own economic well-being. In the early 1990s the American people continued to yearn for what Reagan had given them: a low-cost illusion of greatness combined with the reality of prosperity, at least for the American middle classes who comprised the bulk of a dwindling electorate. George Bush had given them neither. He did not deal in illusions and the public did not like a reality that was less than perfect. Bush believed in simple, straightforward, traditional presidency, but that was no longer what the American customer wanted. Under George Bush's successor there would be a return to the sort of style and image-conscious presidency which Reagan had fostered and which the voters increasingly preferred to the real political issues.

TEN

Bill: A Nation Laughs

The 1992 presidential election marked a watershed in the history of the presidency. That election was contested by three men from very different backgrounds: George Bush, war hero, President, and victor in the Gulf; Bill Clinton, his Democratic rival from Arkansas; and Ross Perot, the maverick billionaire who considered that the American people needed to be offered a fresh alternative to the stale politics of Republican versus Democrat which was steadily failing the United States. Bush represented the generation which had held the presidency since 1945. His credentials as a war hero endowed him with an appeal similar to that of Eisenhower or Kennedy. Clinton and his vice-presidential candidate Al Gore were both in their forties and represented the postwar baby-boom generation. During the course of the campaign questions about Clinton's avoidance of military service in Vietnam were to be raised, and allegations would be made that Clinton conducted extramarital relationships. To further complicate the situation Clinton would also have to answer allegations that in his youth he had smoked marijuana. Clinton dodged these awkward questions, while Bush concentrated on emphasizing his foreign policy triumphs, largely ignoring the economy just as it was becoming a real issue with the electorate. The Bush campaign was harmed by splits in the Republican Party and by the failure of the Republican machine to recognize that the continued long-term decline of voter identification with political parties, as personality replaced politics, called for new campaign tactics involving focus groups and continuous feedback on the shifts and swings in the mood of the public. The founding fathers had designed a Constitution in which the presidency, through the device of the electoral college, would be freed from the temper of the electorate. Never mind the tempers: by 1992 technology and the spin doctors were capable of putting presidential candidates in fear of the most transitory whims of the people. In the 1992 campaign the Clinton campaign team recognized the shifts taking place in American society and responded accordingly, in the process establishing a new style of campaigning.

Clinton's age and the nature of his campaign suggested something new and fresh: Bush's campaign suggested more of the same old style of politics. If Bush appeared to be part of the same generation that had presided during the imperial presidency, then Clinton was part of the generation which had brought it to its knees in the 1960s and 1970s. Perot's third party challenge to the established order also signaled that the presidency had arrived at a watershed in its history. Just what the nature of this watershed might be remained to be seen. The outcome of this election campaign confirmed that an important shift had taken place in US politics. Clinton won the election with 370 electoral college votes, backed by 44,909,889 popular votes to Bush's 168 votes in the electoral college, and 39,104,545 popular votes. The Democrats were back in the White House for the first time in 12 years.

This was a startling victory. In March 1991 a poll by *Time* magazine had found a 90 percent approval rating for Bush as president. In a matter of months that had been completely overturned. The old generation had been dismissed and the new had been welcomed into office. That was significant enough, but what was truly amazing about the election was the showing of Ross Perot. He failed to gather a single electoral college vote, but picked up 19,742,267 popular votes. There had been third party candidates before, but Perot differed from them because of the platform on which he campaigned. Perot was not championing segregation or states' rights, which had been the traditional third party platform since 1948: instead he had called into question the very nature of presidential politics and the type of presidential candidate put forward by the big party machines. That almost twenty million Americans had been willing to support such a platform showed considerable dissatisfaction with the political system.

In many ways the election turned on the question of leadership. Bush's leadership was perceived as strong on foreign policy, but weak on the economy. Clinton's leadership credentials were still more dubious: there were a number of questions about his personal history and he had little experience of leadership. He also lacked foreign policy expertise. Clinton, however, seemed to offer something new for a post-Cold War era. The baby boomers identified him as one of their own, and Clinton at least seemed to be aware of the economic difficulties facing America. Bush did not seem to know or care. Perot, meanwhile, was seen by a broad spectrum of the electorate as being a charismatic and capable leader. He had the attraction of being from outside mainstream American politics. Clinton also had some of this appeal. He may have been an experienced politician but at least he appeared to stand outside of the Washington circle.

Clinton had been born in Hope, Arkansas, on August 19, 1946. As a boy in the summer of 1963 he met President Kennedy, a fact to which the pro-Clinton lobby were to draw attention again and again. Part of Clinton's political image had been built around identifying him with Kennedy: he was presented as the young Democrat, the outsider, the man who triumphed against the odds, the man who seemed to embody the dawn of a new era, the man who would keep America strong and ensure increases in living standards for its citizens. Other potential similarities between the two men, especially those that involved women, were downplayed. In his youth Clinton attended Georgetown University, studying for a bachelor of arts degree in international studies. In addition, he worked on behalf of Senator William Fulbright of Arkansas. The Democratic Senator was chairman of the Senate Foreign Relations Committee, playing a leading role in pushing the Gulf of Tonkin Resolution through Congress. He later became an influential opponent of the war in Vietnam. In part thanks to his work for Fulbright, Clinton similarly came out against the war. Like Fulbright, Clinton went to Oxford University on a Rhodes scholarship. In 1969 he enrolled in the Army Reserve Officer's Training Corps at the University of Arkansas where he was attending the Law School. Clinton was fortunate in that, although he was available for service in Vietnam, in the draft lottery he received a high number and was not called up. In 1970 Clinton moved on to the Law School at Yale where he met his future wife,

Hillary Rodham. In 1973 both graduated: Clinton went to teach at the School of Law at the University of Arkansas; Hillary went to Washington where she worked for the staff of the House of Representatives during the Nixon impeachment. Hillary in her work for the House staff, and Clinton in his work for Fulbright, each played their own small part in the downfall of the imperial presidency. They married in 1975, by which time Clinton had already run for Congress in Arkansas, narrowly failing to beat the Republican John Paul Hammerschmidt.

In 1976, the year of the bicentennial, Clinton was elected Arkansas Attorney-General. Two years later, aged just thirty-two and with 63 percent of the vote, he won the race to become Governor of Arkansas. His administration was noteworthy for educational and welfare reform. By 1980, however, he had alienated sufficient voters in Arkansas to lose the election for the governorship to the Republican challenger Frank White. Clinton went back into legal practice in Little Rock, Arkansas, until he regained the governorship in 1982. He was to hold that office until he was elected president. In 1991 a poll of governors declared him to be the nation's most effective governor as his welfare, education, and economic reforms proved spectacularly successful. This endorsement provided a useful springboard from which to make a run for the presidency.

Clinton's story in securing the Democratic nomination and going on to win the White House is the stuff of modern political folklore. Accused of draft dodging, marijuana smoking and an affair with nightclub singer Gennifer Flowers, he still triumphed on November 3, 1992, against an incumbent president who was thought to have a an unassailable lead in the polls. Clinton's road to the White House was cleverly satirised in the 1998 film *Primary Colors*, with John Travolta as the affair-prone governor from the South who had avoided the Vietnam draft. Clinton's unexpected victory, and the return to the White House of the first Democratic president since 1980, made him an icon of the late twentieth century. He was no Jack Kennedy, but in certain lights he might just about pass for him.

What was truly fascinating about the Clinton presidency was that, although it lasted for two terms, in retrospect it seemed to have undergone a gentle decline from the moment he was first elected in 1992. During his first term he faced particular difficulties over domestic policy, but despite these he went into his campaign for re-election in 1996 with a solid lead in the polls. His Republican opponent, Robert Dole, again represented the old order overthrown in 1992. Wounded during World War Two, he had behind him a distinguished record in Congress and in 1976 had been nominated as Gerald Ford's running mate. Subsequently he had made two unsuccessful attempts to win the Republican Party nomination for the presidency. With the American economy prospering in 1996, Dole was always facing an uphill struggle. He also had trouble trying to show the voters that, despite his age, he could still match Clinton's dynamism. A Republican Congressmen, former member of the Bush administration, and, more importantly, ex-Buffalo Bills football player, Jack Kemp was brought in to add some youthful vigor and glamor to the Dole campaign. When, however, Dole stumbled and fell off the platform into the crowd during one of his public engagements many considered it a deeply symbolic slip. One Clinton aide would later write:

> Dole secured the nomination . . . but he couldn't develop any momentum. When he tried to use his position as majority leader to pass popular tax cuts and force a Clinton veto, Democrats pinned him down on the Senate floor . . . Then he tried to reignite his run by resigning from the Senate. Although his farewell speech was the most moving rhetoric of the campaign its political benefits did not linger. On the campaign trail he looked lost, almost sad, a man homesick for Capitol Hill (Stephanopoulos, 1999, p. 415).

Despite promises of sweeping tax cuts, Dole could not overhaul Clinton. On November 5, Clinton emerged the winner with 379 electoral college votes to Dole's 159. The President had gained 49 percent of the popular vote, Dole 41 percent and Perot, running again as a third party candidate, 8 percent. Voter turnout was a disappointing 49 percent. The president had been elected by a minority of a minority. His status as a minority president was unenviable, and the electorate further complicated his situation by electing Republican majorities in both houses. Within two years of his re-election, Congress would try to impeach him and, even though he survived, he faced a credibility deficit with the American people for the remaining two years of his office. Clinton's presidency, the last of the twentieth century, was to confirm that, no matter how virile the incumbent, the office for a variety of reasons had declined into semi-impotency. Ideally, the people wanted a president to give them illusions of greatness to cling to, but failing that they would settle for competent management of the economy and a cautious foreign policy.

A major part of Clinton's political difficulties stemmed from a steady drift toward the right by the American electorate after 1992. In the mid-term elections in 1994, after Clinton's ambitious plans to tackle the problem of healthcare had run into sufficient opposition for them to be abandoned, there was a landslide in favor of the Republicans, who promised tax cuts, rather than threatening voters with having the federal government spend their money for them. The Republicans' appeal to the electorate in 1994 was based around the promise of a new "Contract with America" which they would implement if elected. The Contract with America aimed in part to roll back the federal state: to cut government regulation and to give more autonomy to ordinary Americans through cutting taxes to enable them to keep more of their own money. The contract was an attack on the federal government and presidential power. It sought to return the United States to what Republicans saw as some sort of pre-modern era, in which presidential activism was limited. In detail the contract promised a series of measures such as: an amendment to force the federal government to live within its means; new legislation to contain violent criminals, including more prisons and the death penalty for violent offenders; welfare reform; greater protection of children, including enforcing child-support payments; tax cuts for families to strengthen the family as the basis of society; raising the earning limits of senior citizens; cutting government regulations affecting small businesses; reform of the legal system; and imposition of a legal limit on the number of years that Representatives and Senators could represent their area in Congress. Within one hundred days of winning control of Congress the Republicans had passed twenty-six bills putting into force elements of the Contract with America. Only four of these bills were, however, to become law, the most important of which were a bill to increase defense spending and a crime bill imposing new penalties for child abusers and pornographers. In making this progress the Republicans in Congress behaved in particularly partisan ways. In November and December 1995 there were government shutdowns as a result of their tactics. Certain nonessential parts of the federal government were shut down as the Republicans tried to pressure Clinton into a climbdown. However, the American public blamed the Republicans rather than Clinton for the inconveniences suffered. The Republican tide appeared to ebb, helping Clinton to a second term of office.

Although one further key element of the contract became law, after Clinton's re-election in 1996 the fervour of the Republican revolution appeared to pass. The Republican Party drifted back toward the centre right. Their desire to reduce radically the size of the federal government and to make it less obtrusive in the lives of ordinary Americans had not been shared to the extent they had wished by the American people. But despite his re-election, in his second term of office Clinton effectively found himself overseeing a moderate Republican legislative agenda. Even before his re-election, in August 1996, Clinton gave his approval to legislation ending the welfare system established by Franklin Roosevelt. Responsibility for maintaining the poor was handed over to the states who were also given federal funds. In addition, under the new scheme no family would be allowed to remain on welfare for more than five years, and it was envisaged that adults would be required to work for their welfare within two years of starting on it. In his second term appointments, as Madeline Albright was appointed as Secretary of State, the first woman to hold the post, Clinton also signaled a shift to the right.

Another shift which had been developing since 1994 was emphasized after Clinton's re-election. Foreign policy increasingly predominated over domestic policy. In some ways this was a natural outcome of the system of presidential terms. By 1994 Clinton had carried his domestic agenda about as far forward as it could go. The shift was a reaction to Republican success and the Contract with

America, which meant that the domestic agenda was largely set by a right-wing Congress. And while the bulk of the Republican Contract with America program was aimed at domestic policy, it also contained an explicit attack on Clinton's foreign policy. The National Security Revitalization Act drawn up by the Republicans promised to reinvigorate national defense. It recognized that since 1992 American military strength had declined and aimed at reversing that trend. It promised to reaffirm the commitment to the "Star Wars" program and to an expanded North Atlantic Treaty Organization. The policy of using US troops in United Nations operations was attacked, and the Act called for an end to the practice of placing US troops under UN command. Most interestingly of all, the NSRA called for the repeal of the 1973 War Powers Act, because in the eyes of the Republicans the act interfered with the president's ability to exercise his role as commander-in-chief. Thus at the same time as the Republicans were criticizing the policies of a Democratic president, they also sought to give him and future presidents greater freedom of action. The NSRA was in part a recognition that the balance of power had shifted too far away from the presidency as a result of the Vietnam War and the mistrust generated by Watergate. Like so many other parts of the Contract with America, the NSRA did not become law.

The National Security Revitalization Act was largely a response to the complexities and shifts in American foreign and military policy which had taken place since 1992. International affairs at this time were in a state of considerable flux. With the end of the Cold War the old familiar pattern of East–West relations had gone and a new direction was required for American foreign policy. Bush had started to try and find that direction with his new world order, but it would be up to Clinton to build on his predecessor's victory in the Gulf. The American public, however, well aware of the end of the Cold War, could not be relied on to play their part in a mission to build up a new world order. To them the Cold War had been won and it was time to concentrate on matters at home. The end of the Cold War meant peace and the American public had shown their enthusiasm for Bush's call to build a new world order by voting him out of office. The only problem was that the world was in some ways a more dangerous place than at the height of the Cold War. The situation required the exercise of strong presidential foreign policy: the American public thought that with the Cold War won less activism was in order.

In Europe, communism and East–West tension had contained ethnic and nationalistic hatreds that dated back more than a thousand years. With the end of communism and the Cold War those tensions surfaced with a vengeance. Czechoslovakia split into two, the former USSR and Yugoslavia into many more parts. The regimes in Poland, Albania, and Romania, and the rest of Eastern Europe, faced massive difficulties as they attempted to overhaul their countries and transform them into market economies. This gave rise to major economic and social difficulties, especially in Russia which maintained powerful nuclear and conventional forces. Clinton gave the new regimes in Eastern Europe considerable verbal encourage-ment and further helped them by allowing the sharing of US expertise and training. But what they really needed was cold hard cash. The situation was akin to that which faced Truman in 1947. Fifty years later, however, there was to be no Marshall plan despite the possibility that the economies of Eastern Europe might collapse, that a fascist or communist movement might gain power in one of the states, or that nuclear, chemical, or biological technology or weapons might be sold or stolen from the ill-supervised facilities of former Eastern bloc countries. American policy toward the new regimes was characterised by a dangerous naivety and an underestimation of the perils that lurked below the surface. For example, US foreign policy invested very heavily in the personality of Boris Yeltsin, who in June 1991 became president of the Russian Federation. Yeltsin's serious heart trouble, and other difficulties inside Russia, hampered the drive toward democracy and the market leading to social hardship, economic collapse and political problems. By common consent Yeltsin, for much of his presidency, was a dead man at the wheel and his behavior at times gave cause for concern and amusement. But because of the failure to supply US money to help the Russians restructure their economy, Clinton had to rely on Yeltsin. This was not a particularly secure base on which America could build its policy toward Russia.

While Clinton had to build on the foundations of policy toward Eastern Europe that George Bush had started to lay down, he was also beset by the continuing legacy of Bush's victory in the Gulf War. The Middle East peace process was given impetus by the victory and in 1993 the Israeli Prime Minister, Yitzhak Rabin, and the leader of the Palestine Liberation Organization, Yassir Arafat, managed to draw up an agreement giving Palestinians self-rule within Israel. The Clinton administration had played an important part in brokering the deal, and the President would subsequently devote considerable efforts to maintaining the Middle East peace accords, such as when in late 1996 outbreaks of violence in Israel–Palestine threatened to sink the agreement. But if the Gulf War had paved the way for an agreement on the Palestinian question then it left the situation in Iraq increasingly problematic. Saddam Hussein, the Iraqi leader, maintained his hold on power and was determined to defy the will of the international community and the United States. His failure to comply with the armistice agreement of 1991 led Clinton to authorize air strikes against military targets in Iraq in September 1994 and again in the summer of 1996. Saddam's refusal to cooperate with United Nations weapons inspectors investigating the extent of Iraq's weapons programs, especially with regard to nuclear, chemical, and biological capabilities, posed a grave challenge to the stability of the region and to the concept of the new world order. The air strikes did not cost American lives, but nor were they effective. Saddam continued to hinder United Nations investigation into Iraqi development programs of weapons of mass destruction and America was unwilling to risk the lives of its service personnel to punish him effectively. The airstrikes were little more than a mild chastisement for his misbehavior. The omnipotence and yet impotence of the United States was striking. The US taxpayer provided its military with some of the most expensive and destructive weaponry in the world, but the American public was unwilling to risk the loss of an important part of these weapons: the human element. Following the large airstrikes of 1996, Clinton settled down into a low-intensity war against Saddam. Airstrikes against military sites, particularly suspected air defenses, continued on a small and desultory scale to the end of his presidency. They went largely unreported in the world's media.

Reluctance to risk the lives of US service personnel also dogged American foreign policy in other areas, especially Haiti and Somalia. In 1993 Clinton gave American backing to the democratically elected premier Jean Bertrand Aristide who had been ousted by the military. Clinton's actions were in part motivated by a growing flood of Haitian refugees who were setting sail in a variety of craft in an attempt to reach Florida. Unless order could be restored in Haiti it seemed likely that Haitians would continue to try to enter the United States only for the lucky ones to be picked up by the American coastguard and returned to Haiti or taken to the American base at Guantanamo Bay in Cuba. For the unlucky ones death by drowning in the Caribbean waited. Humanitarian, practical, and ideological reasons thus compelled Clinton to take the initiative over Haiti. Restoring democracy there accorded with America's beliefs in her own mission in the world, and at the very least it might prevent humanitarian tragedies in Haiti and on the high seas, part of the cost of which had to be borne by the Department of Defense. In 1994 Clinton secured a United Nations resolution permitting him to use force to reinstate the former president. With this backing Clinton threatened to use American military power against the generals in Port au Prince. Faced with the prospect of invasion, the generals allowed former president Jimmy Carter into the country to talk to them. By October 15 Carter had persuaded the generals to relinquish their hold on power. American troops were permitted to land, which they started to do on September 19; Aristide was returned to power, and the influence of the military curbed. On March 31, 1995, the American occupation came to an end and peacekeeping was entrusted to a United Nations force under the command of an American general. The operation was a considerable success. Yet in the process Robert Dole, Clinton's Republican rival-to-be in the 1996 presidential elections, declared openly that restoring Aristide to power was not worth a single American life and that the American people wanted more restraint in the use of troops abroad. Dole had only voiced a feeling common to many Americans, but for a man of his stature and seniority to voice it sent a powerful signal.

The missionary zeal in American foreign policy was in part responsible for the settlement of the problem of Haiti, but it also led to a far less successful episode in the record of the Clinton administration. By the early 1990s the East African state of Somalia was dogged by famine and by civil war between rival armed clans. Despite the severity of the famine, which would leave over 100,000 Somalis dead, international efforts to relieve the suffering proved ineffective. The fighting between the different Somali militias made the distribution of aid dangerous, and at times simply impossible. This had led Bush on December 4, 1992, to launch Operation Restore Hope to use American military power to enable the relief effort to continue. American forces started landing in Somalia on December 9. The commitment was an unhappy bequest to Bush's successor. Just as United Nations troops had found themselves in conflict with clan forces, so too did American troops. During an operation in downtown Mogadishu against the forces of Mohammed Farah Aidid a number of Americans were killed and their mutilated bodies openly paraded through the streets. The images of dead soldiers on American television shifted public opinion decisively against the intervention. Let the Somalis have their civil war, faction fighting, and famine: a hundred or even a hundred thousand dead Somalis were not worth the death of a single American, seemed to be the general attitude. Aidid knew that, after Vietnam, America was unwilling to pay a price in blood for the success of a foreign policy or military initiative. In October 1993 Congress began debating the operations in Somalia. To head off public criticism, Clinton responded by setting a date for the eventual withdrawal of American forces. American military power had been humbled. Somalia had presented a number of dilemmas for Clinton. The military intervention had resulted from the finest motives and on the global scale the death of a number of American service personnel was outweighed by the immense number of lives that were saved by the institution of effective famine relief. The public had at first backed Operation Restore Hope, but American casualties had led them to turn strongly against it. American public opinion had appeared remarkably fickle, even perverse, making it difficult to exercise strong presidential leadership in that field.

This same problem faced Clinton over what to do about the fighting which followed from the disintegration of Yugoslavia in 1991. In June of that year the republics of Croatia and Slovenia had broken away from Yugoslavia to become independent states. In response to fighting between Serbia which, along with Montenegro, continued as the rump state of Yugoslavia, and Croatia, Serbs in the Republic of Bosnia-Herzegovina began a war of conquest against their fellow Bosnian Muslims and Croats. The fighting throughout the former Yugoslavia resulted in numerous atrocities, especially in Bosnia where Serbs used terror tactics to ethnically cleanse Muslim communities from land claimed by the Serbs. Just fifty years after the Holocaust against the Jews, another minority population was being exterminated. Since any side intervening in the fighting in Bosnia risked very heavy casualties and an open-ended commitment to the region, Clinton, the North Atlantic Treaty Organization, and the European Community preferred to remember the dead of fifty years ago rather than take military action to contain Serb aggression. This was despite the fact that, while on the campaign trail, Clinton had talked of using force to restore order in Bosnia. Once he became President things changed, as he perceived difficulties at home and abroad. The limitations imposed on presidential power were starkly obvious from the viewpoint of the Oval Office. Clinton threatened action, but knew that America did not really care. There were no vital, or even significant, American interests at stake in the former Yugoslavia. The Clinton administration, however, did help to broker a peace deal between the different ethnic groups in Bosnia. The Dayton Peace Agreement was initialed at Wright-Patterson Air Force Base on November 21, 1995, and signed in Paris on December 14. The accord brought peace to a shattered land, and US troops were to be used to maintain the agreement, although ethnic hatreds meant that it was a less than easy peace. Some 20,000 US troops went to Bosnia as part of a 60,000 person peacekeeping force organized by NATO. Throughout the episode, the American public was both outraged by Serb atrocity and decisively against a large-scale military intervention by American forces. Such entanglements threatened to derail Clinton's domestic agenda. He was only too well aware that the Great Society had been undermined by the Vietnam War. He did not want Bosnia to undermine his program of domestic reform.

However, the dangers of failing to stand up to the aggressive intentions of dictators were dramatically underlined even as peace came to Bosnia. Political scientists have often asserted that the holders of the presidency from 1945 to the early 1970s were prone to something called the Munich syndrome: the belief that unless the United States vigorously responded to acts of international aggression dictators would only be encouraged in their expansionism. The failure to tackle Serb aggression in Bosnia in the early 1990s led in 1998 to Serbian attempts to ethnically cleanse the Kosovo region of the Serb Republic which was populated by a predominantly Muslim, ethnically Albanian population. Kosovo is the cradle of Serb identity, being important for historical, religious, and economic reasons, and since 1980 the Serbs had been using ever more violence to repress the Kosovar Albanians. By the early 1990s the guerrilla Kosovo Liberation Army was contesting control of the region with the Serb police, paramilitary units, and army. In 1998, as the Kosovars escalated their military efforts, the Serbs decided to settle the problem by resorting to the tactics of ethnic cleansing which had worked so well in Bosnia. By the middle of March 1998 thousands of refugees were flooding out of Kosovo into Macedonia and Albania. The West warned the Serb leader Slobodan Milosovic to halt the campaign of murder. But after Bosnia, Milosevic doubted the resolve of the West, and it was only when the first airstrikes were launched by NATO on March 24 that the Serbs conceded that the threat to them was more than bluster. Nevertheless it took 80 days for the American-led forces to secure a Serb withdrawal from Kosovo. The American public clearly feared a ground war and the opinion polls suggested that Clinton would get little support for such an endeavor. Knowing this, Milosevic preferred to sit tight and wait for US forces to take the casualties which he felt that the American public would not stomach, and which would lead to an American climbdown. With the exception of the loss of one American aircraft and the capture of three American soldiers, there were no such casualties, but Milosevic demonstrated an acute understanding of the weakness of American foreign and military policy. It was only when on June 3 his own generals, fearing a NATO invasion of Kosovo, advised him to end the war, that Milosevic finally agreed to end the presence of the Serb military in Kosovo. However, the lesson of Milosevic's behavior was inescapable. The United States could not stomach casualties in pursuit of American foreign policy. The United States was perceived as weak in the eyes of this Balkan dictator.

Foreign affairs offered Clinton the chance to offset his domestic impotence, only for the opportunities to be squandered by the failure of the White House to create the illusion of good, in the form of omnipotent American military power, battling the evils of Serbian and Somali warlords. What was worse was that Clinton's weakness as President was to be underlined in other ways. Scandal continued to dog the President and the First Lady. In 1993 a congressional investigation was launched into allegations of financial irregularities concerning the involvement of the Clintons in a failed business venture back in Arkansas – the so-called Whitewater affair. The 1978 Ethics of Government Act, passed under the influence of Watergate, had created the Office of Special Prosecutor, which was renamed in 1988 the Office of Independent Counsel. The Office was to investigate any allegations of financial impropriety against senior public officials, and in 1994 independent counsel was asked to investigate Whitewater. The investigation rumbled on for months, apparently getting nowhere, but refusing to die. The efforts of independent counsel established that Hillary Clinton had been involved in dealing with some of the legal aspects of the Whitewater deal, but there was no evidence that she had in any way acted improperly. Even so, the whiff of corruption refused to go away. Then on January 20, 1998, the White House learned that the *Washington Post* was going to run a story saying that the President had asked an aide to lie to lawyers about an alleged affair in the long-running Paula Jones case. In 1994 Jones had filed a civil action against Clinton claiming that she had been sexually harassed by him during his period as governor of Arkansas. Lawyers in the Jones case attempted to establish whether or not the alleged incident with their client was part of some wider pattern of aberrant behavior on the part of the accused. Despite Clinton's repeated denials of wrongdoing and efforts to evade prosecution on the grounds that a private litigant could not bring a lawsuit against a serving president, the investigation continued. Allegations of wrongdoing by Clinton were also being probed by the independent Counsellor Kenneth Starr, who, as well as being responsible for investigating Whitewater, was also inquiring into certain other issues such as allegations of improper handling of FBI files. The Jones case and the Starr investigations appeared to be going nowhere until the *Washington Post* got its story on January 20.

That evening Clinton issued strenuous denials against the allegations, but that did not stop the newspaper from running the story on the following day. It was alleged that Clinton had had a sexual relationship with a White House intern called Monica Lewinsky who was in her early twenties. The president had denied that he was, or had been, involved in extramarital activities with federal or state employees to lawyers in the Jones case. Furthermore, it was alleged that the President had asked Lewinsky to lie about the relationship in order to avoid embarrassment and to avoid giving help to Paula Jones in her lawsuit. After the allegations had been made Clinton repeatedly denied wrongdoing, culminating with his famous public statement: "I did not have sexual relations with that woman, Miss Lewinsky." However, Clinton's denials were not sufficient to prevent the extension of the jurisdiction of the Office of Independent Counsel to cover the Lewinsky allegations.

When the Starr Report on the Lewinsky allegations was released on the Internet on September 11, 1998, it revealed that the President had begun a sexual relationship with Lewinsky on November 15, 1995, and that they had been physically intimate some ten times. The relationship had been casual and had ended in December 1997. The 453 page report was graphic in sexual detail because Clinton had tried to hide behind tight legalistic definitions of sexual behavior. Legally Clinton may have been correct in his opinion that he had not, indeed, had sexual relations "with that woman, Miss Lewinsky." But morally, and so far as the rest of the country was concerned, their relationship had involved sexual relations. The exposure of the Lewinsky relationship was a serious embarrassment to the presidency: Clinton had lied to his cabinet, the nation, his friends, and his family about the true nature of his relationship with the young woman. Suddenly the world was able to read the most intimate details of the life of the President. But Starr considered that the affair had raised possible grounds to impeach Clinton. He listed eleven possible grounds including lying under oath in the Jones case, lying to the grand jury about his relationship with Lewinsky, obstructing justice, tampering with a potential witness, and abusing his constitutional authority by failing to cooperate with the investigation.

The Lewinsky affair also highlighted the loneliness of the President wrestling with private and public agonies. Lewinsky's relationship with the President was only in very small part about sex. Their sexual encounters were few and far between, given the duration of the relationship, and were largely unfulfilling for both parties. But Clinton had a very deep emotional need for Lewinsky. He could unburden himself to her, and share with her the painful decisions that confronted him as President. The sexual element in their relationship was simply a further form of stress relief from the pressures of the presidency. Most people chose to laugh at the relationship between Clinton and Lewinsky, then but most people could not imagine what it would be like to be president. The Lewinsky episode showed the kind of strains put on the President, showed the isolation, showed the torment. Yet so ridiculed was the office which Clinton occupied that the American public chose to laugh at him, rather than find the smallest grounds for sympathy. The British author Andrew Morton highlighted the neglected aspect of the Lewinsky affair in his biography of Monica:

Far from using her as a mere sexual plaything to be discarded at whim, the fifty-year-old President seemed to have a much deeper need for this girl in her early twenties. As the months went by Monica came to know the man behind the public mask, a flawed figure riddled with doubt and wrestling with guilt, yet emotionally needy, vulnerable and ultimately alone. The politician who used to play his saxophone late into the night as a refuge against loneliness, would instead pick up the phone to call Monica Lewinsky (Morton, 1999, p. 83).

On December 19, 1998, the House of Representatives voted to impeach Clinton. On the charge that Clinton had lied under oath before the grand jury the House voted against Clinton by 228 votes to 206, with five Democrats voting with the Republicans. The second and third articles of impeachment, charging Clinton with perjury in the Paula Jones case, and abuse of presidential power in trying to stop aides from testifying to the Grand Jury, were thrown out by 221 votes to 212. It was then left to a Senate trial to determine whether or not Clinton should be removed from office. As the preparations for the trial, set to begin on January 7, 1999, continued, Clinton agonized over what to do next. He knew that the country, and with it the western world, would be plunged into a leadership vacuum by a Senate trial. At the height of Watergate Nixon had warned that the process of impeachment held severe dangers for the United States. After having decided to resign, Nixon reflected that to let the country go through the process of impeachment would not be fair "I would be a part-time president" (Woodward and Bernstein, 1976, p. 441). However, in 1999 Clinton felt no obligation to act as Nixon had done and resign to spare the nation, and Congress was willing to risk the perils of impeachment. This reflected badly on both parties.

The trial was beset by political maneuvering and complex legal arguments, as well as a growing perception that the attempt to impeach Clinton would fail as not enough Democratic Senators would side with the Republicans. Thus the American public waited impatiently for a conclusion to be reached. As proceedings in the Senate dragged on into February, the sentiments of most Americans were voiced by Richard Llamas, a spectator at the trial, who jumped to his feet in the gallery and shouted: "God Almighty, take the vote and get it over with." Senate obliged on Friday, February 12. There were not enough votes to remove Clinton from office, and there were clear signs that Republican Senators had become steadily more concerned that the American public regarded the whole thing as an expensive charade foisted on the country by a vengeful Republican Party. On the first article of impeachment covering perjury, Clinton was acquitted by 54 votes to 46 with 9 Republicans voting with the Democrats, and on the second, involving the charge that Clinton had obstructed justice, the President escaped with a 50–50 split in the vote with 5 Republicans joining the Democrats. The Starr investigation had cost $40 million, convulsed the nation, and ultimately failed to secure the downfall of the President. Like some Broadway show, the Lewinsky affair had been dramatic and showy, but ultimately, despite the cost, a great popular hit had not emerged and the audience had deserted it in their droves. One thing, however, was certain: the Lewinsky affair would provide the inspiration for a future Hollywood production, and the studio would doubtless edit down the role of Congress to put right what had gone wrong in audience terms with the live version.

The attempt to impeach President Clinton again highlighted the issue of presidential power. No president had ever before had such intimate details of his private life brought before the American public. No president had ever been so publicly humiliated by the pornographic detail of a publication such as the Starr Report. In the midst of the investigation, the White House had asserted that drawing up articles of impeachment against the president constituted a sort of *coup* against the American public by a Republican Party which aimed to overturn the results of two presidential elections. The Republicans had pursued Clinton with a kamikaze-like zeal even though in the process they suffered greater damage. In the November 1998 elections the Republicans were surprised when they failed to do well and Republican losses led Newt Gingrich to resign as Speaker of the House. For Clinton, too, resignation would have been the easy option. It would have saved him considerable time, trouble, and above all money. By the end of the trial the Clinton family had incurred debts of $8 million in legal expenses. That $8 million would keep Mr Clinton in the White House for just two more years. At least the Democrats could claim some sort of victory out of the mess of impeachment, but only in the sense that they had been the party to suffer least damage. Congress meanwhile could take little comfort in the episode. The American public had shown a deep and very worrying boredom with events on Capitol Hill. If the American people could not get excited about only the third attempt to impeach a president in American history, then what would they take an interest in? The public's apathy toward national politics was demonstrated once again, and the hypocrisy of some of Clinton's accusers in Congress, who led less than entirely blameless lives themselves, was the subject of a little old-fashioned muckraking journalism. Bob Livingston, the Republican Speaker-Elect in the House of Representatives, was forced to resign, after rumors about his extramarital activities were the subject of an investigation by the magazine *Hustler*. Three other prominent Republicans were also forced to admit illicit relationships during the months of media frenzy surrounding the investigation into the President's activities with Monica Lewinsky. In the eyes of ordinary Americans, national politics was immeasurably cheapened by revelation after revelation. During Watergate the *Washington Post* had played a key role in unearthing presidential wrongdoing: by the late 1990s national politics was a suitable subject for rather "lower-brow" publications.

It was all so reminiscent of twenty years earlier. Nixon had been unmasked as a liar and now, so too was Clinton. Nixon had many things to his credit – so did Clinton. Under his administration the budget had moved out of deficit and into surplus and the number of Americans claiming welfare had fallen dramatically. In the cases of both Nixon and Clinton they would be remembered for scandal. However, there were important differences. In the early 1970s Nixon could expand the war in Vietnam and order the Christmas bombing of Hanoi. In the late 1990s Clinton dared not risk the life of a single American soldier. In the 1970s the international stakes were too high for Nixon to behave in any way other than he did in his conduct of US foreign policy. In the 1990s the domestic political stakes were too high for Clinton to behave in anything other than the most circumspect way. More dramatically, the Watergate affair shocked Americans whose beliefs in presidential power and probity were dispelled by Nixon's Machiavellian approach to the opponents of his regime. With the Lewinsky affair the nation simply laughed at the goofball antics of their chief executive. Both men did wrong, but Nixon remained respected and feared in some quarters while Clinton was regarded as a common jerk. The continued decline of the presidency after 1974 was strikingly apparent in the comparisons which could be drawn between attitudes of the American public between 1974 and 1999.

The restoration of the presidential image which Ford and Carter had begun and which Reagan had built upon, until the Iran-Contra debacle, was exposed as being at best partial and transitory. The American public did not seem to care. Such was their indifference to the political system that by the 1990s the president could be elected with the votes of about a quarter of the electorate. That electorate viewed the political leadership of their country with scarcely disguised contempt. Superior campaign machines, rather than superior candidates, were what seemed to turn presidential elections, and the emphasis on personality had become a beauty contest where the best cosmetics won the day. The electorate were also more self-interested. The state of the American economy mattered more than anything else. This cost George Bush the White House in 1992, and it was what made the electorate willing to forgive Clinton in the midst of the Lewinsky affair. Politicians were expected to lie, or dissemble as Clinton would put it. The American public could accept that. What they could not accept was incompetence on bread and butter economic issues: the issues which made Ford, Carter, and Bush vulnerable despite the relative successes of their presidencies. The American people might not have known it, but in their contempt for politicians and the presidency they were moving back toward a nineteenth-century model of presidential behavior. The prime task of any president was not to do anything wrong, and if that meant foregoing the chance of getting something right with a little activism then so be it. Even in the dying months of the Clinton administration, as media attention shifted away from Clinton and to his possible successors in January 2001, history could be seen replicating itself. As the electorate drifted to the right, the Republican front-runner, George Bush Jr., the son of the former president, was assailed by allegations that he had avoided participation in the Vietnam War thanks to the influence of his father, and that in his youth he had taken cocaine. This did not matter except to the media searching for a good story. By the year 2000 Americans had largely resigned themselves to expect that candidates willing to stand for the presidency must be flawed in some vital respect. The electorate had come to recognize that presidential hopefuls might project the illusion of greatness, as had Reagan and

Clinton, but sooner or later illusion would be dispelled by the realities of arms to Iran or the Lewinsky episode. In the public view, figures like Washington, Jefferson, Lincoln, even Truman and Eisenhower, appeared like wholesome figures from some lost golden age, and there was perhaps the unspoken assumption that the only good presidents were dead presidents.

CONCLUSION

Presidential Power at the Turn of the Twenty-First Century

In the 1960s, at the height of the imperial presidency and the Cold War, Gene Roddenberry wrote an episode of *Star Trek* that was strikingly imaginative about what he saw as the possible future of the United States. In that episode the crew of the USS *Enterprise* visit a planet divided between two pre-industrial warring races, the Comms and the Yangs. It transpires that the world of the Comms (the communists) and the Yangs (the yankees) was largely destroyed in a catastrophic war fought centuries before. The Yangs have almost totally lost their identity but the Declaration of Independence and the Stars and Stripes remain sacred objects. Garbled passages of the Declaration of Independence are being recited by a people who do not know what the words mean, except that they are in some way holy and that they require reverence and worship. Nearly forty years on from that episode of *Star Trek*, Roddenberry's view of the future remains prescient. A catastrophic war has not been visited on the United States, but the continuing attitude of some toward the Constitution and the body politic of the USA mirrors that portrayed by the Yangs toward the Declaration of Independence. The Constitution remains a holy document, but all that it enshrines, especially the American political system, is in crisis. In the 1970s the presidency was mistrusted. By the 1990s it was mistrusted, ridiculed and considered irrelevant to their lives by a significant number of Americans. Participation in presidential elections had fallen to worryingly low levels with it being possible, as in the case of Clinton in 1996, for a president to be elected with a minority share of the vote. With a turnout of less than 50 percent Clinton was elected by a minority of a minority. When one also considers that a significant minority of US citizens are, in any case, not registered voters the implications for American democracy become staggering.

The foundations on which American democracy rests are crumbling. The illusions used by presidents to conceal their activities, and the illusions about presidential history fostered by the academic establishment have played a vital role in this process. Joan Hoff was arguing as early as Clinton's first term:

> We seem to have allowed the creation of a type of postmodern presidency beyond citizenry control. Why? . . . First, at certain levels, the American political system inherited from the days of Andrew Jackson in the nineteenth century is working in less democratic ways than ever before. Second, for a variety of reasons, since World War II a romanticized version of the modern presidency has been shaped largely by historians and political scientists, and they and the journalists in agreement with them . . . impose this skewed image on the public mind (Hoff, 1994, p. 13).

When participatory democracy appears to be dying in the United States, how can the US act as the international champion of democracy? To the outside world America no longer appears as a democracy but as a competitive oligarchy in which a nebulous political, social, and economic elite compete to see which of their number will rule as president. The emergence of ruling clans such as the Kennedys or the Bushs appears symptomatic. The American people look on as largely disillusioned bystanders, and the future looks even bleaker. In September 1999 a survey by Project Vote Smart, formed in 1990 in response to the perceived crisis of American democracy, found that only 65 percent of young Americans aged between eighteen and twenty-five years old intended to *register* to vote. Only 45 percent, less than half the youth of America, were definitely intending to become active members of a participatory democracy. The survey also found that almost a quarter of young Americans had no faith whatsoever in any level of the American political system, and that mistrust of the federal government was almost total. The mistrust between presidency and people was also emphasized in the run-up to the presidential elections in the year 2000 by the threat to bring a class action alleging that in the 1980s agencies of the federal government had assisted South American drugs barons to import cocaine into the United States. Those drugs barons, whose operations were allegedly assisted by the Central Intelligence Agency, Department of Justice and others, in turn supported the Contra rebels in Nicaragua, and the resultant crack cocaine epidemic in the United States helped to weaken black communities. The collateral effect of this was, it was argued, to keep the ghetto in its place. That a president, and the federal government, could be accused of such crimes is indeed indicative of the weakening of the "United" States. Unconquerable on the battlefield, the United States appears to be slowly dissolving from within as acid mistrust erodes faith in the institutions which made it great. What is worse is that the mistrust is not irrational. Evidence from various government agencies does indeed suggest that in the 1980s drug traffickers had been assisted to various degrees by the federal government. This opens up a fascinating Pandora's box. Did Reagan, the then President, know what was happening in the name of the American people? As Reagan's Vice-President, with particular responsibility for intelligence matters, was George Bush Sr. implicated in the trafficking operations? Did Bill Clinton, as Governor of Arkansas, know that his state was being used to land drugs from South America? The implications were indeed grave but, even if it eventually transpires that there is no case to answer, public belief in the presidency and the federal government will have been further eroded. The image of American politics which emerges from such allegations is deeply disturbing. As William Rees Mogg, a British observer of the American political scene, put it in the London *Times* on September 13, 1999: "Hollywood and the Internet tell Americans that there is really only one Establishment, a monster with two heads, one Democrat and one Republican."

Prominent Americans are also willing to affirm this image of the United States in the grip of a twin-headed monster. Hollywood star Warren Beatty told his audience at the Beverly Hilton on September 29, 1999, to "speak up for the people that nobody speaks for," and suggested that there was little to choose between the two main parties. He said that the Democratic Party was "enslaved by big money" and that it was "more interested in profits than people, investments but not environment." The leadership of the Democratic Party was attacked for making "political bargains that have left 100 million Americans behind." Implicit in Beatty's speech was the notion of the two-headed monster which had left the American voter disempowered and disillusioned.

That disillusionment and mistrust have meant that the presidency can no longer function effectively. Harry Truman was probably right when he suggested that the power of presidency lies in the ability to suggest, to give moral leadership, to persuade rather than coerce. The imperial presidency coerced the people until the people refused to be coerced, and in that process of revolt relations between the rulers and the ruled have been soured to the point where a recovery of trust between the two was likely to be transitory. There would always be an Iran-Contra, Whitewater or Lewinsky affair to prove to the American public that their mistrust of the presidency was well placed. With successive presidents having lost the authority to govern and being compelled to be particularly circumspect in their conduct of foreign and military policy, the US people instinctively grope back toward the notion of guardianship or caretaker presidency. They want a president who does nothing wrong rather than an activist presidency which gets some things wrong and some things right. This creates a certain paradox: the American people have generally tended to favor an activist presidency and among he greatest presidents by popular consent were those who were the most active. In the circumstances of the late 1990s, however, the American people see little prospect of decent leadership from either wing of the establishment, and prefer to forgo leadership altogether than fall victim to its flaws.

In the revolt against presidential power and the drift back toward a guardianship presidency it has been all too easy to forget why the modern presidency emerged. It has also been easy to overlook the fact that, without the kind of presidency founded by Roosevelt and Truman, the United States, and indeed the free world, would have fallen to communism after World War Two. As the bases of British power were destroyed in two world wars so the role of world leadership fell to the United States and its president. In the aftermath of injustices like the McCarthy hearings, following the losses in Korea and Vietnam, and secure in the knowledge that the Cold War was won by the United States, it is all too easy to underestimate or downplay the threat from the Soviet Union. In 1945, also, the United States faced a power under Joseph Stalin that had enslaved and killed millions of its citizens for ideological reasons. In 1921 the backward Russian economy had been in tatters. By 1945 it was second only to the United States in its industrial output. At the end of World War Two the United States faced a power which had overwhelmed the German military machine, which controlled Eastern Europe, and which had Western Europe apparently at its mercy. This power had demonstrated its willingness to sacrifice millions of lives for strategic or tactical advantage, and it was well versed in the use of internal subversion and external military threats to secure its own interests. The threat to the USA was massive and insidious. The President of the United States and his successors had to choose whether to stand up to this threat, or to allow events to take their course.

For most of the late 1940s and early 1950s the United States was all that stood between western Europe and a communist takeover. In Asia, too, the United States stood between postwar regimes in South Korea, Thailand, Japan and elsewhere and communist expansionism. That threat had to be met, from Berlin to Tokyo, but meeting it would cost lives from Inchon to Pleiku and beyond. That was recognized by Truman and by the Presidents who followed him. In the process of fighting the Cold War the presidency became more powerful as the United States became more powerful. World leadership and global challenges meant strong leadership at home in the United States and the enhancement of the foreign policy aspect of the presidency. The increasing sophistication and speed of modern weaponry also meant challenges to the president's role as commander-in-chief. Strict adherence to the Constitution was difficult to square with a set of dangers ranging from the possibility of a Soviet nuclear attack, through armed conflicts of limited scope, to wars waged by proxy as in the case of the Bay of Pigs fiasco. In the eighteenth century, the nature of warfare could allow for the idea of

Congress declaring war on an enemy of the United States. By the late twentieth century there was not time to resort to the correct constitutional procedure and, in any case, in the circumstances of war by proxy, or all-out thermonuclear conflict, asking Congress for a declaration of war was preposterous. The United States had to adapt to the changing world after 1945 and so too did the presidency.

But as support for the Cold War in the United States waned in the 1960s and 1970s the presidency became beleaguered, trying to conduct an increasingly unpopular struggle. Nixon's plumbers originated from the leak of the Pentagon papers, and Nixon's presidency went wrong as he tried to conclude peace with honor in Vietnam, whereas the American public were for peace at almost any price. The Cold War had changed the presidency, making it more powerful and an omnipresent feature of people's lives across much of the globe. In the 1970s the American public concluded that, on balance, the changes had not been for the best.

What if Truman and his successors had not risen to the challenge posed by the Soviet Union, however? What if the Cold War had not been fought and the United States had pursued an isolationist policy? The outcome hardly bears thinking about. Like the question "What would have happened if the Nazis had won World War Two?", the answer to some questions of alternative history are too terrifying to contemplate. The price of preventing these alternative outcomes had to be paid in blood. There was no alternative, and there were also hidden costs. One of these was the enhanced power of the executive branch. It is worth noting that in war it is almost invariably the case that the executive gains in power at the expense of the legislative. The British experience is instructive here. In Britain after World War One there was a concentration of power in the hands of the government, especially in the hands of Prime Minister David Lloyd George. Members of Parliament questioned whether Lloyd George, by administrative innovations such as the prime minister's secretariat, and the cabinet secretariat, was not usurping the authority of fellow ministers and of Parliament itself. Such innovations were vital reforms to enable the existing governmental structure to meet the challenges of war and its disturbed aftermath. In the United States, Truman's creation of the architecture of what has been described as the national security state allowed the United States to withstand the challenge of the Cold War, but similarly generated a host of suspicions.

After World War One there was a revolt against Lloyd George in the UK, and against the process of centralizing power which he appeared to represent. This led to his downfall in 1922. In the United States the revolt against the centralization of power in the presidency took longer, but was nonetheless effective. With Nixon's resignation the era of the imperial presidency drew to a close, although under Bush a few of its echoes continued to reverberate. The image of presidential authority was seriously tarnished by Watergate and the moral authority of the office was seriously undermined. Congressional challenges such as the War Powers Act chipped away at the powers of the presidency. Turmoil, drift, and a sense of powerlessness were inevitable consequences of the final debacle in Vietnam. The Ford and Carter administrations were condemned to historical mediocrity before they had begun.

Ronald Reagan knew that freedom cost lives, but he also knew that the American public was unwilling to pay the human cost of fighting communism. So instead he fought communism with the taxpayer's dollars, a large dose of rhetoric, and small-scale military actions. As he pushed the Soviet Union into an arms race that would bankrupt it, he reassured the American people of their greatness, and the American military rebuilt its self-belief by limited strikes against Libya, Grenada, and Panama. Operation Desert Storm in 1991 completed the rehabilitation of American military power which had become manifest under Reagan. But by that stage the Cold War was drawing to a close and there was ever less need for the kind of national security presidency set up by Truman and continued by his successors. The Clinton presidency, like those of Ford and Carter, was always going to be beset by difficulties because of changing circumstances. But with the economy doing well, and a Pax Americana prevailing over much of the world, it took Clinton's libido and his business dealings to pose a threat to his presidency.

The future of the presidency after Clinton is problematic. To the US public there appear to be no pressing issues demanding strong executive leadership. Their mistrust of the political establishment, especially the presidency and the federal government, is manifest everywhere. Indeed some commentators thought that Clinton's trial marked a congressional coup against the presidency. The British journalist Andrew Sullivan, writing in the *Sunday Times* on December 13, 1998, considered:

> In the wake of the cold war, the impeachment of President Clinton could mark a transition. It is a Congressional power-grab. Now that the existence of the free world does not hinge on the man in the Oval Office, Congress does not feel required to take his power as seriously. We are returning to the late 19th century, when the president was almost incidental to the politics of the country and his . . . role diminished into an almost ceremonial function.

The Russians are not about to overrun New York and the economy sails serenely on. The engine of the world economy carries on running smoothly despite economic difficulties elsewhere. Without the kind of issues which call for strong presidency the American people can afford to see their leaders humbled and ridiculed. But the question must be whether the body politic of the United States can continue to see the gulf of mistrust between rulers and ruled deepen any further. Instead of asking this question the establishment prefers to engage in internal feuds while the people turn against it. The Starr Report was perhaps the greatest humiliation ever heaped upon an American president. Congress feels that it has the time to indulge in the sport of impeachment. Nero is reputed to have fiddled while Rome burned. In the 1990s Washington is perhaps not burning, but the establishment is certainly fiddling. But there may be dangers developing, as yet invisible to most commentators, that will face the United States. In the twenty-first century the nation may find itself faced with dangers as yet unforeseen, these dangers which might overwhelm a country that had relaxed its vigilance after facing down the communist threat in the Cold War. Alternatively a new threat might unite the people into accepting a return to dynamic and decisive presidential leadership. These dangers could overwhelm the

United States at the moment when after the Cold War the US seems most powerful.

During Clinton's trial some British commentators questioned whether the United States could continue to play the role of superpower. Robert Harris, writing in the *Sunday Times* on January 10, 1999, argued:

> To perform the role of superpower demands precisely the qualities now most under threat in America: a strong executive and a united people. It also demands something else: a willingness to take casualties – and the fact that America, quite understandably, is no longer prepared to pay this price is . . . reason . . . to question the USA's long-term global role.

Harris argued that America had grown complacent – a classic symptom of imperial decadence straight out of Gibbon's *Decline and Fall of the Roman Empire*. The developing threats to the interests of the United States may be diverse and difficult to evaluate, but they are real. Environmental catastrophe offers a variety of nightmare scenarios that could face the United States after the year 2000. The countries that made up the former Soviet Union could pose a variety of financial and military threats to American interests. Middle Eastern and domestic terrorism remains an ever present danger. Lastly, the economy could implode as spectacularly as it did in 1929, when it took the considerable political skills of Franklin D. Roosevelt to revive effective presidential leadership and find a path toward stability. Whichever of these dangers confronts the United States, one thing is certain: the position of the presidency has been so undermined in the closing years of the twentieth century that the danger will have to reach crisis point before it can be dealt with effectively. Only when a disaster such as the Great Depression confronts the American people will there again be the political will to support strong presidential action.

A further developing theme of American politics at the end of the twentieth century has been the decline of support for liberal internationalism. By the 1980s to be accused of being a liberal was the equivalent of being called a communist in the 1950s. More damagingly, by the 1990s many in the Republican Party were questioning whether America should continue to pay the cost of being the world's policeman. There was a noticeable ebbing of support in the Republican Party for continued involvement in the United Nations and a growing desire for America to pursue an international policy based solely on US interests. Evidence of a sea-change in American politics and foreign policy became spectacularly apparent in mid-October 1999 as Congress refused to endorse a nuclear test ban treaty which had already been signed by Clinton. Designed to halt the proliferation of nuclear weapons by banning their testing, the treaty was comprehensively rejected by a Republican-dominated Congress. Some British observers blamed the Lewinsky effect on American politics. Ben Macintyre, writing in the London *Times* on October 16, argued:

Not content with her already baleful effect on political and popular culture, Monica Lewinsky has now undermined global stability, raised the spectre of a nuclear arms race, enraged her nation's closest allies and helped to push through the most emphatic American rejection of an international agreement since the Treaty of Versailles was voted down 80 years ago. . . . Monica burnt up the middle-ground in American politics. Last January Clinton proclaimed a wide-ranging policy agenda in his state of the Union address, but today there seems little prospect of creative compromise with Congress on issues such as trade, foreign policy, budgets, education and social programs. Clinton's last 14 months in office are set to become a tale of sound and fury legislating nothing, or very little. Partisan politics have skewed America's world role before. Woodrow Wilson was detested by the Republicans who took over Congress in 1918 and then voted down the Treaty of Versailles, ensuring that the US did not join the League of Nations. That decision had profound consequences for the world, as may this week's repudiation of the test ban treaty. But the contrasts with 1918 are also telling: the Versailles treaty was rejected in the US after one of the great intellectual and moral debates of the century, following a war of searing significance; the test ban treaty was put to death in haste and anger, with scant deliberation, after a fight over the President's girlfriend.

The international effect of the rejection of the test ban treaty was indeed severe. The British journalist Will Hutton, writing in the British newspaper the *Observer*, proclaimed an end to the liberal internationalism which had been a feature of successive administrations since 1945. He issued a warning to America's allies:

> The US has not ratified the land-mines treaty. It will not accept the provenance of the International Criminal Court. It has not accepted targets for the reduction of noxious emissions at either the Rio or Kyoto earth summits. It has fired cruise missiles unilaterally and with no attempt at justification in international law at targets in Afghanistan and the Sudan. It will not make common cause over tightening international financial regulation. It has become ever more hawkish over trade disputes. The Senate vote refusing to ratify the test ban treaty was but the latest and most dangerous manifestation of a trend that has been growing since the Reagan years. The US is turning nasty. For many in Britain, this is hard to accept. The US has been the reliable good guy in the West's Manichean fight first against fascism and then communism. It has guaranteed our security, kept its markets open to our goods and set the pace for the social revolutions that have defined the age. The idea that America could put itself comprehensively on the side of wrong in its international relationships is inconceivable. These are our allies, our friends and fellow English speakers; they feel like an extension of ourselves. We urgently need to revise that view. The US is a foreign country. It is also, although its own commitment to its un-imperial Constitution makes it reluctant to admit it, an imperial power at the centre of a global empire. Since the collapse of the Soviet Union, US military, financial, corporate and technological might has no equal; it can do precisely what it likes and on the terms it likes.

As America in its politics and foreign policy seems to change, the world looks on with concern and fear. Isolationism and a moribund presidency seem the likely outcomes of the drift of US politics toward the right.

It was against this background of rising despair that I undertook a journey to Chicago in February 2000. I wanted to get past the views of the historians, political scientists, and journalists to those of the people. As the immigration officer at O'Hare reminded me on learning why I was visiting the United States, Chicago and the State of Illinois have played a significant role in presidential history, which is why I had selected it as my destination. A middle-of-the-road city politically, Chicago was a good vantage point from which to take a snapshot of opinion. As license plates in Chicago proclaim, Illinois is the birthplace of Lincoln, the man who saved the Union. In more recent times, on November 3, 1948, the *Chicago Daily Tribune* had famously but wrongly proclaimed Truman's defeat at the hands of Dewey, and on September 26, 1960, the Kennedy–Nixon TV debate came from the city. Kennedy's success in the debate gave his campaign a momentum that proved impossible to stop, although there were later allegations that in the election the Democratic machine in Chicago had been busy stuffing the ballot boxes with thousands of fraudulent ballot papers. In August 1968, the city was convulsed by violence outside the Democratic Convention. In the following year began the trial of the Chicago Seven as Abbie Hoffman, Jerry Rubin, Tom Hayden and others stood trial for conspiracy to incite the riots of the previous year. The trial and the daily demonstrations in the city symbolized the growing divisions in US society over the Vietnam War. A quarter of a million men and women from Chicago and its environs were to fight in the Vietnam conflict and 964 Chicagoans would die in Southeast Asia during the course of the war. As the presidency went so badly wrong in the early 1970s Chicago bore witness to the process. On August 9, 1974, the *Tribune* brought out a special edition containing a full, 246,000 word transcript of the Watergate tapes which Nixon had been compelled to hand over. The Republican *Tribune* had called for Nixon to resign or be impeached as support for Tricky Dicky withered across Illinois and the Midwest. Events in Chicago after Nixon's resignation also seemed indicative of the general pattern of national history as cynicism about the presidency, and perhaps about all politicians, spread. Chicago offered a useful standpoint from which to survey contemporary American opinion.

Armed with only a tape recorder I spent my days wandering the snowy city striking up a conversation here and there, seeking out how ordinary Americans (if there is such a thing) felt about the presidency at the end of the twentieth century. The picture was overwhelmingly bleak. The lady giving away newspapers near the offices of the *Chicago Sun-Times* was only too pleased to talk to me:

> The best people don't stand for the Presidency. Why should they? They only get shot at and abused. Could you cope with that scrutiny of your private life? Anyway they're all corrupt. Can you name one who hasn't got or had a mistress? Have you read the stuff about Jefferson and his black lover? I tell you it's been going on right from the start.

She didn't know whether she would be voting in the 2000 presidential elections although it was plain that she had voted in every previous contest. Her comment that the "best people" don't stand for president was a theme I heard again and again over the following days. Quite what the "best people" did instead of running for public office somehow remained unclear. Despite the assertions of the presidential hopefuls, no-one was prepared to believe their claims of moral integrity, that they would not lie to the American public. The scale of voter cynicism was overwhelming and depressing. Despite the increasing sophistication and responsiveness of the techniques of political campaigning in the United States, the candidates appeared to lack the most basic assets of all in politics – conviction and public trust.

Some of my interviewees were less interested in the personalities and more interested in the constitutional balance. "It's Congress that runs the country, not Bill," said the construction worker. "Bill has been too busy with other things if you catch my drift." "Alan

Greenspan really runs the show, 'cept he don't tell no-one," said the bank worker. The personal assistant was even more forthcoming:

> The President doesn't matter a damn to most of us. He does the foreign policy stuff. People in the Midwest find that a hard thing to relate to. The laws Congress passes down, what happens at the state level and in Cook County Illinois is what interests me. Maybe the people in New York care about that sort of thing more.

I tackled her and others about the possibility of reform. She was of the opinion that there was no need for political reform despite her recognition of the obvious flaws in the system.

> So long as people have the right to vote, or the right not to vote, they are happy. That is the great thing about this country – opportunity and equality before the law. Sure there is no real equality, but the fact that the principle of equality is enshrined in law is a pretty powerful symbol. People can use the legal system to defend their rights. Same with the Presidency. Just because people don't vote for it don't mean that they are not interested in it. There might be a degree of apathy, but depending on the issue and the candidates that could change very quickly. The system works just fine and if people choose not to vote then that's part of America's libertarian mentality.

To a certain extent I could agree with her. If one was a member of America's white middle classes that had done so well out of the economic boom in the mid- to late 1990s, then perhaps a certain amount of complacency was in order. There were no pressing political issues, and with the presidential front-runners committed to broadly similar policies perhaps it did not matter who became president. The economy would just go rolling on under the watchful eye of Alan Greenspan.

But below the middle classes lay sectors of society whose involvement with the economic boom of the 1990s was at best peripheral. "Excuse me sir, will you be voting in the presidential

259

elections later this year?" I asked an African-American selling fruit to passing motorists at a busy intersection. It seemed that here was a man trying to live the American dream. In going to the fruit wholesaler and buying produce to sell on at a profit I thought I had found a man trying to get to somewhere from nowhere. Maybe that was the case, but his responses to questions about the American political system made me question my initial thoughts. He was going to vote in the election, but he didn't know who for, didn't seem to know who was standing, didn't know the kind of issues being raised in the campaign. But he was definitely going to vote. Given the struggles of African-Americans to get the vote it was a kind of duty on him to vote. I gave him a couple of bucks and left him dodging in and out of the traffic trying to sell his fruit to the office workers hurrying downtown.

His vote, maybe all the votes, would not change things, but he had to vote all the same. I heard a similar tale from a homeless man who was not registered to vote. He seemed resigned to his position in life and considered that social reform through the political system was an impossibility. "Been this way all time, always gonna be like this, won't ever change. The people with the money, they are the ones who run this country, and that kinda counts me out." Another interesting example of the a-politicization of the poorest sections of American society was provided by the African-American woman who hustled me in the grounds of Chicago University for a couple of dollars for a bus ride home. I gladly gave her the money, figuring her feet must be as cold as mine tramping through the snow. She seemed well dressed, indeed rather better dressed than me. In my old army boots, and ex-Swedish army overcoat, I looked like a fat version of Travis Bickle without the serious haircut. But as I talked to her I saw the ravages of drugs in her eyes. The way they watered wasn't just because of the cold. Her body was weeping for the lost soul within. Just how lost she was became apparent as we talked politics: "Sure I'm gonna vote. Bob Dole I guess." I didn't have the heart to tell her that her Bob would not be standing for the presidency this time.

As I neared the end of my stay I was gripped by a real sadness. I had not talked to anyone who expressed any hope at all about the presidency and the American political system more generally. I thought to myself that surely in the young, those not yet old enough to vote, I would find the antidote to the cynicism which seemed all-pervasive. Walking down East 57th Street I heard an English voice. A family, with an ex-patriate English mother, was heading into one of the bookshops. I followed them in and struck up a conversation in the American history section. Strangely, they had visited my part of Great Britain only last year. The woman confirmed much of what I had heard already – "the good don't run, the job's too big for any one." I asked the lady's daughters whether they would vote when they had the opportunity. They said they would but, rather like one of my earlier interviewees, only because of the struggle that it had taken to get American women the vote. Perhaps sensing my dismay at yet another largely negative response the eldest daughter, who was twelve or thirteen, asked me what was wrong. Her accent was the most bizarre combination of English and American that I had ever heard. She was truly a product of two cultures: The one mine, the other that which I was in part studying. Faced with her question, I told her of my findings over the previous days. I was truly surprised by her reaction. Instead of simply shrugging her shoulders she rounded on me forcefully telling me that she had hope. Things could get better and she believed that she could make a difference. She wasn't thinking of a run for the presidency or some other entry into politics, in order to save her family the inevitable pain, but she did want to become a journalist. She really did think she could make a difference and wanted me to know it and believe it. In a strangely touching moment she reached out and shook my hand warmly. We must have made a bizarre sight, a three hundred pound, 33-year-old English academic embraced by a slender teenage girl. I still don't know quite why she did it, but I sensed a profound understanding. Somewhere in this girl, and in the thousands like her, lay the possibility of a brighter, less cynical future.

That evening at dinner with a group of American academics I discussed my experiences with a professor in his sixties. Maybe it was because he was an expert in Buddhism, but his outlook on life was the same as the young woman I had met earlier in the bookshop. They shared the same youthful vigor and belief in change. I only hoped that if I made it to his age that I could have such a positive outlook. "Young man, you just met your second optimist of the day." He was true Democrat, a believer in Clinton and a believer in Al Gore. He believed in the presidency, believed that it could do good, largely trusted its powers. His soul did not appear to bear the scars of Watergate, Vietnam, Iran-Contra, or Zippergate. They were firmly in the past so far as he was concerned and he embraced the present and the future with a trust and a glee that was childlike in its beauty, strength, and simplicity. The presidency and the political system did work.

Arriving at O'Hare the following morning I felt far happier than I had twenty-four hours earlier. I had found hope on the streets of America. And there tucked away in a corner at the American Airline's terminal was an explanatory display about how O'Hare international airport had been named after Edward Butch O'Hare who had shot down five Japanese aircraft in 1942. He had been awarded the Congressional Medal of Honor for his exploit, only to be posted as missing in action in the following year. Somehow this reminder of American idealism and sacrifice from an earlier era was curiously reassuring to a visitor from overseas. It was a powerful echo from a time when people had similarly been cynical about the ability of the presidency and the political system to deliver reform and meet the challenges facing America. Roosevelt had given the people hope at the height of the depression and, backed by the bravery of O'Hare and others, he had gone on to lead them to victory in World War Two. Boarding the aircraft I was filled with a sense that, given the underlying idealism and commonsense of the American public, and the incredible resilience of the institution of the presidency over the past two hundred years, the United States, in an ironically British way, would continue to muddle through despite whatever problems are to be faced in the twenty-first century.

Select Bibliography

PRIMARY SOURCES

Apple, R.W., 'Introduction', *The Tower Commission Report*, Bantam, New York, 1987.

Benn, Tony, *Diaries 1973–1976*, Arrow, London, 1989.

Benn, Tony, *Diaries 1980–1990*, Arrow, London, 1994.

Beschloss, M.R., *Taking Charge: The Johnson White House Tapes, 1963–1964*, Simon & Schuster, London, 1997.

Carter, J., *Keeping Faith: Memoirs of a President*, University of Arkansas Press, Fayetteville, 1995.

Collins, J. *Imbalance of Power: An Analysis of Shifting US, Soviet Military Strengths*, Presidio Press, California, 1978.

Dean, J., *Blind Ambition*, Simon & Schuster, New York, 1976.

Eisenhower, D.D., *The White House Years – Mandate for Change 1953–1956*, Heinemann, London, 1963.

Eisenhower, D.D., *The White House Years – Waging Peace: 1956–1961*, Doubleday & Company Inc., New York, 1965.

Ferrell, R. H., *Off the Record: The Private Papers of Harry S. Truman*, University of Missouri Press, Columbia, 1980.

Glennon, J.P., *Foreign Relations of the United States, 1958–1960*, vol.I, Vietnam, United States Government Printing Office, Washington, 1986.

Glennon, J.P., *Foreign Relations of the United States, 1964–1968*, vol.1, Vietnam, 1964, United States Government Printing Office, Washington, 1992.

Hechler, K., *Working with Truman: A Personal Memoir of the White House Years*, University of Missouri Press, Columbia, 1996.

Johnson, L. B., *The Vantage Point: Perspectives of the Presidency 1963–1969*, Weidenfeld & Nicolson, London, 1972.

Kissinger, H., *Years of Renewal*, Weidenfeld & Nicolson, London, 1999.

Kutler, S. I., *Abuse of Power: The New Nixon Tapes*, The Free Press, New York, 1997.

LaFantasie, G.W., *Foreign Relations of the United States, 1964–1968*, vol. II, Vietnam, January–June 1965, United States Government Printing Office, Washington, 1996.

MacGregor Burns, J., *To Heal and to Build: The Programs of President Lyndon B. Johnson*, McGraw-Hill, New York, 1968.

McNamara, R. S., *In Retrospect: The Tragedy and Lessons of Vietnam*, Random House, New York, 1995.

Mailer, N., *Miami and the Siege of Chicago*, Penguin, New York, 1968.

Mailer, N., *The Presidential Papers*, Panther, St Albans, 1976.

May, E.R. and Zellikow, P. D., *The Kennedy Tapes: Inside the White House during the Cuban Missile Crisis*, The Belknap Press of Harvard University, Massachusetts, 1997.

Miller, M., *Plain Speaking: An Oral Biography of Harry S. Truman*, Coronet Books, London, 1974.

Morris, R., *Richard Milhous Nixon: The Rise of an American Politician*, Henry Holt & Co., New York, 1990.

Nixon, R.M., *The Memoirs of Richard Nixon*, Book Club Associates, London, 1978.

Nixon, R.M., *The Real War*, Warner, New York, 1980.

North, O., *Under Fire: An American Story*, HarperCollins, London, 1991.

Reagan, N., *My Turn: the Memoir of Nancy Reagan*, Weidenfeld & Nicolson, London, 1989.

Ruane, K., *The Vietnam Wars*, Manchester University Press, Manchester, 2000.

Schultze, G., *Turmoil and Triumph: My Years as Secretary of State*, Charles Scribner, New York, 1993.

Starr, K., *Report: the Findings of Independent Counsel Kenneth W. Starr*, Public Affairs, New York, 1998.

Stephanopoulos, G., *All Too Human: A Political Education*, Hutchinson, London, 1999.

Strober, G.S. and Stober, D.H., *Nixon: An Oral History of His Presidency*, Harper Perennial, New York, 1994.

The White House Transcripts: Submission of Recorded Presidential Conversations to the Committee on the Judiciary of the House of Representatives by President Richard Nixon, Bantam Books, New York, 1974.

Toledano, R., *One Man Alone: Richard Nixon*, Funk & Wagnalls, New York, 1969.

Truman, Harry S., *Memoirs*, 2 vols, Doubleday, New York, 1955–6.

Truman, Margaret, *Harry S. Truman*, William Morrow, New York, 1973.

Warren, R.P., *All the King's Men*, Prion, London, 1999.

Wofford, H., *Of Kennedys and Kings: Making Sense of the Sixties*, Farrar Straus Giroux, New York, 1980.

Woodward, H., Bernstein, C., *The Final Days*, Secker & Warburg, London, 1976.

SECONDARY SOURCES

Aitken, J., *Nixon: A Life*, Weidenfeld & Nicolson, London, 1993.

Alexander, C.C., *Holding the Line: The Eisenhower Era, 1952–1961*, Indiana University Press, Bloomington, 1975.

Ambrose, S.E., *Eisenhower*, 2 vols, Simon & Schuster, New York, 1983-4.

Ambrose, S.E., *Nixon*, 3 vols., Simon & Schuster, New York, 1987-91.

Ambrose, S.E., "The Presidency and Foreign Policy", *Foreign Affairs*, Winter 1991–2, pp. 120–37.

Ambrose, S. E. and Brinkley, D. G., *Rise to Globalism: American Foreign Policy since 1938*, Penguin, New York, 1997.

Select Bibliography

Barilleaux, R.J. and Stuckey, M.E., *Leadership and the Bush Presidency: Prudence or Drift in an Era of Change?*, Praeger, Westport, 1992.

Bates, M., *The Wars We Took to Vietnam: Cultural Conflict and Storytelling*, University of California Press, Berkeley, 1996.

Bernstein, I., *Guns or Butter: The Presidency of Lyndon Johnson*, Oxford University Press, New York, 1996.

Beschloss, M., *Mayday: Eisenhower, Krushchev and the U-2 Affair*, Harper & Row, New York, 1986.

Beschloss, M., *Kennedy v. Krushchev: The Crisis Years 1960–63*, Faber & Faber, London, 1991.

Bischof, G. and Ambrose, S.E., *Eisenhower: A Centenary Assessment*, Louisiana State University Press, Baton Rouge and London, 1995.

Bourne, P.G., *Jimmy Carter: A Comprehensive Biography from Plains to Postpresidency*, Scribner, New York, 1997.

Brandon, H., *The Retreat of American Power*, The Bodley Head, London, 1972.

Brendon, P., *Ike: The Life and Times of Dwight D. Eisenhower*, Secker & Warburg, London, 1987.

Brogan, H., *Kennedy*, Longman, Harlow, 1996.

Buzzanco, R., *Vietnam and the Transformation of American Life*, Blackwell, Massachusetts, 1999.

Cannon, J. *Time and Chance: Gerald Ford's Appointment with History*, University of Michigan Press, Ann Arbor, 1998.

Caridi, R.J., *The Korean War and American Politics: The Republican Party as a Case Study*, University of Pennsylvania Press, Philadelphia, 1968.

Caro, R.A., *Years of Lyndon Johnson*, 2 vols, Knopf, New York, 1982–90.

Chang, L. and Kornbluh, P., *The Cuban Missile Crisis 1962*, The New Press, New York, 1992.

Chomsky, N., *Rethinking Camelot: JFK, the Vietnam War, and US Political Culture*, Verso, London, 1993.

Cunliffe, M., *American Presidents and the Presidency*, Fontana, London, 1972.

Dallek, R., *Lyndon Johnson and His Times 1961–1973*, Oxford University Press, Oxford, 1998.

Davis, V., *The Post Imperial Presidency*, Transaction Books, New Brunswick, 1980.

Donovan, R.J., *Conflict and Crisis: The Presidency of Harry S. Truman*, University of Missouri Press, Columbia, 1996.

Donovan, R.J., *Tumultuous Years: The Presidency of Harry S. Truman, 1949–53*, Norton, New York, 1982.

Emery, F., *Watergate: The Corruption and Fall of Richard Nixon*, Jonathan Cape, London, 1994.

Evans, H., *The American Century*, Jonathan Cape, London, 1998.

Fink, G., *The Carter Presidency: Policy Choices in the Post-New Deal Era*, University of Kansas Press, Kansas, 1998.

Fursenko, A. and Naftali, T., *One Hell of a Gamble: Krushchev, Castro, Kennedy and the Cuban Missile Crisis, 1958–1964*, John Murray, London, 1997.

Select Bibliography

Garson, R. and Bailey, C., *The Uncertain Power: A Political History of the United States since 1929*, Manchester University Press, Manchester, 1990.

Giglio, J., *The Presidency of John F. Kennedy*, University of Kansas Press, Kansas, 1991.

Glad, G., *Jimmy Carter: In Search of the Great White House*, Norton, New York, 1980.

Goldman, M.S., *Richard M. Nixon, The Complex President*, Facts on File Inc., New York, 1998.

Greenstein, F., *The Reagan Presidency: An Early Assessment*, The Johns Hopkins University Press, Baltimore, 1983.

Halberstam, D., *The Best and the Brightest*, Random House, New York, 1977.

Hamby, A., *Harry S. Truman and the Fair Deal*, D.C. Heath, Massachusetts, 1974.

Hamby, A., *Man of the People: A Life of Harry Truman*, Oxford University Press, New York, 1995.

Hamilton, N., *JFK: Reckless Youth*, Arrow, London, 1987.

Harrison, R., *State and Society in the Twentieth Century America*, Addison Wesley Longman, London, 1997.

Hastings, M., *The Korean War*, Michael Joseph, London, 1987.

Hayden, T., *Trial*, Jonathan Cape, London, 1971 (first published 1970).

Haynes, R.F., *The Awesome Power: Harry S. Truman as Commander in Chief*, Louisiana State University, Baton Rouge, 1973.

Hersh, S., *The Dark Side of Camelot*, HarperCollins, London, 1998.

Hess, S., *Organizing the Presidency*, The Brookings Institution, Washington, 1976.

Hoff, J., *Nixon Reconsidered*, HarperCollins, New York, 1994.

Hughes, R., *American Visions: The Epic History of Art in America*, A.A. Knopf, New York, 1997.

Irwin, R., *The Loneliest Campaign: The Truman Victory of 1948*, New American Library, New York, 1948.

Johnson, H.B., *Sleepwalking through History – America in the Reagan Years*, W.W. Norton, London, 1991.

Kaufman, B.I., *The Presidency of James Earl Carter*, University of Kansas Press, Lawrence, 1993.

Kessler, R., *Inside the White House*, Simon & Schuster, New York, 1996.

King, A. (ed.) *The New American Political System*, American Enterprise Institute, Washingon, 1978.

Kissinger, H., *Diplomacy*, Simon & Schuster, London, 1994.

Koenig, Louis (ed.) *The Truman Administration: Its Principles and Practice*, New York University, New York, 1956.

Kolko, G., *Vietnam: Anatomy of War 1940–1975*, Unwin, London, 1986.

Lacey, M. J. (ed.) *The Truman Presidency*, Cambridge University Press, Cambridge, 1991.

LaFeber, W., *The American Age: United States Foreign Policy at Home and Abroad since 1750*, Norton & Co., London, 1989.

Lasky, V., *JFK: The Man and the Myth*, Macmillan, New York, 1963.

Levantrosser, W. F., *Harry S. Truman: the Man from Independence*, Greenwood, Connecticut, 1986.

266

McCoy, D. R., *The Presidency of Harry S. Truman*, University of Kansas Press, Kansas, 1990.

McCullough, D., *Truman*, Simon & Schuster, New York, 1992.

McDonald, F., *The American Presidency: An Intellectual History*, University of Kansas Press, Kansas, 1994.

Martel, G., *American Foreign Relations Reconsidered, 1890–1993*, Routledge, London, 1994.

Medland, W.J., *The Cuban Missile Crisis of 1962: Needless or Necessary*, Praeger, New York, 1988.

Mervin, D., *Ronald Reagan and the American Presidency*, Longman, London, 1990.

Mervin, D., *George Bush and the Guardianship Presidency*, Macmillan, Basingstoke, 1998.

Morris, E., *Dutch: A Memoir of Ronald Reagan*, HarperCollins, London, 1999.

Morris, K.E., *Jimmy Carter: American Moralist*, University of Georgia Press, Athens, 1996.

Morton, A., *Monica's Story*, Michael O'Mara Books Limited, London, 1999.

Moynihan, D., *Secrecy: The American Experience*, Yale University Press, New Haven, 1998.

Muslin, H.L. and Jobe, T.H., *Lyndon Johnson: The Tragic Self: A Psychohistorical Portrait*, Insight Books, New York, 1991.

Nalty, B.C., *The Vietnam War*, Smithmark, New York, 1996.

Neustadt, R. E., *Presidential Power with Reflections on Johnson and Nixon*, John Wiley, New York, 1976.

Pach, C.J. and Richardson, E., *The Presidency of Dwight D. Eisenhower*, University of Kansas Press, Kansas, 1991.

Palmer, D. R., *Summons of the Trumpet*, Presidio, California, 1978.

Parmet, H.S., *Richard Nixon and His America*, Smithmark, New York, 1990.

Paterson, T.G., *Meeting the Communist Threat: Truman to Reagan*, Oxford University Press, Oxford, 1988.

Paterson, T.G. (ed.), *Kennedy's Quest for Victory: American Foreign Policy, 1961–1965*, Oxford University Press, New York, 1989.

Pemberton, W. E., *Harry S. Truman: Fair Dealer and Cold Warrior*, Twayne, Boston, 1989.

Primary Colors, Universal Studios, 1998.

Ready, George, *The Twilight of the Presidency*, World Publishing, New York, 1970.

Richardson, H., *The Presidency of Dwight D. Eisenhower*, University of Kansas Press, Kansas, 1991.

Schaller, M., *Reckoning with Reagan: America and its President in the 1980s*, Oxford University Press, New York, 1992.

Schandler, H.Y., *The Unmaking of a President: Lyndon Johnson and Vietnam*, Princeton University Press, Princeton, 1977.

Schell, J., *The Time of Illusion*, Vintage Books, New York, 1976.

Schieffer, B. and Gates, G., *The Acting President*, E.P. Dutton, New York, 1989.

Schlesinger, A.M., *The Bitter Heritage: Vietnam and American Democracy 1941–1966*, André Deutsch, London, 1967.

Schlesinger, A. M., *The Imperial Presidency*, André Deutsch, London, 1974.

Schlesinger, A.M., *The Cycles of American History*, André Deutsch, London, 1987.

Seymour-Ure, C., *The American President*, Macmillan, Basingstoke, 1982.

Shaw, M., *Roosevelt to Reagan: The Development of the Modern Presidency*, C. Hurst & Company, London, 1987.

Shesol, J., *Mutual Contempt: Lyndon Johnson, Robert Kennedy, and the Feud that Defined a Decade*, W.W. Norton & Company, New York, 1997.

Sidey, H., *John F. Kennedy: Portrait of a President*, André Deutsch, London, 1964.

Skowronek, S., *The Politics Presidents Make: Leadership from John Adams to George Bush*, Harvard, Massachusetts, 1993.

Smith, H., *Reagan: the Man, the President*, Pergamon Press, New York, 1980.

Sorensen, T., *Kennedy*, Hodder & Stoughton, London, 1965.

Steinberg, A., *The Man from Missouri: the Life and Times of Harry S. Truman*, Putnam, New York, 1962.

Strober, D.H. and Strober, G.S., *Reagan: The Man and His Presidency*, Houghton Mifflin, New York, 1998.

Swanson, S., *Chicago Days: 150 Defining Moments in the Life of a Great City*, Contemporary Books, Illinois, 1997.

Tower, J., *The Tower Commission Report*, Bantam Books, New York, 1987.

Underhill, R., *FDR and Harry: Unparalleled Lives*, Praeger, Connecticut, 1996.

Vidal, G., *Empire*, André Deutsch, London, 1987.

Whelan, R., *Drawing the Line: The Korean War 1950–53*, Faber & Faber, London, 1990.

White, M.J., *Kennedy: The New Frontier Revisited*, Macmillan, London, 1990.

White, M.J., *The Cuban Missile Crisis*, Macmillan, London, 1996.

White, T.H., *America in Search of Itself: The Making of the President 1956–1980*, Jonathan Cape, London, 1983.

Whittaker, D., *United Nations in the Contemporary World*, Routledge, London and New York, 1997.

Wildavsky, A., *The Beleaguered Presidency*, Transaction Publishers, New Brunswick, 1991.

Wills, E.S., *A Necessary Evil: A History of American Distrust of Government*, Simon & Schuster, London, 1999.

Wintle, J., *The Vietnam Wars*, Weidenfeld & Nicolson, London, 1991.

Wright, S., *Meditations in Green*, Abacus, London, 1985.

Index

Index

Index

Pearl Harbor 20, 61
Pennsylvania 128, 211
Pentagon *see* Defense, Department of
Perot, Ross 224–6, 228
Persian Gulf 211, 215, 219; Gulf War 216–23, 231, 219
Philadelphia (PA) 35, 167
Pleiku vii, 111–12, 250
Poindexter, John 196–7, 200
Powers, Francis Gary 65
Presidents and the Presidency of the United States: assassinations 7–8, 11, 70–1, 73–4, 90–5, 97, 100, 120, 153, 202; Assassination Records Review Board 94–5; unsuccessful attempts 186–8, 209; Camp David 65; Commander-in-Chief of US armed forces 5, 10, 20–1, 42, 46–7, 115, 142, 161–2, 199, 211, 215, 219, 231, 250; ethical and moral issues xiii, 8, 24, 70, 77, 85, 90, 126, 131, 143–5, 147–8, 151, 167–8, 175, 182, 224, 227, 238–44, 248–9, 252, 258; executive privilege 54, 69; "fireside chats" 19–20, 169; Head of State role 52, 253; health problems 17, 24, 53, 70–1, 100, 122, 145, 186–7, 198–9, 202–4, 209; immunity claim 239; impeachment viii, 8–9, 29, 76, 143–4, 157, 202, 227, 229, 240–2, 253–4; inauguration 18–19, 36–7, 74, 169, 179, 183; "imperial presidency" ix, 6, 70, 91, 101, 133, 154, 169, 176, 183, 202, 206, 225, 227, 246, 249, 252; powers, extent of and limitations on vii, x, 1–3, 5–6, 8–9, 12, 18–19, 25, 28–30, 36, 42–3, 48, 52, 54–5, 60, 69, 70–1, 73–4, 76, 78, 89, 111, 114–15, 117, 121, 123, 127, 128–9, 141, 146–8, 157, 159, 161–2, 171, 173, 176, 196, 201, 203, 219–20, 236, 241–2, 246–54; presidential elections 2–3; (1892) 5; (1900) 10; (1904) 13–14; (1932) 18; (1940) 20–1; (1944) 21, 22, 24; (1948) 34–6, 181; (1952) 26, 49–51, 181; (1956) 51–2, 181; (1960) 70–3, 75, 126, 181; (1964) 98–9, 101, 106, 113, 120, 181; (1968) 120, 123, 125–8, 130–1, 136, 181; (1972) 135, 140, 143, 150; (1976) 156–7, 164–8, 175, 181–2, 228; (1980) 173–4, 177–9, 182, 184, 208; (1984) 193–4, 209; (1988) 209–11; (1922) 206, 223–6, 244; (1996) 228–30, 234, 246; (2000) 244, 248, 258, 260; voter apathy xi, 93, 166–7, 179, 194, 211, 224, 228, 242, 244, 246–7, 258–61; primary elections 2; (1952) 50; (1960) 72; (1968) 125, 181; (1976) 164, 166,
181; (1980) 174, 178, 208; (1988) 209–10; (2000) xii; religion 71, 88, 100, 165, 178; State of the Union address 12, 101, 218, 255; term of office 2–4, 6, 28, 230; veto on legislation 8, 27–9, 34, 47, 74, 135, 161–2, 164; Vice-Presidents 8, 10–11, 22–3, 50, 71–2, 77, 92, 97, 100, 105, 123, 125–6, 131, 150–6, 163, 178, 202–3, 205, 208–10, 248; White House 2, 8, 17, 20, 22–3, 34, 45, 48, 53, 60, 73, 77, 81–2, 89, 97, 101, 109, 116, 121, 123, 126, 130, 136, 142–4, 147–8, 150–1, 153, 160, 165, 169–70, 174, 178, 182–3, 185, 193, 196, 198–9, 208–9, 211, 223, 225, 227, 238, 242, 244; Oval Office 137, 142, 177, 236, 253; White House advisers and staff x, 77, 80, 86, 131–2, 144–6, 185, 187, 196–7, 200, 202–5, 239
Press (US) xi, 3, 9–11, 19–20, 53, 72, 128, 144–6, 154, 193, 201, 243, 247, 261; *Chicago Daily Tribune* 257; *Chicago Sun-Times* 258; *Hustler* 243; *New York Journal* 9; *New York Times* 144; *New York World* 9, 20; *Observer* (London) 256; *St Louis Post Dispatch* 20; *Saturday Evening Post* 79; *Sunday Times* (London) 253–4; *The Times* (London) 248, 255; *Time* 105, 168–9, 182, 211–12, 255; *Washington Post* 143, 145–6, 238–9, 243
Price Administration, Office of 133
Project Vote Smart 247
Progressive Party 14
public opinion (US) xi, 1, 10, 19–20, 28–9, 40–1, 43, 46–9, 53, 56, 91–5, 116, 119–23, 127–8, 137, 142, 146–7, 157–8, 164, 166–7, 173–7, 186, 192, 198–9, 202, 206, 211–12, 218, 220–1, 223, 225, 229–30, 235–6, 240–5, 248–9, 251–3; public opinion polls 3, 54, 84, 99, 150, 167, 173, 225, 237, 247
Pulitzer, Joseph 9, 20

Rabin, Yitzhak 233
Ray, James Earl 125
Reagan, Jack 179
Reagan, John 179
Reagan, Nancy 181, 197
Reagan, Nelle 179
Reagan, Ronald Wilson, US President (1981–9) viii, xiii, 24, 164, 174, **176–204**, 205–6, 208–11, 215, 218, 220–1, 223, 244, 248, 252, 256
Regan, Donald 185
Reichstag 121
Republican Party xii, 8–11, 14, 17–19, 21, 25–7, 30, 34, 36–9, 43, 47, 49–52, 54, 60–3, 69, 79–80, 98, 100, 126, 130, 147, 151, 153, 164, 168, 172, 174, 177–8, 181–2, 184, 186, 188, 206–10, 224, 227–31, 241–3, 248–9, 255; Chicago Convention (1952) 50–1; "Contract with America" 229–31; Convention (1980) 208; Kansas City Convention (1976) 164; Republican National Committee 208
Robertson, Pat 210
Rockefeller, Nelson 150, 154, 156, 163
Roddenberry, Gene 246
Rome 195, 253
Roosevelt, Franklin Delano, US President (1933–45) x–xi, 6, 17–28, 31, 47–8, 50–2, 55, 63, 69, 72–3, 98, 100, 102, 106, 115, 178, 187, 189, 198, 230, 249, 254, 262
Roosevelt, Kermit 55
Roosevelt, Theodore, US President (1901–9) 9–16, 19, 21, 24, 55, 72, 74, 177, 215
Rose, Gary ix–x
Rubin, Jerry 257
Rumsfield, Donald 155
Rusk, Dean 75–7, 108
Russia 13, 133, 214, 232

Saigon 55, 96, 109, 119
San Francisco (CA) 104; San Francisco Conference 31
Schlesinger, Arthur ix, 42, 75, 115, 147
Scorsese, Martin 167
Seale, Bobby vii–viii, x
Secretary of State, *see* State Department
segregation in schools xii, 66–9, 134–5, 225
Seoul 55
Serbia 236–8
Seymour-Ure, Colin 28, 173
Shaw, Clay 121
Shepard, Robert 222
Shultz, George 183, 197, 201
slavery xi–xii
Somalia 234–5, 238; Operation Restore Hope 235
Sorensen, Ted 73
South America, *see* Latin America
South Carolina xii, 35–6
Southeast Asia Treaty Organization (SEATO) 58, 112
Southern States, "The South" xii, 8, 35–6, 66–7, 81, 100, 104, 106, 130, 134, 165
Southwest Texas State Teachers' College 99
Soviet Union 26, 30–2, 34–5, 37–8, 40–1, 43–5, 48, 54, 56, 59, 61–6, 72,

273

Index

77, 79, 81–3, 85–8, 97, 118, 127,
141, 148, 158, 171–3, 177, 184,
189–92, 194–5, 204–5, 212–14,
217–18, 221–2, 232, 250–1, 253–4,
256
Space Program, *see* National
Aeronautics and Space
Administration
Spain 9–11, 16; Spanish-American War
(1898) 9–12, 16, 21
Special Prosecutor, Office of 238
spies 38–9
Sputnik space satellites 62–3
Square Deal policy 12
Stalin, Joseph Vissarionovitch 30, 32,
35, 41, 61, 250
Stanton, Edward 8
Star Wars program 191, 194, 231
Starr, Kenneth 239, 242; Starr Report
x, xiv, 239–40, 242, 253
State Department 39–40, 42–3, 58, 65,
75, 78, 112, 132–3, 163, 197,
216–17; Secretary of State 39, 42,
75, 88, 108, 128, 141, 155, 173,
183–4, 197, 217, 230; "shuttle
diplomacy" 148
Stevenson, Adlai 49, 51
Stewart, James 23, 180
Stone, Oliver 91–4
Strategic Arms Limitation Talks (SALT)
141, 148, 172
Strategic Arms Reduction Treaties
(START I and II) 214
strikes, *see* labor unions
submarine warfare 15, 20, 165, 172
Sudan 256
Sullivan, Andrew 253
Supreme Court (US) 4, 19, 66, 220
Syria 193, 217

Taft, Robert A. 49–51
Taft, William Howard, US President
(1909–13) 14, 49, 215
Taiwan 37, 41, 44, 59
taxation 19, 23, 27, 41, 44, 63–4, 81,
101, 103, 131, 134–5, 160–1, 178,
181, 187–8, 193, 204, 210, 212–13,
228–9, 233, 252
Tehran 173, 195–7, 215–16
terrorism 192–3, 195, 204, 254
Texas xiii–xiv, 99, 126, 141, 207, 211
Thailand, 141, 250
Thatcher, Margaret 187
Thurmond, Strom 35–6
Tojo, Hideki 21
Tonkin, Gulf of 108–10, 120; Gulf of
Tonkin Resolution, *see* Congress
Tower, John 211
Transportation, Secretary of 155, 211
Treasury, Department of the 163, 185;
Federal Reserve Board 160; Treasury,

Secretary of the 185
Truman, Harry S., US President
(1945–53) ix–xi, 3, 11, 20, **21–49**,
51–2, 54–5, 63, 69–70, 73, 76,
110–11, 115, 142, 156, 181, 198,
204, 232, 245, 249–52, 257; Truman
Doctrine 31, 40–1, 43, 48, 54, 69
Turkey 32, 85–7

United Nations Organization (UN) 31,
36, 41, 44–7, 59, 94, 112, 115, 170,
177, 185, 192, 207, 217–19, 221,
231, 233–5, 255; UN Resolution
#678, 218; UN Security Council 41,
192
United States armed forces 15–16,
26–7, 40–2, 45–7, 54–5, 63, 78, 107,
156, 192, 194, 218–20, 223, 233,
235–7, 252; Air Force 44, 55, 57, 61,
107, 112, 116–17, 120, 139–41,
171, 192, 220, 233, 243; Army 15,
22, 44, 47, 50, 54, 68–9, 89, 107,
113, 115–16, 136–7, 161, 215, 226,
234–5; 14th Infantry Regt vii; 2nd
Missouri Field Artillery Regt 22;
Coastguard 234; Delta Force 173–4,
176, 215; Marine Corps 14, 16, 113,
119, 159, 177, 192–3, 199; Navy 9,
13, 20, 37, 44, 78, 83, 85, 100,
108–10, 115, 126, 133, 152, 165,
171–2, 195, 206; *C. Turner Joy* USS
108–11; *Maddox* USS 108–11;
Maine USS 9–10; *PT-109* USS 71;
Ticonderoga USS 109
Urban Affairs, proposed Department of
81

Vance, Cyrus, 173
Vandenberg, Arthur 43
Venezuela 12–13
Versailles, Treaty of 16–17, 255–6
Vietnam vii, ix, xiii, 2, 38, 47, 57–8,
61, 70–1, 87–90, 92, 96–7, 101–2,
106–28, 130–1, 133, 136–44,
147–50, 152–3, 156–62, 164–7, 169,
171, 174, 176, 179, 182, 192, 196,
202–4, 215, 219–20, 224, 226, 231,
235, 237, 243, 250–2, 257, 262;
antiwar movement (US) 116–19,
121–2, 124–5, 128, 130–1, 137–8,
140, 144, 146, 226, 257; draft
dodgers 157–8, 171, 224, 227, 244;
My Lai massacre 136; North
Vietnam, 58, 88, 107–10, 111–12,
138, 158, *see also* Hanoi;
"Linebacker" operations 139–40;
Operation Rolling Thunder 112;
Paris Accords 148; peace
negotiations 140–1; prisoners-of-war
141–3; South Vietnam, 58, 88–90,
106, 108, 110, 112, 131, 138, 158,

see also Saigon; Tet Offensive
119–20, 125; Viet Cong 111–14,
119, 137
Villa, Pancho 15
Volunteers in Service to America
(VISTA) 104

Wall Street crash (1929) 17–18
Wallace, George 128–30
Wallace, Henry 23, 35–6
War, Secretary of 8, 76
Warren, Earl, Chief Justice 66; Warren
Commission Report 93–4, 121, 153
Warsaw Pact 61
Washington (DC) 16, 32, 37, 42, 46,
66, 86, 97, 99, 116, 121, 126, 134,
137, 143, 148, 167, 175–6, 185–6,
206, 211–13, 226–7, 253
Washington, George, US President
(1789–97) 1, 6–7, 13, 25, 30, 245;
Washington Monument 150
Watergate affair ix–x, xii, 93, 127,
143–51, 153–8, 162, 164–6, 168–9,
175–6, 179, 182, 184, 197, 201–4,
208, 231, 238, 241, 243, 252, 257,
262
Weinberger, Caspar 184, 197
welfare policies 17, 19, 33, 73–4, 81,
101–4, 106, 119, 127, 134–5, 166,
169, 180–1, 188–9, 212–13, 227,
229–30, 243, 255
West Point Military Academy 22, 50
Whitewater affair 238–9, 249
Wilson, Edith Bolling Galt 17
Wilson, Woodrow, US President
(1913–21) 14–17, 20–1, 29, 98,
215, 255; Wilson's Fourteen Points
15–16
Wisconsin 39, 54
Wofford, Harris 76
women's rights 135, *see also* civil rights
Woodward, Bob 143, 146–7
World War I (1914–18) 12, 15–17,
20–2, 25–6, 29, 34, 50, 133, 249,
251–2, 256
World War II (1939–45) xiv, 6, 20–1,
23–6, 30–1, 34, 37, 49, 57, 63, 68,
70, 75, 100, 116, 126, 142, 152,
180, 184, 192, 217, 228, 247,
249–51, 262
Wyman, Jane 180

Yale University 152, 206–7; Law
School 147, 155, 226
Yeltsin, Boris 214, 232
Young, Andrew 170
Yugoslavia 232, 235

Zapata Offshore Company 207
Zapata Petroleum Company 207
"Zippergate" 262